W9-AGZ-019

# ARMAGEDDON

## Appointment with Destiny

## GRANT R. JEFFREY

Best-selling author of *Creation*

WATERBROOK
PRESS

ARMAGEDDON
PUBLISHED BY WATERBROOK PRESS
2375 Telstar Drive, Suite 160
Colorado Springs, Colorado 80920
*A division of Random House, Inc.*

All Scripture quotations, unless otherwise indicated, are taken from the *King James Version.* Scripture quotations marked (NIV) are taken from the *Holy Bible, New International Version*®. NIV®. Copyright © 1973, 1978 by International Bible Society. Used by permission of Zondervan Publishing House. All rights reserved.

ISBN-13: 978-0-921-71440-8

Copyright © 1997 by Grant R. Jeffrey

All rights reserved. No part of this book may be reproduced or transmitted in any form or by any means, electronic or mechanical, including photocopying and recording, or by any information storage and retrieval system, without permission in writing from the publisher.

WATERBROOK and its deer design logo are registered trademarks of WaterBrook Press, a division of Random House, Inc.

*Armageddon* was originally published by Frontier Research Publications in 1997.

Library of Congress Cataloging-in-Publication Data
Jeffrey, Grant R.
Armageddon: Appointment with Destiny

1. Armageddon   2. Eschatology   3. Israel
1. Title

Printed in the United States of America
2004

10  9  8  7  6  5  4  3

# COMMENTS ON GRANT JEFFREY'S
## SEVEN BEST SELLING BOOKS

ARMAGEDDON     MESSIAH
APOCALYPSE     THE PRINCE OF DARKNESS
FINAL WARNING     THE SIGNATURE OF GOD
              HEAVEN

"Grant Jeffrey has written an extraordinary new book, *The Signature of God*, that provides astonishing proof that the Bible was inspired by God. Grant is recognized as the leading researcher in Bible Prophecy today."
**Hal Lindsey, Hal Lindsey Ministries**

"*Prince of Darkness* was written by acclaimed Bible Prophecy teacher Grant R. Jeffrey. This unequaled masterpiece is the result of 30 years of intense research. It will stir you and inspire you as few books have. . . . It is extremely well written — extraordinarily researched and fascinatingly presented . . . this is the best book I have ever read on this subject."

"Grant's book *Messiah* is one of the finest fact-jammed prophecy books I've ever read. . . . It is well written, solidly scriptural, fully documented and extremely easy to read and understand . . . this astounding book will enlighten and inspire you and your friends."
**Jack Van Impe, Jack Van Impe Ministries**

"Grant Jeffrey . . . is now a bestselling author throughout North America. . . . His breakthrough book was his first, *Armageddon: Appointment With Destiny*. . . . Bantam Books later picked it up, and it turned out to be their No. 1 religious best seller in 1990."
**Philip Marchand, Book Review Editor, Toronto Star, Aug. 1, 1992**

"We need to have a biblically-based outlook on Bible prophecy. That's why we are featuring Grant Jeffrey in our magazine. His book *Armageddon: Appointment With Destiny* explores the amazingly accurate fulfillment of past prophecies, and examines the prophecies that relate to this time period leading to the Second Coming of Christ."
**Jerry Rose: Past President, National Religious Broadcasters**

"*Armageddon: Appointment With Destiny* has been our hottest single religious title. . . . We took it on with tremendous enthusiasm because there was something very exciting about the way Grant wrote, and it was something that we thought might go beyond the traditional religious audience."
**Lou Arnonica, Vice Pres. Bantam Books, New York Times, Oct. 22, 1990**

"We are excited about Grant Jeffrey's new book. . . . Now the book with the latest information on prophetic fulfillment, the book of the nineties, is *Armageddon: Appointment With Destiny*. It will show that God is in control and, most importantly, it will also prove to be a powerful witnessing tool to those who need Christ."     **David Mainse: Host, 100 Huntley Street**

A Special Message from the Publisher Regarding
the 1997 Revised and Enlarged Edition of
*Armageddon: Appointment With Destiny*
By Grant R. Jeffrey

Grant Jeffrey's book, *Armageddon: Appointment With Destiny*, became an instant international bestseller when it was published for the first time in 1989. During the last eight years, over half a million readers were fascinated by the brilliant and original research presented by Mr. Jeffrey in his well-written exploration of the phenomenal accuracy of Bible prophecies. This book went through eleven printings and has been published in numerous languages including Spanish, Korean, Japanese, and Chinese. Many of the greatest Bible prophecy teachers and writers have endorsed *Armageddon*. Hal Lindsey, this century's most popular prophecy writer, wrote that "Grant Jeffrey is recognized as the leading researcher in Bible Prophecy today."

However, over the last eight years since *Armageddon* first appeared, the world has been shocked by massive political, military, and economic changes. These major events include the collapse of the USSR, the rise of China as a new economic and military superpower, and the troubled peace process in the Middle East between Israel and her enemies. Many readers have written to ask questions about how these events and trends impact the fulfillment of the Bible prophecies leading to the return of Jesus Christ as the Messiah.

In response to these requests, Grant has thoroughly revised, updated, and enlarged his book *Armageddon: Appointment With Destiny* by adding more than eighty new pages of up-to-the-minute research on how world events are setting the stage for the earth-shaking cataclysm known in the Bible as the Battle of Armageddon. This newly revised and expanded edition of *Armageddon* will allow readers to go behind the headlines and the news soundbites. Readers will gain an in-depth understanding of the prophetic importance of the vital news stories and developments in Washington, Moscow, Beijing, and Jerusalem.

We trust you will enjoy this thought-provoking and important study on the fascinating prophecies that are being fulfilled in our generation.

The Publisher

# Table of Contents

# Acknowledgements

A book like *Armageddon: Appointment With Destiny* is the result of the reading and inspiration of thousands of books, articles, and commentators, plus countless hours of Bible study over the last thirty years. Although almost one hundred volumes are referred to in the footnotes and selected bibliography, these books represent only a fraction of the authors who have influenced and challenged my thinking. However, the inspired Word of God is the major source for my studies as reflected in this book.

My parents, Lyle and Florence Jeffrey, instilled in me a profound love for the Lord and His Word and have continually encouraged me in this project.

I would like to dedicate this book to my loving wife, Kaye, who is a faithful partner in our ministry and publishing house. She is a continual encouragement, my partner and the inspiration to my efforts to share my research with others.

I trust that the information revealed in the following pages will encourage you to carefully study the prophecies found in the Word of God and increase your personal faith in the Lord Jesus Christ as your Savior.

Grant R. Jeffrey,
Toronto, Ontario
July 1997

# Introduction

Does the Bible reveal future events that will vitally affect the lives of each of us in the next decade?

Has God actually set "appointments with destiny" for Israel, Russia, and America?

Do the ancient prophecies of the Bible reveal the time of the final Battle of Armageddon?

Will Israel rediscover the lost Ark of the Covenant and rebuild its beloved Temple in the last days?

The Bible's answer to these questions is a resounding "YES."

All of these questions and many more will be discussed in the fascinating light of original biblical and historical research. Unlike some books on prophecy you may have read, this book will challenge you with intriguing new ideas and research that has never been published previously.

The theme of this book is that throughout history God has set precise, prophetic "appointments with destiny" for Israel, the Gentile nations, and for individuals. God has manifested His sovereignty and prophetic foreknowledge through these predictions and their precise fulfillment. These prophecies and their incredibly accurate fulfillment prove the divine inspiration of the Scriptures. In addition, the evidence in this book strongly suggests that God has set prophetic appointments for our generation which will also be fulfilled "at the time appointed."

As you observe this phenomenon of divine time cycles and mysterious biblical anniversaries governing the life of Israel and the nations, I believe you will be filled with a sense of wonder that God has exercised His sovereign control over the rise and fall of empires to accomplish His purposes throughout human history.

It is fascinating to observe that all of these prophetic time cycles converge in our lifetime, the generation that is now poised to participate in the most climactic struggle in human history. This struggle for the soul and destiny of mankind has spanned all of the generations since Adam. We will witness the incredible conclusion of this conflict in the cataclysmic events during the next few years. It is no exaggeration to state that man is now faced with spiritual, environmental, political, and military choices that will determine the very survival of our human race. As we face this intense crisis over the next decade, it is important to realize that all of these events were foreseen by the prophets of the Bible thousands of years ago. Whether we personally believe it or not, God has His hand upon this world and He has set from the beginning of time an appointment with destiny for mankind that cannot be evaded or postponed.

Throughout recorded history, humanity has struggled with a burning desire to know its future destiny. We have focused our hopes and fears on our future. The sociologists have found that every tribe and culture throughout history has been fascinated with prophecy, despite the abysmal failure rate of all known prophecies outside of the Bible. In this frightening period of history, as we approach this new millennium, people's interest in the destiny of mankind is heightened by the undeniable fact that, for the first time in history, intelligent men can actually envision the catastrophic ending of all our hopes and dreams as a result of world war, plague, or environmental disaster.

Man stands today on a path that seems to lead step by step towards the worst horrors of all our nightmares. Before us lies an abyss containing the possibilities of nuclear war, famine, chemical and biological warfare, dictatorship, rising terrorism, and the collapse of morality and those family values that make life worthwhile.

Is there any hope for humanity? Is there any intelligent basis for believing that man will survive and go forth to build a secure, prosperous, and just society in which our human potential will finally be realized?

The answer to these questions is yes, there is still hope. It is not a hope based on wishful thinking, but rather a firm confidence that beyond all the frightening prospects lies a land, "a paradise lost," which mankind has searched for with tears and suffering through all these past generations. There is a basis for a realistic hope for tomorrow. We have not been left in total darkness about our future. The fascinating prophecies of the Bible tell us why mankind is facing this present crisis. Furthermore, the ancient prophets revealed the final outcome of this crisis, including the earth-shaking events that will culminate in the Battle of Armageddon. The message of the prophets offers us hope in the tremendous promises of the messianic age that will be fulfilled when Jesus Christ returns to establish His Kingdom on earth forever.

The same God who prophesied the precise details of Israel's history, which have already been fulfilled, has also told us clearly about the dangers mankind will face during "the last days." God revealed a great amount of information through His prophets about the approaching holocaust that all mankind fears and dreads. However, the Lord has also revealed the marvelous future that will immediately follow the Battle of Armageddon, when Jesus Christ will establish His long-promised Kingdom. He prophesied that He will create a paradise on earth and in heaven for each of us who will put our trust in Jesus Christ. While it is true that the immediate future contains awesome and tragic events as the result of man's sinfulness and God's judgment, this terrible crisis will be followed by the one-thousand-year Kingdom of God on earth known as the Millennium — the greatest period of peace, happiness, and prosperity that man has ever known.

Prophecy is not simply another branch of theology for a Christian. Our personal view of prophecy is found at the heart of our faith. Our perception of God's unfolding purpose in human history will reflect itself in our understanding of the revelation of the prophetic truths of the Bible. The fundamental principles we use to interpret Scripture in general are intimately linked to the principles we use to interpret the prophetic portions of Scripture.

An important principle to remember is that God has never abandoned His Covenant with Israel. Jesus Christ will finally accomplish His sovereign purpose in history when He returns to earth to usher in the long-awaited messianic kingdom. Historically, over the last two thousand years, many in the Church have "written off" Israel and ignored the eternal covenant promises that God made to His Chosen People, the Jews. Many scholars have mistakenly taught that God rejected and abandoned Israel forever when the majority of Israel rejected Jesus Christ as their Messiah. However, the apostle Paul warned the Church against this tragic error: "For I would not, brethren, that ye should be ignorant of this mystery, lest ye should be wise in your own conceits; that blindness in part is happened to Israel, until the fullness of the Gentiles be come in. And so all Israel shall be saved: as it is written, There shall come out of Sion the Deliverer, and shall turn away ungodliness from Jacob" (Romans 11:25–26). God has promised that He will still accomplish all of His promises to Israel.

The primary focus of this book is to present an interpretation of the unique prophecies concerning Israel and the nations; it does not focus directly on the prophecies about the Church. Naturally, as a committed Christian, I am vitally concerned with Christ's command to each believer to be a witness to the world and to understand His prophecies about the role of the Church, the Rapture of the saints, and our future life in heaven. These subjects are developed at length in my second book, *Heaven: The Mystery of Angels.*

*Armageddon: Appointment With Destiny* explores the astonishing precision in the accurate fulfillment of past prophecies. In addition, it examines the prophecies leading up to the Second Coming of Christ that are being fulfilled in our generation. The book will present evidence that those prophecies of the Bible which have already been accomplished were fulfilled to the letter. Since this is true, why is it so difficult for some people to believe that the prophecies regarding future events will also be fulfilled literally? Many liberal theologians suggest that we should now interpret the language of these prophecies as myth or allegory. They naturally suggest that nothing definite can or should be concluded regarding the interpretation of these prophecies related to unfolding world events.

It is certainly true that there is a spiritual meaning and principle behind all prophetic portions of Scripture. However, every single prophecy that has had its fulfillment recorded in Scripture was fulfilled with precise accuracy down to the smallest detail. It is inconsistent and illogical to propose that we should now interpret the biblical prophecies in a nonliteral or allegorical manner. Rather, in light of the precise fulfillment of past prophecies, we can have confidence that the future prophecies about the "last days" will also be fulfilled as precisely as the hundreds of past predictions regarding Christ's life, death, and resurrection. Therefore, I have interpreted these "last-day" prophecies in a literal sense because both the historical fulfillment and the literal method of interpretation of prophecies by Christ and the apostles in the New Testament indicate that this is the correct method. A small sample of these precise literal fulfillments is found in chapter 1.

As we consider the critical importance of these prophetic events related to the Second Coming, it is natural for Christians to inquire as to when this will occur. Does the Bible give any indication of the generation when these appointed prophetic events shall come to pass? The answer is a resounding yes! As we look back at the history of the last four thousand years of history in light of Scripture, we are confronted by a strange phenomenon. Despite the apparently random nature of historical dates and events, a curious pattern of astonishing complexity emerges when we examine the biblical prophecies regarding the nation of Israel and their precise fulfillments. More than forty of the most significant events in Israel's history have occurred precisely to the day on the anniversaries of the feast days of the biblical calendar, such as the Feast of Passover. The odds against this phenomenon occurring by random chance are staggering.

God's sovereign control over the events of human history and His prophetic foreknowledge of future events are clearly manifested in the pages of the ancient Scriptures as He sets these prophetic appointments for Israel. Then, as each time cycle concludes, the Lord keeps the appointment by bringing the prophesied event to pass at the appointed time.

This amazing phenomenon, together with proofs of the precise fulfillment of many other prophecies, suggest that we do not have to live in darkness regarding the major events that will occur before the Second Coming of Christ. The apostle Peter attests to the value of prophecy: "We have also a more sure word of prophecy; whereunto ye do well that ye take heed, as unto a light that shineth in a dark place, until the day dawn, and the day star arise in your hearts" (2 Peter 1:19).

During the closing days of Christ's ministry on earth, He warned us about the terrible events that would constitute the "signs of the times" leading up to the Battle of Armageddon and His Second Coming. He then gave His disciples a clear prediction of when these events would occur — at the rebirth of the nation Israel. "Now learn a parable of the fig tree; When his branch is yet tender, and putteth forth leaves, ye know that summer is nigh: So likewise ye, when ye shall see all these things, know that it is near, even at the doors. Verily I say unto you, This generation shall not pass, till all these things be fulfilled" (Matthew 24:32–34). The fig tree was used six times throughout the Bible as a prophetic symbol of the nation Israel.

On May 15, 1948, after almost nineteen hundred years of devastation and persecution, Israel became a nation — in the precise year foretold by the prophet Ezekiel over twenty-five hundred years earlier. Therefore, based on Christ's promise in Matthew 24:32–34, our generation is the first group of Christians in history with a sound foundation for believing that, within our natural life span (forty to seventy years), we will witness the amazing events concerning the Second Coming of Christ described in the final chapters of this book. We are the first generation in history that can, in light of the firm scriptural authority of Matthew 24:32–34, respond in confidence to Christ's command, "And when these things begin to come to pass, then look up, and lift up your heads; for your redemption draweth nigh" (Luke 21:28).

# 1

# *The Precision of Prophecy*

I am God, and there is none like me, Declaring the end
from the beginning, and from ancient times the things that
are not yet done, saying, My counsel shall stand, and I will
do all my pleasure.                              (Isaiah 46:9–10)

One of the strongest evidences of the divine inspiration of
Scripture is the phenomenon of fulfilled prophecy. The Bible is
unique among the religious books of mankind in that it dares to
predict future events in great detail. Other religious writings, such
as the Koran or the Veda, do not contain detailed, specific prophecies. The reason for this is that it is impossible to consistently
prophesy specific future events with real accuracy unless you are
God. Only in the Bible do we find hundreds of detailed prophecies
concerning various nations, events, and individuals covering
thousands of years.

Modern-day secular prophets do make predictions, but they
have a very poor record of accuracy. The more specific their
prediction, the more certain it is to be wrong. Anyone who
attempts to prophesy specific events will be confronted by the
staggering odds against success created by the inescapable laws of
mathematical probability. Human wisdom fails to accurately predict even a simple fifty–fifty proposition, such as which team win
a football game.

To appreciate fully the difficulty of making detailed prophecies such as those found in the Bible, let us consider the comparatively simple task of predicting the precise score of tomorrow's football game between the Los Angeles Rams and the New York Jets.

There is one chance in two that the L.A. Rams will beat the N.Y. Jets. That's fairly easy to guess correctly. But what will be the final score? Assuming that most football scores are between 1 and 50, the chances of guessing correctly that the L.A. Rams will have a particular final score (say 42 points) at the end of the game are one chance in fifty. The same odds, one chance in fifty, also apply for predicting the N.Y. Jets' final score. Therefore, to sum up the risk of basing our reputation on predicting tomorrow's exact football score, we simply multiply the probabilities: 2 x 50 x 50 = 5000 possible score totals. This analysis shows that there is only one chance in 5000 that you will correctly pick the precise final score. This is why you would not bet a month's pay, let alone your reputation, on predicting the exact score of the game.

When you consider the difficulty of predicting accurately such a simple thing as the final score of tomorrow's football game, you can readily understand why only God Himself would dare to risk His claim to the divine inspiration of His Word, the Bible, on such a foolish undertaking — humanly speaking — as predicting future events in great detail.

Current so-called "prophets," such as those you read about in magazines, understand the odds against making such accurate predictions. They are too "wise" to risk their reputations for their psychic abilities by attempting to publicly predict the actual score of a football game. Such "prophets" are content to predict, for instance, that "someone who is either a member or friend of the royal family will come close to death or injury in the next few years." Considering that there are, perhaps, as many as twenty people in the royal family, the odds are roughly one in three that such an event will transpire, given such a vague prediction.

If anyone connected with the royal family, even a friend, is injured, the newspapers will claim this to be "an amazing psychic success," and the "seer's" reputation will remain secure for those who are easily impressed. If these "prophets" could truly predict events with any degree of accuracy, any stockbroker would be delighted to show them how they could easily earn millions of dollars each month on the stock market.

David Hocking, in his April 8, 1985, radio broadcast, *Biola Bible Class*, reported on a fascinating article entitled "The Shattered Crystal Ball." This study analyzed the accuracy of the ten top psychics whose prophecies were published over a three-year period, 1976–1979. The study compared all of the published predictions with their subsequent success or failure rate. The results are certainly intriguing: 98 percent of all of their predictions were totally incorrect! Only 2 percent of their predictions were fulfilled. However, some predictors were much less accurate than their colleagues: six out of the ten psychics were wrong 100 percent of the time as recorded in the study.

The other four accurate psychics made only one correct prediction each during the three-year study. Their crystal ball is indeed shattered. Yet, despite this hopelessly poor record, millions of citizens spend hard-earned dollars on psychics and channellers, looking for guidance in their confused lives. These inaccurate prophets not only deceive their clients, but they also tend to promote false, occult beliefs such as spiritualism, channelling, and other New Age occult practices.

However, when we examine the prophecies in the Bible we encounter a different phenomenon of staggering mathematical proportions. The Bible contains hundreds of incredibly accurate predictions of events, verified by historians and archeologists, that defy mathematical probability. God declares boldly in His Word that these prophecies and their fulfillments are His signature upon the Bible and His verification that the Bible is truly the inspired (God-breathed) Word of God.

Over twenty-five hundred years ago, God hurled forth His challenge to false prophets and false religions. and thus far there has been no credible response to His challenge.

"'Present your case,' says the Lord. 'Set forth your arguments,' says Jacob's King. 'Bring in your idols, to tell us what is going to happen. Tell us what the former things were, so that we may consider them and know their final outcome. Or declare to us the things to come, tell us what the future holds, so we may know that you are gods'." (Isaiah 41:22–23 NIV).

The Lord declares that accurate prophecy belongs to God alone and that He alone can prophesy accurately the future of mankind. The precision of fulfilled prophecy thus becomes not only an irrefutable proof of God's foreknowledge and sovereignty, but it also proves conclusively that the Bible is the revelation of God's truth regarding man's sinfulness and need for salvation. We are confronted with the claims of Christ regarding our sinful rebellion and His pardon which He purchased for us by His death and resurrection.

"Remember the former things of old: for I am God, and there is none else; I am God, and there is none like me, declaring the end from the beginning, and from ancient times the things that are not yet done, saying, My counsel shall stand" (Isaiah 46: 9–10).

### The Laws of Probability

Statistical theory shows that if the probability of one event occurring is one in five and the probability of another event occurring is one in ten, then the probability of both events being fulfilled in sequence is five multiplied by ten. Thus, the chance of both events occurring is one in fifty.

Consider one area of specific prophecy and its fulfillment. Throughout the Old Testament, there are hundreds of prophecies in which God promised that He would send a Messiah to save humanity from their sins. To illustrate the precision of biblical prophecy, let us examine three specific predictions made by three different prophets and their detailed fulfillment in the life of Jesus Christ hundreds of years later. We will examine, as well, the probability or odds of these events occurring by chance alone so that you can see how impossible it is that these prophecies were made by man's wisdom.

| *The Prediction and the Event* | *Probability* |
|---|---|
| 1. The Messiah would come from the tribe of Judah, one of the twelve tribes descended from Jacob (Genesis 49:10; Luke 3: 23–24) | 1 chance in 12 |
| 2. He would be born in Bethlehem (Micah 5:2; Matthew 2:1) | 1 chance in 200 |
| 3. He would be betrayed for thirty pieces of silver (Zechariah 11:12; Matthew 26:15) | 1 chance in 50 |

The Combined Probability: 12 × 200 × 50 = one chance in 120,000

Thus, there is only one chance in 120,000 that any man would fulfill all three prophecies by chance. For those who believe that Jesus simply arranged the events of His life to fulfill these predictions, I would respectfully point out the difficulty most of us would have in arranging our ancestors, the particular city of our birth, and the exact price in silver of our betrayal.

## The Prophecies about the Messiah and the Laws of Probability

Of the many hundreds of prophecies concerning the promised Messiah, some four dozen are quite specific. Including several of the prophecies already mentioned, the following is an analysis of eleven messianic predictions made more than four hundred years before they were fulfilled.

The odds I have assigned in this chapter are obviously arbitrary estimates. Some of my readers will find that the odds I have suggested are too liberal or too conservative in some cases. What odds would you assign for the accuracy of these predictions coming true by chance, rather than by divine sovereignty? If you have other suggestions for the odds for any particular predictions, substitute your own estimates and recalculate the mathematical probabilities that these eleven prophecies were fulfilled by chance alone. Regardless of your estimates, the combined mathematical probabilities are staggering.

*The Eleven Predictions:*        *The Odds Against This Occurring:*

The promised Messiah would

1.   Be born in Bethlehem                Probability: 1 in 200
*Old Testament Prediction:*
"But thou, Bethlehem Ephratah, though thou be little among the thousands of Judah, yet out of thee shall he come forth unto me that is to be ruler in Israel" (Micah 5 2).
*New Testament Fulfillment:*
"Jesus was born in Bethlehem of Judea in the days of Herod the King" (Matthew 2:1).

2. Be preceded by a messenger              Probability: 1 in 20
*Old Testament Prediction:*
"The voice of him that crieth in the wilderness, Prepare ye the way of the Lord, make straight in the desert a highway for our God" (Isaiah 40:3).

*New Testament Fulfillment:*
"In those days came John the Baptist, preaching in the wilderness of Judea, and saying, Repent ye: for the kingdom of heaven is at hand" (Matthew 3:1–2).

3. Enter Jerusalem on a colt                    Probability: 1 in 50
*Old Testament Prediction:*
"Rejoice greatly, O daughter of Zion; shout, O daughter of Jerusalem: behold, thy King cometh unto thee: he is just, and having salvation; lowly, and riding upon an ass, and upon a colt the foal of an ass" (Zechariah 9:9).
*New Testament Fulfillment:*
"And they brought him to Jesus: and they cast their garments upon the colt, and they set Jesus thereon. And as he went, they spread their clothes in the way. And when he was come nigh, even now at the descent of the mount of Olives, the whole multitude of the disciples began to rejoice and praise God with a loud voice for all mighty works that they had seen" (Luke 19:35–37).

4. Be betrayed by a friend                    Probability: 1 in 10
*Old Testament Prediction:*
"Yea, mine own familiar friend, in whom I trusted, which did eat of my bread, hath lifted up his heel against me" (Psalms 41:9).
*New Testament Fulfillment:*
"And while he yet spake, lo, Judas, one of the twelve, came, and with him a great multitude with swords and staves, from the chief priests and elders of the people. Now he that betrayed him gave them a sign, saying, Whomsoever I shall kiss, that same is he; hold him fast. . . . And Jesus said unto him, 'Friend, wherefore art thou come?'" (Matthew 26:47–50)

5. Have His hands and feet pierced                    Probability: 1 in 100
*Old Testament Prediction:*
"The assembly of the wicked have enclosed me: they pierced my hands and my feet" (Psalm 22:16).
*New Testament Fulfillment:*
"And when they were come to the place, which is called Calvary, there they crucified him, and the malefactors, one on the right hand, and the other on the left" (Luke 23:33).

6. Be wounded and whipped by His enemies    Probability: 1 in 25
*Old Testament Prediction:*
"But he was wounded for our transgressions, he was bruised for our iniquities: the chastisement of our peace was upon him; and by his stripes we are healed" (Isaiah 53:5).
*New Testament Fulfillment:*
"Then released he Barabbas unto them: and when he had scourged Jesus, he delivered him to be crucified" (Matthew 27:26).

7. Be sold for thirty pieces of silver        Probability: 1 in 100
*Old Testament Prediction:*
"And I said unto them, If ye think good, give me my price; and if not, forbear. So they weighed for my price thirty pieces of silver" (Zechariah 11:12).
*New Testament Fulfillment:*
"What will ye give me, and I will deliver him unto you? And they covenanted with him for thirty pieces of silver" (Matthew 26:15).

8. Be spit upon and beaten            Probability: 1 in 10
*Old Testament Prediction:*
"I gave my back to the smiters, and my cheeks to them that plucked off the hair: I hid not my face from shame and spitting" (Isaiah 50:6).
*New Testament Fulfillment:*
"Then did they spit in his face, and buffeted him; and others smote him with the palms of their hands" (Matthew 26:67).

9. Have His betrayal money thrown in the
Temple and given for a potter's field        Probability 1 in 200
*Old Testament Prediction:*
"And the Lord said unto me, Cast it unto the potter: a goodly price that I was prized at of them. And I took the thirty pieces of silver and cast them to the potter in the house of the Lord" (Zechariah 11:13).
*New Testament Fulfillment:*
"And he cast down the pieces of silver in the temple, and departed, and went and hanged himself. And the chief priests took the silver pieces, and said, It is not lawful for to put them into the treasury, because it is the price of blood. And they took coun-

sel, and bought with them the potter's field, to bury strangers in" (Matthew 27: 5–7).

10. Be silent before His accusers                    Probability: 1 in 100
*Old Testament Prediction:*
"He was oppressed, and he was afflicted, yet he opened not his mouth: he is brought as a lamb to the slaughter, and as a sheep before her shearers is dumb, so he openeth not his mouth" (Isaiah 53:7).
*New Testament Fulfillment:*
"And when he was accused of the chief priests and elders, he answered nothing. Then said Pilate unto him, Hearest thou not how many things they witness against thee? And he answered him never a word; insomuch that the governor marvelled greatly" (Matthew 27:12–14).

11. Be crucified with thieves                    Probability: 1 in 100
*Old Testament Prediction:*
"He hath poured out his soul unto death: and he was numbered with the transgressors; and he bare the sin of many and made intercession for the transgressors" (Isaiah 53:12).
*New Testament Fulfillment:*
"Then were there two thieves crucified with him, one on the right hand, and another on the left" (Matthew 27:38).

The Combined Probability:
One chance in 10 to the 19th power
or
One chance in 10,000,000,000,000,000,000

In other words, there is only one chance in 10 billion times a billion that the prophets could have accurately predicted these eleven specific prophecies by chance alone, or that any one man's life could fulfill these detailed prophecies by chance alone; in fact, it is obviously impossible!

Regarding the estimates I have given for the probability of these specific events occurring purely by chance, let us consider the first prophecy of Micah's that was written more than seven hundred years before its fulfillment, that the promised Messiah would be born in the insignificant village of Bethlehem. I have assigned a probability of one chance in two hundred to the possibility of Israel's King being born in this little village by chance alone. In Israel, as in all other countries with monarchies, virtually all of the kings were born in their capital, Jerusalem, and almost never in a small agricultural village.

Let us assume then that the odds of a king being born in the countryside rather than in the capital city are one in ten, which is a very conservative estimate. Since Israel had thousands of small villages, the odds against picking the correct village by chance alone, are conservatively one in one thousand. Therefore, to be realistic, the odds against correctly predicting the birthplace of the promised King are one in ten (the odds on the capital versus a rural village); to this figure we multiply one chance in one thousand (the odds on picking the right village). This produces a combined probability of one chance in ten thousand. However, in an attempt to be very conservative, I have assigned the probability as only one chance in two hundred, instead of one chance in ten thousand, a figure which could easily be justified.

The prophecy of Jesus having "his hands and feet pierced," for example, is given odds of 1 in 100. This prediction in the Psalms was made more than five hundred years before the Roman Empire invented crucifixion as an unusual and barbaric method of execution. The prophecy that He would be wounded and whipped by his enemies is given odds of 1 in 25. This also is very conservative in that few kings in history have been subjected to whipping by their enemies. The prophecy of His silence before His accusers is given odds of 1 in 100. The number of leaders and teachers who have been unjustly accused and executed, and who have chosen to remain silent and not defend themselves, is minuscule. Even if we were guilty, most of us would loudly defend ourselves against our accusers if we were faced with torture, whipping, and death by agonizing crucifixion, let alone if we, like Christ, were innocent of the charges.

Another point should be considered by those who are mathematically inclined and who feel that my assigned probabilities are too high. Even if you assign the most conservative numbers possible to these combined prophetic probabilities about the life of Jesus the Messiah, you will still be confronted with a probability so staggering in its magnitude that it is impossible to honestly convince yourself that these things occurred by chance. In the unlikely event that you are still not convinced, you should consider that we have listed only eleven of the forty-eight major prophecies given in the Old Testament about the promised Messiah.

## The Bible's Precise Prophecies Prove That It Is the Word of God

When we consider all forty-eight of the specific Messianic prophecies, the odds against any one life fulfilling these predictions by chance alone are simply astronomical. In order that we might grasp, with absolute certainty, the reality of this prophetic proof that Jesus Christ is the promised Messiah and Son of God, consider the following illustration:

1. The odds of the prophets of the Bible correctly guessing all eleven prophecies is 1 chance in 10 to the 19th power. That is only one chance in 10 billion times 1 billion.

2. Let each chance in 1 to the 19th power (10 billion times a billion) represent an area of the ocean floor only 1/20 of an inch square (the size of one printed letter on this page). The entire remaining parts of the earth's ocean floor will represent all of the other chances against Jesus fulfilling these eleven prophecies by chance.

3. To see just how "lucky" the biblical prophets had to be to predict those eleven significant events, imagine that someone dropped a diamond ring from a plane somewhere over one of the oceans. You wager that you can locate it with just one try, using a long line and a fishhook. You can wander over earth's oceans (197,000,000 square miles of surface) in your boat for as long as you like. When you feel lucky, stop, drop the line, and try to hook the diamond ring that is lying thousands of feet below you on the ocean floor. You only get one try. Your odds of finding the lost ring are precisely equal to the odds against the biblical prophets correctly predicting those eleven specific details in the life of Jesus Christ, the promised Messiah.

With such odds against you, would you bet one month's salary that you would find the ring? I doubt that you would risk your money on such impossible odds. Yet, sadly, every year millions will die who have bet their lives and their eternal destinies on the "chance" that fulfilled prophecy and the Bible are not reliable and that, therefore, they can safely ignore the claims of Christ upon their lives.

"For God so loved the world, that he gave his only begotten Son, that whosoever believeth in him should not perish, but have everlasting life. He that believeth on him is not condemned: but he that believeth not is condemned already, because he hath not believed in the name of the only begotten Son of God" (John 3:16,18).

This book will focus primarily on the interpretation of the predictive elements of the message of the biblical prophets. However, the role of the prophet and his message is much broader than simply the prediction of spiritually significant future events. There are three Hebrew words used in the Bible to describe a prophet: *ro'eh*, *hozeh* and *nabi*. In combination, they reveal that his role includes both that of the seer as well as an exhorter of personal and national righteousness. Prophecy includes a declaration of God's sovereign design as it unfolds itself in human history and His call to our obedience to that revealed will, both individually and corporately. In summary, the message of the prophet is two-fold: First, it declares God's coming judgment of sin, and secondly, it declares the hope in the immediate and ultimate triumph of God's truth and purpose. Both the past and the future are united together in the message of the prophet through the prophetic revelation that God is guiding human history toward that day when the kingdoms of this world will truly become the kingdoms of Christ.

Several important principles of biblical prophetic interpretation are reflected in this book that have developed from my twenty-five years of Bible study and teaching: (1) Take all Scripture in its ordinary, usual, and common-sense meaning unless the context makes it clear that the statement is symbolic. (2) Symbolic language in one passage is usually interpreted by a more literal meaning in another biblical passage. (3) God has consistently prophesied and set appointed times for Israel and the nations that have been fulfilled to the exact day as predicted. The Lord has always dealt with Israel in relation to specifically appointed time periods and the Promised Land. (4) However, in dealing with the Church, Scripture reveals no appointed time period pinpointing the "day or the hour" of the Rapture, when Christ takes the believers to heaven. (5) The message of the prophet is both for his own time and for all the generations that follow him. It's purpose is not simply to provide information, but rather to challenge our behavior and our life priorities in light of Christ's lordship of our present as well as our future.

While it is certainly true that many details in the unfolding plan of God in history will not be known until they come to pass, four factors encourage us to examine the prophecies that point to events leading up to the time of Christ's return to set up His Kingdom: (1) God puts great importance on His prophecies: over one quarter of the Bible is prophetic, and He directs us to study His Word; (2) fulfilled prophecies, such as the ones in this chapter, encourage us to believe that future prophecies will be fulfilled in a similar, literal manner; (3) Christ criticized the religious leaders of His day for failing to pay attention to the prophecies and failing to "discern the signs of the times"; (4) the apostle Paul specifically reminds Christians that while it is true that "the Day of the Lord so cometh as a thief in the night" to unbelievers, believers are exhorted to heed another important truth: "But ye, brethren, are not in darkness, that that day should overtake you as a thief. Ye are all the children of light, and the children of the day: we are not of the night, nor of darkness. Therefore let us not sleep, as do others: but let us watch and be sober" (1 Thessalonians 5: 4–6).

These factors encourage us to carefully and prudently examine those prophecies that clearly relate to our generation.

In the following chapters we will look into some exciting prophecies that have already been fulfilled to the exact day. However, the final chapters should prove very interesting as we look into those prophecies that still remain to be fulfilled in our generation.

God will continue to fulfill His ancient prophecies as He has in the past. The Lord Himself says, "For I am the Lord, I change not" (Malachi 3:6). We will also analyze those appointments with destiny that God has set for Israel and the nations, based on the ancient biblical calendar, and discover indications of when these final events will come to pass.

# 2

# Daniel's Seventy Weeks: Israel's Time of Visitation

Seventy weeks [490 years] are determined upon thy people and upon thy holy city, to finish the transgression, and to make an end of sins, and to make reconciliation for iniquity, and to bring in everlasting righteousness, and to seal up the vision and prophecy, and to anoint the most Holy. Know therefore and understand, that from the going forth of the commandment to restore and to build Jerusalem unto the Messiah the Prince shall be seven weeks, and threescore and two weeks: the street shall be built again, and the wall, even in troublous times. And after threescore and two weeks shall Messiah be cut off, but not for himself: and the people of the prince that shall come shall destroy the city and the sanctuary; and the end thereof shall be with a flood, and unto the end of the war desolations are determined. And he shall confirm the covenant with many for one week: and in the midst of the week he shall cause the sacrifice and the oblation to cease.                                            (Daniel 9:24–27)

Nebuchadnezzar, King of Babylon, conquered Jerusalem in 606 B.C. and returned home with a group of royal captives, including a young man named Daniel. According to Babylonian custom, these Jewish captives received special training in all the wisdom and knowledge of this pagan empire to prepare them to serve as royal advisors. Daniel distinguished himself by his exemplary character, his wisdom, and the tremendous prophetic gifts that God had bestowed upon him due to his faithfulness. As a result of these prophetic abilities, Daniel was elevated from the position of a captive Jewish slave to ultimately become the First Minister of Babylon, the greatest empire in ancient history.

While Daniel was taken to Babylon with the other captives, his contemporary, the prophet Jeremiah, continued to prophesy to the remainder of the Jewish people living under the Babylonian army of occupation in Jerusalem. Jeremiah declared that "this whole land shall be a desolation, and an astonishment; and these nations shall serve the king of Babylon seventy years" (Jeremiah 25:11).

In 538 B.C., after living for almost seven decades in Babylon, Daniel read Jeremiah's prediction and knew that the seventy years of the Babylonian Captivity would end within two years in 536 B.C. He began to pray and ask God to reveal to him the future of the Jewish people. While he was interceding on behalf of his people and Jerusalem, God answered by sending His angel Gabriel to give him "skill and understanding" about the future course of history. Daniel received one of the most amazing visions ever given to man. This vision of the Seventy Weeks of years foretold to the precise day when Israel would reject and "cut off" their Messiah. In addition, his vision looked forward almost two thousand years to the Messiah's Second Coming to set up His everlasting Kingdom. It is an unusual prophecy because the time frame given is so specific and clear. Daniel 9:24–27 records the details of this revelation. (See the verses at the beginning of this chapter.)

In 1895, Sir Robert Anderson, a gifted biblical scholar and the head of Scotland Yard, wrote a fascinating review of Daniel's prophecy of Seventy Weeks. In a masterful work, *The Coming Prince*, Anderson proved that the portion of Daniel's prophecy that begins with, "From the going forth of the commandment to restore and to build Jerusalem unto the Messiah the Prince shall be seven weeks [sevens], and threescore and two weeks [sevens]" was fulfilled to the exact day 483 biblical years (each year equaling 360 days) after it commenced.

In considering the chronology of prophecy, it is important to remember that the length of the prophetic year differs from our calendar year. The Jewish year during biblical times was lunar-solar and had only 360 days. The solar year (365.25 days), which we live by, was unknown to the nations in the Old Testament. According to the *Encyclopedia Britannica* and *Smith's Bible Dictionary on Chronology*, Abraham continued to use a year of 360 days in his original Chaldean homeland. The record of the history of Noah's flood confirms that a thirty-day month was used in the book of Genesis (150 days are recorded as the five-month interval between the seventeenth day of the second month and the seventeenth day of the seventh month). Sir Isaac Newton related that "all nations, before the just length of the solar year was known, reckoned months by the course of the moon, and years by the return of winter and summer, spring and autumn; and in making calendars for their festivals, they reckoned thirty days to a lunar month, and twelve lunar months to a year, taking the nearest round numbers, whence came the division of the ecliptic into 360 degrees." (see Appendix A on the 360-day biblical year.)

Therefore, if we wish to understand the precise times involved in the fulfillment of prophecy, we still need to use the same biblical lunar-solar year of 360 days that the prophets themselves used. If the prophet Daniel made an appointment to meet someone in one year, he would arrive in 360 days, not 365 days. The failure to understand and utilize the true biblical year of 360 days has prevented a clear understanding of Daniel's vision of the Seventy Weeks and many other prophecies that contain a time element. This is borne out in the book of Revelation where John's vision refers to the Great Tribulation. John describes the last three and one-half years as precisely 1260 days (Revelation 12:6); "a time, times and half a time," where a "time" in Hebrew stands for one year of 360 days (verse 14); and "forty two months" of thirty days each (13:5). All of these references reaffirm that the 360-day biblical year is the one by which we must calculate biblical prophecy.

### Summary of Anderson's Calculation of Daniel's Seventy Weeks

First, Anderson stated that the commencement point of the vision is "the commandment to rebuild the walls of Jerusalem," which begins in Daniel 9:25. This decree was issued by the Persian

King Artaxerxes Longimanus "in the month of Nisan, in the twentieth year" of his reign, according to Nehemiah 2:1. "The first day of the month of Nisan," according to the *Talmud* (a collection of writings that constitute Jewish civil and religious law), is the New Year for the computation of the reign of kings and for festivals. The 1st of Nisan in King Artaxerxes' twentieth year was computed by the Royal Observatory, Greenwich, United Kingdom, as March 14, 445 B.C."

Second, "from the commandment to restore and to build Jerusalem" given on March 14, 445 B.C., there is a period of seven "weeks" (7 × 7 = 49 years ), and sixty-two "weeks" (62 × 7 = 434 years) which total 69 weeks of years ( 69 × 7 years = 483 biblical years). This period of 483 biblical years equals 173,880 days (483 × 360 days = 173,880 days).

Third, at the end of the sixty-nine "weeks" (483 years), or 173,880 days, there will be a time when, according to Daniel, the "Messiah will be cut off." On the tenth day of Nisan, April 6, A.D. 32, on Palm Sunday, Jesus Christ entered Jerusalem and presented Himself as "the Messiah" in fulfillment of this prophecy. (See "The Date of Christ's Ministry and Crucifixion" in the appendix.)

On that significant day the Messiah rode into Jerusalem on the back of a foal. His disciples recognized Him as the Messiah and proclaimed, "Blessed be the King that cometh in the name of the Lord: peace in heaven, and glory in the highest" (Luke 19:38). However, the Pharisees and most of the people refused to acknowledge Him as their Messiah. They called out to Jesus, "Master, rebuke thy disciples" (verse 39). But Jesus replied to the Pharisees that "if these should hold their peace, the stones would immediately cry out." Luke then describes the poignant scene as Jesus approached Jerusalem:

> He beheld the city, and wept over it, saying, If thou hadst known, even thou, at least in this thy day, the things which belong unto thy peace! But now they are hid from thine eyes. For the days shall come upon thee, that thine enemies shall cast a trench about thee, and compass thee round, and keep thee in on every side, and shall lay thee even with the ground, and thy children within thee; and they shall not leave in thee one stone upon another; because thou knewest not the time of thy visitation.
> (Luke 9:41–44)

In the preceding passage, Jesus emphasized the fact that this day, the tenth day of Nisan, April 6, A.D. 32, was a very important day for Israel. This was the "time of thy visitation," their decision day, in which Israel had to decide whether or not to accept Jesus as their prophesied Messiah-King. Despite the acclaim of Jesus' disciples and some of the country's citizens, the reaction of the nation's religious and political leaders to their time of visitation was to reject their Messiah. Five days later this rejection culminated in the crucifixion of Jesus and the postponement of the promised Kingdom for now almost two thousand years.

In A.D. 70, less than forty years after Christ's prophecy, the Roman army besieged Jerusalem, killing more than one million of her inhabitants. The Roman legions leveled the city of Jerusalem, totally fulfilling Christ's prophecy that "they shall not leave in thee one stone upon another"(Luke 19:44). The fearsome cry of the people, "Let him be crucified" (Matthew 27:23) and "His blood be on us, and on our children" (Matthew 27:25) had its tragic fulfillment, according to Flavius Josephus in his *Wars of The Jews* (bk. 5, chap. 11, sec. 2), during the final siege of Jerusalem in A.D. 70 when the hills surrounding Jerusalem were studded with thousands of crosses as far as the eye could see.

To sum up these calculations, Daniel's vision spoke of a total of seventy "sevens" or seventy "weeks" of years, equalling 490 biblical years. This period of time, beginning with the command to rebuild the walls of Jerusalem (March 14, 445 B.C.) until the Messiah was "cut off" (April 6, A.D. 32, the tenth of Nisan) is seven "sevens" plus sixty-two "sevens," equaling sixty-nine "weeks of years" (173,880 days). This prophecy was fulfilled to the exact day. As a reminder, in calculating the duration in years between any date B.C. (before Christ), to any date A.D. (*anno Domini*, in the year of our Lord), one year must always be omitted. Therefore, the time lapse between Passover in 1 B.C. and the next passover in A.D. 1 is only one year, not two years, because there is no such year as 0 B.C.

For those who want to confirm these calculations for the period of the 69 "weeks" by working back from our calendar dates, there is another way to calculate. Follow these computations with a calculator. From March 14, 445 B.C. (the date of the command to rebuild Jerusalem) to March 14, A.D. 32 is 476 years of 365 days each, or 173,740 days. Add the 24 days from March 14, A.D. 32 until April 6, A.D. 32 (Palm Sunday, the "cutting off" of

Messiah) — twenty-four days. Then add the 116 leap days that occurred during this period (calculated by the Royal Observatory, Greenwich, United Kingdom) — 116 days. These numbers added together (173,740 + 24 + 116 = 173,880) total 173,880 days, the exact duration of Daniel's 69 "weeks" of years.

The first sixty-nine "weeks" of Daniel's vision were fulfilled to the very day. The seven-year Tribulation Period, the last Seventieth Week of seven critical years, remains to be fulfilled in our generation (see figure 1).

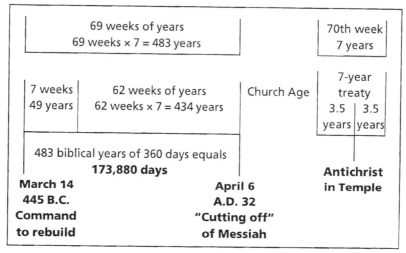

*DANIELS'S VISION OF THE 70 WEEKS*
*Figure 1*

When we thoughtfully consider the incredible accuracy of Daniel's prophecy, how could we possibly doubt that the remaining "week" of seven years, the Seventieth Week of years, will be fulfilled just as precisely?

The final week of Daniel 9:27 is the climactic seven years towards which all of Jewish and Gentile human history has been inexorably focused. When Israel rejected Jesus Christ as their promised Messiah on Palm Sunday, April 6, A.D. 32 — "the time of thy visitation" on the last day of Daniel's sixty-ninth week of prophecy — God's prophetic clock was stopped. The Lord postponed the prophesied Kingdom for almost two thousand years.

An analogy of this postponement of the promised Kingdom can be found in the parallel situation some fifteen hundred years earlier when Israel stopped at the very edge of the Promised Land and awaited the report of the twelve tribal leaders who spied out Canaan. If Israel had believed and obeyed God at that time, they could have immediately gone in to possess the Promised Land. However, the tragic history in Exodus tells us that through their disobedience and disbelief in God's promises, the people rejected both God's Word and His leader, Moses, and sought to stone him and Aaron. This rejection by the people led to the forty years in the wilderness and the loss of that entire generation who died without seeing the fulfillment of the original conditional promised possession of the land of Canaan. The entry into the Promised Land was postponed until a new generation had grown up in the wilderness and were ready to believe God's promises and receive the prophesied Kingdom. In a similar manner, the nation of Israel again missed their time of visitation and failed to recognize their Messiah in A.D. 32. As a result the Jewish people have now waited almost two thousand years to return to the Promised Land. Only at this point will they hear the steps of their Messiah approaching to finally usher in their long-awaited Kingdom.

During this interval between the ending of Daniel's sixty-ninth week (A.D. 32) and the beginning of the final Seventieth Week, God has created a Church of both Jews and Gentiles from all nations. Their purpose is to witness to all the world and to offer God's salvation to any who will accept Jesus Christ as Lord and Savior.

Also during this period, Daniel's prophecy that "war and desolations" would continue until the end has been tragically fulfilled. Yet, God promised that Israel would ultimately be saved. Paul prophesied that "blindness in part is happened to Israel, until the fullness of the Gentiles be come in. And so all Israel shall be saved" (Romans 11:25–26).

Daniel 9:24 specifically tells us that "seventy weeks" are decreed for Daniel's people, the Jews. The first sixty-nine weeks of years dealt with the Jewish people and God's witness to the world through His "chosen people." In a similar manner, the central focus of this final Seventieth Week of seven years will again be on God's dealing with Israel and the utilization of the 144,000 Jews to witness to the world of the coming Messiah and His Kingdom, as described in chapter 11.

God will never leave the world without a witness. After the

resurrection of the Church (the miraculous rapture of Christians to heaven), God will focus again on His people, Israel, who will rebuild the Temple. Christ promised that "this gospel of the kingdom shall be preached in all the world for a witness unto all nations; and then shall the end come" (Matthew 24:14). This "gospel of the kingdom" will be similar to the message delivered by John the Baptist and preached by Jesus during His three and one-half years of ministry, which ended on Palm Sunday, the end of the sixty-ninth week of years.

John the Baptist preached, "Repent ye: for the kingdom of heaven is at hand. For this is He that was spoken of by the prophet Esaias, [Isaiah], saying, The voice of one crying in the wilderness, Prepare ye the way of the Lord, make his paths straight" (Matthew 3: 2-3). And, "From that time Jesus began to preach, and to say, 'Repent: for the kingdom of heaven is at hand'" (Matthew 4:17).

# 3

# Ezekiel's Vision of the Rebirth of Israel in 1948

This shall be a sign to the house of Israel. Lie thou also upon thy left side, and lay the iniquity of the house of Israel upon it: according to the number of the days that thou shalt lie upon it thou shalt bear their iniquity. For I have laid upon thee the years of their iniquity, according to the number of the days, three hundred and ninety days: so shalt thou bear the iniquity of the house of Israel. And when thou hast accomplished them, lie again on thy right side, and thou shalt bear the iniquity of the house of Judah forty days: I have appointed thee each day for a year.

(Ezekiel 4:3–6)

It appears that in God's divine purpose, many of the details of the last days were sealed in prophetic visions in such a way that they could not be clearly discerned prior to their accomplishment. Each prophecy must be interpreted carefully in the light of the rest of Scripture. A sincere student of the Word must be very careful when he moves from the clear, broad outlines of prophecy (e.g., the restoration of Israel and the revival of a tenfold division of the Roman Empire) to the specific forecasting of exact times and the sequences of events of the latter days.

To illustrate the problem: consider the four different prophecies about the earthly home of Jesus Christ. He is described in the Old Testament as (1) being born in Bethlehem, (2) coming forth out of Egypt, (3) being a Nazarene, and (4) being presented as the King of the Jews in Jerusalem. On the face of it, these four prophecies seem totally contradictory, and yet each one of them was fulfilled to the letter in Christ's life. He was born in Bethlehem, spent several years in Egypt, was raised in Nazareth, and was presented in Jerusalem as their King.

While there was some expectation and knowledge of details surrounding Christ's birth before that day, (for example, that it would take place in Bethlehem), it was only after the events had occurred that believers could search the Old Testament and discover just how large a number of detailed prophecies had been fulfilled to the letter in the life, death, and resurrection of Jesus.

A basic principle of Scripture is that times are always specified in great detail for Israel, but never for the Church. We would look in vain for any date or calculation that reveals the time of the Rapture. God has specifically hidden this time. It is the failure to appreciate this fact that has led to so much error in prophetic interpretation.

In this chapter, I will confine my observations to a single event that has taken place in recent history that has tremendous implications — the rebirth of Israel. "Henceforth there is laid up for me a crown of righteousness, which the Lord, the righteous judge, shall give me at that day: and not to me only, but unto all them also that love his appearing" (2 Timothy 4:8).

Israel's relationship to the land is a major focus of prophecy, both fulfilled and unfulfilled. God prophesied precisely when the Jews would return to the Promised Land on two past occasions: after her captivity in Egypt and following her captivity in Babylon.

## Israel's First Captivity and Return

On the 14th day of Nisan, the exact day that would later become the date of Passover, the Lord appeared to Abraham to give him the Covenant for the Promised Land. God also prophesied that Abraham's descendants would be in affliction and bondage for a period of 430 years.

"And he said unto Abraham, Know of a surety that thy seed shall be a stranger in a land that is not their's, and shall serve them, and they shall afflict them four hundred years" (Genesis 15:13). The mistreatment of the seed of Abraham (his descendants) began just thirty years after God gave Abraham the promise of the land. "And the child [Ishmael] grew, and was weaned: and Abraham made a great feast the same day that Isaac was weaned. And Sarah saw the son of Hagar the Egyptian, which she had born unto Abraham, mocking. Wherefore she said unto Abraham, Cast out this bond woman and her son: for the son of this bond woman shall not be heir with my son, even with Isaac" (Genesis 21:8–10). This jealous mocking of Isaac by his older brother, Ishmael, began the affliction of Abraham's seed in Canaan and eventually ended four centuries later in bondage in Egypt and in the killing of male infants (Abraham's descendants) by the Egyptians. "Now the sojourning of the children of Israel, who dwelt in Egypt, was four hundred and thirty years. And it came to pass at the end of the four hundred and thirty years, even the selfsame day it came to pass, that all the hosts of the Lord went out from the land of Egypt" (Exodus 12:40–41).

On Passover, on the exact day that the 430 years ended, God fulfilled His promise and brought Israel out of the bondage of Egypt to become a mighty nation (see figure 1). The apostle Paul, in his letter to the Galatians, confirmed that God fulfilled His promise to end the captivity precisely 430 years after the promise was given to Abraham (Galatians 3:17).

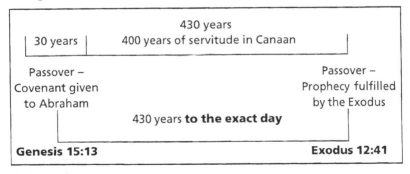

*ISRAEL'S FIRST CAPTIVITY AND RETURN FROM EGYPT*
*Figure 1*

### Israel's Second Captivity and Return

When the Israelites finally reached the Promised Land after their Exodus from Egypt — and after an additional forty years of wandering in the wilderness as punishment for their disbelief — there followed a period of time when Israel submitted to the leadership of God, with only a few lapses during the time of the Judges, the descendants of Abraham. This lasted until the kingdom was divided, following the death of King Solomon.

Years of rebellion against God followed during which the people, led by some of their worst kings, turned to idol worship and other gods. God's constant warnings to His people through His prophets were ignored. The people of the ten northern tribes, called Israel, were the first to be conquered in 721 B.C.: "In the ninth year of Hoshea the king of Assyria took Samaria, and carried Israel away into Assyria" (2 Kings 17:6). Then, from the kingdom of Judah, Jeremiah gave the final prophecy before the people of Judah were also removed from their Promised Land and taken captive to Babylon in 606 B.C.: "And this whole land shall be a desolation, and an astonishment; and these nations shall serve the king of Babylon seventy years" (Jeremiah 25:11).

| 70-year Babylonian captivity | |
| --- | --- |
| Nisan | Nisan |
| 606 B.C. | 536 B.C. |
| | |
| Babylon | Cyrus frees the |
| conquers | Jews to return |
| Israel | to Israel |
| | |
| Daniel 1:1 | Ezra 1:1–3 |

*ISRAEL'S SECOND CAPTIVITY AND RETURN*
*Figure 2*

Seventy years later, in fulfillment of Jeremiah's prophecy, King Cyrus of Persia overthrew the Babylonian Empire and released the Jews, just as the prophecy had foretold. History records that the captivity began in the month of Nisan, 606 B.C. and ended seventy years later, exactly as prophesied, on the first day of Nisan, 536 B.C. (see figure 2 ). Ezra records the decree of King Cyrus: "Who is there among you of all His people? his God be with him, and let him go up to Jerusalem, which is in Judah, and build the house of the Lord God of Israel, (he is the God) which is in Jerusalem" (Ezra 1:3).

However, only a small remnant of the Jews took advantage of the opportunity to leave the Babylonian captivity and return to Israel (fewer than fifty thousand). The vast majority (millions) never returned; they choose, rather, to live in the nation of their captivity.

## Israel's Third and Final Captivity and Return

Throughout the Old Testament there are prophecies of a final return of the Jewish exiles to the Promised Land in the last days. Considering the precision with which God revealed the duration of the earlier dispersions and captivities, it seemed probable to me, as a student of biblical history and prophecy, that hidden somewhere in Scripture there would be a clue revealing the time when the Jews would return from their final worldwide captivity to their Promised Land and once again establish a nation.

The prophet Ezekiel, like Daniel, was carried off to Babylon as a captive. He prophesied there for about twenty years. Also, like Daniel, he was aware from the prophecies of Jeremiah that the captivity in Babylon would last seventy years. All three prophets were contemporaries of each other. When the Lord appeared to Ezekiel in a vision, He gave him the prophecy quoted at the beginning of this chapter:

> This shall be a sign to the house of Israel. Lie thou also upon thy left side, and lay the iniquity of the house of Israel upon it: according to the number of the days that thou shalt lie upon it thou shalt bear their iniquity. For I have laid upon thee the years of their iniquity, according to the number of the days, three hundred and ninety days: so shalt thou bear the iniquity of the house of Israel. And when thou hast accomplished them, lie again on thy right side, and thou shalt bear the iniquity of the house of Judah forty days: I have appointed thee each day for a year.
> (Ezekiel 4:3–6)

In this prophecy we are given a sign and a clear interpretation that each day represents one biblical year. Ezekiel was told that Israel would be punished for a period of 390 years and for 40 years. As prophesied by Jeremiah, at the end of the seventy years

37

of captivity in Babylon during the spring of 536 B.C., in the month Nisan, and under the decree of the Persian king, Cyrus, a small remnant of the house of Judah returned to Jerusalem. The vast majority were content to remain in the pagan Persian Empire as colonists.

From the total decreed punishment of 430 years for Israel's and Judah's sin (390 years + 40 years = 430 years), deducting the 70 years of the Babylonian captivity which ended in 536 B.C., there remains a total of 360 years of further punishment beyond 536 B.C., the end of the Babylonian captivity (see figure 3).

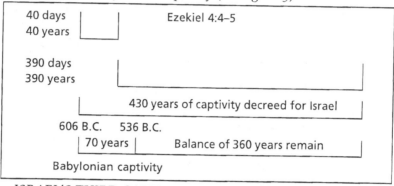

*ISRAEL'S THIRD CAPTIVITY AND RETURN TO THE LAND*
*Figure 3*

However, a close scrutiny of Israel's history fails to yield any significant period that corresponds to this period of 360 years of additional punishment, either at the end of the 430 years or at the end of the 360 years. It should be noted that, historically, Israel did not repent of its sin at the end of the seventy years in Babylon. In fact, even the minority of fifty thousand who chose to return with Ezra to the Promised Land did so with little faith. The larger part of the nation failed to repent of the sin and disobedience that caused God to send them into captivity. The majority of Jews simply settled down as colonists in the Persian Empire (Iraq-Iran).

The solution to the mystery of the duration of Israel's world-wide dispersion and return is found in a divine principle revealed to Israel in Leviticus 26. In this chapter the Lord established promises and punishments for Israel based on her obedience and her disobedience. On four different occasions in this passage, God told Israel that if, after being punished for her sins, she still refused to repent, the punishments previously specified would be multiplied by seven (the number of completion). "And if ye will not yet for all this hearken unto me, then I will punish you seven times more for your sins" (Leviticus 26:18; see also Leviticus 26:21, 23–24, 27–28). In other words, if Israel did not repent, the punishments already promised would be prolonged or multiplied seven times: 360 years × 7 = 2,520 biblical years. Taking God's warning into consideration, the end of the punishment and final restoration to the land would be accomplished in 2,520 biblical years of 360 days each.

The end of the captivity in Babylon, according to the Bible and other historical sources, including Flavius Josephus, is recorded as having occurred in the spring of 536 B.C. This date is the starting point for our calculations: 2,520 biblical years × 360 = 907,200 days. Converting this figure into our calendar year of 365.25 days and dividing 365.25 into 907,200 days we reach a total of 2,483.8 calendar years. (In these calculations we must keep in mind that there is only one year between 1 B.C. and A.D. 1). Therefore, the end of Israel's worldwide captivity would occur after a total of 2,483.8 years had elapsed from the spring of 536 B.C.

| | |
|---|---|
| End of Babylonian captivity in the spring of 536 B.C. | 536 B.C. |
| *PLUS* | + |
| Duration of worldwide captivity (360 biblical years x 360 days = 907,200 days = 2483.8 years) | 2483.8 calendar years |
| End of third captivity The rebirth of Israel | May 15, 1948 |

On May 15, 1948, an event transpired that shocked foreign governments around the world. The Jews proclaimed the independence of the reborn state of Israel, even while six Arab armies simultaneously prepared to invade the tiny country the next day to try to destroy it at its birth. As an old Jewish rabbi blew on the traditional shofar, or ram's horn, the Jewish people celebrated the end of their tragic worldwide dispersion and captivity at the exact time prophesied thousands of years earlier by the prophet Ezekiel (see figure 4).

| 606 B.C. | 536 B.C. | May 15, 1948 |
|---|---|---|
| First period 70 year Babylonian captivity | Second period (to be multiplied by seven) 360 years × 7 = 2520 biblical years (2483.8 calendar years) | |
| Babylonian captivity | Partial return in unbelief | Final return worldwide captivity |

## THE THIRD CAPTIVITY AND REBIRTH OF ISRAEL
*Figure 4*

This great day marked the first time since the days of Solomon that a united Israel took its place as a sovereign, independent state among the nations of the world. As far as I have been able to determine in my research, this interpretation of Ezekiel's prophecy, showing its exact fulfillment on May 15, 1948, has never before been published (see figure 5). Here is a fulfillment of prophecy in our time of such incredible precision that one is forced to marvel at the power of God to foresee and control man's plans and their results.

What does this fact mean to you and me? First, it means that despite the apparent anarchy of the events of our time, God is still on the throne of this universe. He is still in full control of world-wide events. The universe is unfolding precisely as our Lord ordained millennia ago. Second, this revelation about Israel's rebirth in 1948 renews our interest in the words of Jesus Christ recorded in Matthew 24:32–34: "Now learn a parable of the fig tree; When his branch is yet tender, and putteth forth leaves, ye know that summer is nigh: So likewise ye, when ye shall see all these things, know that it is near, even at the doors. Verily I say unto you, This generation shall not pass, till all these things be fulfilled."

### What Is the Significance of the Rebirth of Israel?

Perhaps a few lines from an article by Dr. N. Rabinovich can put this event in a Jewish perspective. After discussing the horrors of the holocaust and the inexplicable silence of God during the annihilation of six million Jews, in an article in the *Jerusalem Post* he goes on to speak of the meaning of Israel:

> The rebirth of Israel is not an indemnity for the unspeakable horrors of the Nazi era and certainly not for the accumulated anguish of seventy-five generations of suffering. The reestablishment of the Jewish state does not

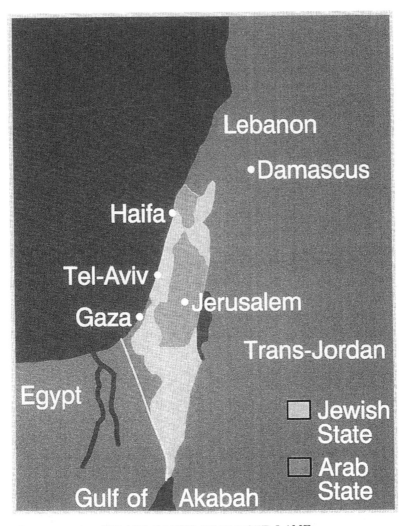

*ISRAEL IN THE PROMISED LAND*
*Figure 5*

solve the dread perplexity of Exile, nor does it spell the quick end of the persistent hatred of the Jew which is the mark of civilization unredeemed. Is the State of Israel the long awaited fulfillment of the prophecies? Surely only a prophet can tell. Are the footsteps of the Messiah resounding over the hills? Who among us can presume to recognize the signs? There is one simple basic fact which is there for all the world to see. It is so utterly simple and so totally obvious that thousands of millions of people all over the globe know it and see it. Israel is, and it bears God's Name and it has restored God's Crown! In the light of this radical truth, all other questions take on a different meaning. . . . The challenges are very great indeed. It has been pointed out that the existence of the state makes possible the fulfillment of two great aims of Torah: the Ingathering of the Exiles and the building of a just society. The achievement of these ends will require all the dedication and ingenuity that all Jews everywhere are capable of, and we hope that their accomplishment may initiate the Messianic era.

The fig tree (Israel) has put forth it's leaves (been reborn), and we who read these words are of "this generation," the one that is alive to see the fig tree budding its leaves. It is our generation that has witnessed the miracle of Israel's rebirth from "the valley which was full of dry bones"(see Ezekiel 37:1). In light of these events, we may join with the prophet John in his closing prayer in the book of Revelation chapter 22:20: "He which testifieth these things saith, Surely I come quickly. Amen. Even so, come, Lord Jesus."

# 4

# *The Appointed Feasts*

And Moses declared unto the children of Israel the feasts
of the Lord .                                      (Leviticus 23:44)

Also in the day of your gladness, and in your solemn days,
and in the beginnings of your months, ye shall blow with
the trumpets over your burnt offerings, and over the sacrifices of your peace offerings; that they may be to you for a
memorial before your God: I am the Lord your God.
                                                  (Numbers 10:10)

In giving the laws for His people, God set several appointed
"feasts of the Lord" for Israel to observe at specific times during
the year (Leviticus 23). These feasts were to be celebrated from
that time in the wilderness when God first gave the Law and
would carry on into the future. The first feast day God established
was the Sabbath day, which is to be observed every week. The
Lord established the following seven feasts in Leviticus 23 that
were to be celebrated annually: Passover, Unleavened Bread,
Firstfruits, Pentecost, Trumpets, Atonement, and Tabernacles.

Each feast commemorated a specific event in God's dealings
with Israel. But that is not all. Looking back from the vantage point
of modern history, we discover that other specific prophesied
events were fulfilled on the exact feast days that God instituted to

commemorate the original historical events. For example, the Feast of Passover commemorated the deliverance of the Hebrew people from the "destroyer angel," who passed over their blood-sprinkled homes as he visited the homes of the Egyptians, taking the lives of the firstborn of every family — humans and cattle. The blood that the Jews were told to put on their door posts had come from a sacrificial Passover lamb. The event that was prophetically prefigured, of course, was the offering of the Lamb of God on Calvary.

Four of the seven feasts we will discuss in the next few chapters have already been prophetically fulfilled, each one on the same day of the month on which God commanded that the feast should be commemorated.

Because of this documented phenomenon, we can expect, therefore, that those prophecies that are still in our future will also be fulfilled on the exact calendar day on which these feasts are celebrated.

## The Appointed Feast Days: "A Shadow of Things to Come"

The apostle Paul spoke of the importance of these special days in his epistle to the church at Colosse. "Let no man therefore judge you in meat, or in drink, or in respect of an holy day, or of the new moon, or of the sabbath days: Which are a shadow of things to come; but the body is of Christ" (Colossians 2:16–17). In these verses Paul was primarily admonishing the church to free itself of legalisms. However, he also clearly revealed that the holy-day feast, the new moon celebration, and the sabbath day were intended by the Lord as prophetic signs of future events.

Some critics suggest that many of the events recorded in the Bible were arbitrarily given dates purposely to correspond to the liturgical festival calendar. However, after years of personal research and the tremendous confirmation of the historical truthfulness of the Bible, as proven by the discoveries of archeology in the last century, I am fully convinced that the biblical accounts are inspired by God and can be taken as accurate records of historical events. Therefore, I have accepted the dates revealed in the Bible as being the correct and literal dates of these events.

As we contemplate the sovereignty of God in this precise alignment of feast days and significant events in Israel's history and future, we should feel a profound sense of wonder. God is truly in charge. God knows the end from the beginning, and He is concerned that we seek to understand His will as He unfolds His plan in human history.

In addition to the seven annual feast days that were proclaimed "as holy convocations," we will look at some other historically important calendar dates in the Jewish biblical year that have also had significant events happen more than once on their exact calendar day. In some cases we can expect prophetic events to be fulfilled on some of these exact dates in the future as well.

As an aid to our study, figure 1 gives a comparison of the Jewish calendar to our modern calendar. These revelations of God become more meaningful if we can see them from our perspective. We will examine only those months in which God commanded feast days be observed in accordance with the Mosaic Law (Exodus 40 and Leviticus 23) and in which fast days were proclaimed, according to the biblical history of Israel. These months include Nisan, Sivan, Tammuz, Av, Tishri, and Chisleu.

### THE BIBLICAL CALENDAR

| | *Jewish months* | *Our equivalent month* |
|---|---|---|
| 1. | Nisan, or Abib | Mar – April |
| 2. | Zif, or Iyar | April – May |
| 3. | Sivan | May – June |
| 4. | Tammuz | June – July |
| 5. | Ab, or Av | July – Aug |
| 6. | Elul | Aug – Sept |
| 7. | Tishri | Sept – Oct |
| 8. | Bul | Oct – Nov |
| 9. | Chisleu | Nov – Dec |
| 10. | Tebeth | Dec – Jan |
| 11. | Sebat | Jan – Feb |
| 12. | Adar | Feb – Mar |
| | Ve–Adar (the Intercalary Month) | |

*Figure 1*

The first four of the annual feasts — Feast of Unleavened Bread, Feast of Passover, Feast of Firstfruits, and Feast of Pentecost — were fulfilled during the first coming of our Lord Jesus Christ. The final three feasts — the Feast of Trumpets, the Feast of

Atonement, and the Feast of Tabernacles — will be fulfilled, it is believed, at the time of our Lord's Second Coming. In the following chapters we will study each feast and the prophecy it symbolizes, as well as the events that have occurred already in Israel's history on the exact calendar day of the feast.

On Rosh Hodesh, the first day of each month of the Jewish calendar, the appearance of even a tiny sliver of the new moon in the night sky signaled the beginning of the month. This first day of the month was announced by blowing the shofar, the ram's horn, in the cities and by the smoke of signal fires on each mountain top. This method announced the beginning of the new month to the most distant villages in Israel: "Blow up the trumpet in the new moon, in the time appointed, on our solemn feast day. For this was a statute for Israel, and a law of the God of Jacob" (Psalm 81:3–5). During the First Temple period, in King Solomon's reign, the High Priest announced the appearance of the new moon. Later, the Sanhedrin (the highest legal authority) announced the first day of the first month to set the calendar for the new year and to set the dates for the seven annual feasts.

### First Day of Nisan

The first day of the month of Nisan was a time for ritual cleansing and new beginnings for the Jews. During the time of the Exodus, God declared that Israel was to change their New Year's Day from the fall to a new calendar system in which the first day of Nisan, in the spring (Mar.–Apr.), would mark the beginning of the calendar year. Nisan, then, became the first month in the Jewish civil calendar. Four events symbolizing cleansing and new beginnings have already transpired in Israel's history on this first, important biblical anniversary. One event still remains to be fulfilled (see figure 2).

### 1. *The Dedication of the Tabernacle in the Wilderness*

Two years after the Exodus from Egypt, Moses was instructed by God to build the Tabernacle. After Moses had completed God's instructions for building and furnishing the Tabernacle, he dedicated it to the Lord. Moses wrote, "it came to pass in the first month in the second year, on the first day of the month, that the tabernacle was reared up" (Exodus 40:17). God told Moses that He would fill the Tabernacle with His presence and His "Shekinah" glory to guide Israel. (Exodus 40:2, 33–34).

---

**Theme: Cleansing and New Beginning**

1. The dedication of the Tabernacle during Exodus

2. The cleansing of the Temple by Hezekiah

3. Ezra and the exiles begin their return to Jerusalem from Babylon

4. The decree is given to Nehemiah to rebuild the walls of Jerusalem

5. The cleansing of the Millenial Temple

---

### THE FIRST DAY OF NISAN
### Figure 2

2. *The Cleansing of the Temple by King Hezekiah*

After King Solomon died, a series of kings led the divided nations of Israel and Judah. Most of them, however, were evil and practiced idol worship. Finally God raised up a righteous leader, King Hezekiah, who "did that which was right in the sight of the Lord, according to all that David his father had done. He in the first year of his reign, in the first month, opened the doors of the house of the Lord, and repaired them" (2 Chronicles 29:2–3).

The sacred House of the Lord was in such ruins that it took weeks to cleanse it fully. "Now they began on the first day of the first month to sanctify" (2 Chronicles 29:17). Two weeks later all Israel gathered to celebrate the Feast of Passover, one of the greatest celebrations in Jewish history.

3. *Ezra Began His Journey to Jerusalem to Rebuild the Nation*

On the first day of Nisan, 457 B.C., the Jewish leader, Ezra, began his journey to Israel, bringing an additional group of returning captives to provide leadership to the rebuilding of the Second Commonwealth. "For upon the first day of the first month began he to go up from Babylon" (Ezra 7:9).

God had commanded him to provide additional leadership to the returned exiles. "And thou, Ezra, after the wisdom of thy God, that is in thine hand, set magistrates and judges, which may judge all the people that are beyond the river, all such as know the laws of thy God; and teach ye them that knew them not" (Ezra 7:25). Nehemiah joined the Jews in Jerusalem thirteen years later (Ezra 7:9).

### 4. *The Decree Was Given to Rebuild the Walls of Jerusalem*

As we mentioned in chapter 2, concerning Daniel's vision of the Seventy Weeks, the Persian King Artaxerxes Longimanus issued a decree that sent Nehemiah to Jerusalem to rebuild the walls of the city. According to Sir Robert Anderson in his book, *The Coming Prince*, this decree was issued on the first day of the month of Nisan, or March 14, 445 B.C. (see Nehemiah 2:1–8). This important date was the beginning point of Daniel's vision of the Seventy Weeks of years.

### 5. *The Cleansing of the Millennial Temple*

This will be an annual Millennium festival that will take place on the first day of Nisan once the Fourth Temple is built in the future. In his writings on the Millennial Kingdom, the prophet Ezekiel discusses the offerings and holy days in the new Millennial Temple: "Thus saith the Lord God; In the first month, in the first day of the month, thou shalt take a young bullock without blemish, and cleanse the sanctuary" (Ezekiel 45:18).

Each of these important biblical anniversary events occurred on the first of Nisan — the first day of the first month of the Hebrew calendar falling in the spring.

### The Tenth Day of Nisan

Sanctification is the theme associated with the tenth day of Nisan. It was the day connected with the setting apart of the Passover Lamb for a holy purpose. There are four major events associated with this special day (see figure 3).

### 1. *The Sanctification of the Passover Lamb during the Exodus*

The first event related to this day occurred at the beginning of the Exodus. Setting aside the unblemished lamb was the first act of the Jewish captives toward freedom from bondage in Egypt. Four days before the great night in which Israel's Passover occurred, Moses instructed them: "In the tenth day of this month they shall take to them every man a lamb, . . . a lamb for an house; . . . your lamb shall be without blemish, . . . And ye shall keep it up until the fourteenth day of the same month" (Exodus 12:3–6).

---

### Theme: Sanctification

1. The sanctification of the Passover lamb during the Exodus

2. Israel crosses the Jordan River and enters the Promised Land

3. Christ "Our Passover Lamb" was "cut off" on Palm Sunday

4. Ezekiel's vision of the Millennial Temple

---

## THE TENTH DAY OF NISAN
### Figure 3

This sanctified lamb, sacrificed four days later on the night of Passover, became the perfect symbol that "Christ our Passover is sacrificed for us" (1 Corinthians 5:7). The Jewish rabbis taught that these four days (between the setting aside of the lamb on the tenth day and the sacrifice on the fourteenth of Nisan) symbolize the four generations of Israel that died in Egypt before the Passover and deliverance.

### 2. *Israel Crossed the Jordan River and Entered the Promised Land*

The second notable incident that took place on the tenth day of Nisan is described in the book of Joshua. After forty years of wandering in the wilderness, the Israelites were finally ready to cross the Jordan River into the Promised Land.

Joshua told the people, "Sanctify yourselves: for tomorrow the Lord will do wonders among you" (Joshua 3:5). Then the story continues, describing how, during this flood season, God caused the Jordan River to stop flowing above the place of crossing so that "the waters which came down from above stood and rose up upon an heap . . . and the people passed over right against Jordan" (Joshua 3:16). Scripture goes on to state that "the people came up out of Jordan on the tenth day of the first month" (Joshua 4:19), forty years after God had miraculously delivered them through the parting of the waters of the Red Sea.

### 3. *Christ, Our Passover Lamb, Was "Cut Off," on Palm Sunday*

As we discussed in a previous chapter, Palm Sunday, the tenth day of Nisan, A.D. 32, is the exact day in which Jesus Christ was finally, irrevocably presented to Israel as their long-awaited Messiah. This truly was Israel's "time of visitation." Although His disciples and some citizens of Jerusalem acknowledged His Kingship, the religious and political leaders (together with the vast majority of the population of Israel) rejected His claim, and the Messiah was "cut off" (Daniel 9: 26). This rejection resulted inevitably in His trial and crucifixion on Passover, thus fulfilling the type of the Passover Lamb that was set aside on the tenth day of Nisan and later sacrificed at the Passover Feast.

### 4. *Ezekiel's Vision of the Millennial Temple*

The fourth event that took place on the tenth day of Nisan was the magnificent vision that was given to the prophet Ezekiel (40:1–2). He had just received an amazing prophecy regarding a cataclysmic battle between the invading forces of Gog and Magog (Russia) and Israel. God showed Ezekiel that He would supernaturally defeat this future invasion. Then a vision was given to the prophet that revealed the building of a tremendous future Temple. He saw Israel finally enjoying, in perfect peace, all of the Promised Land that God originally granted to Abraham and his descendants forever (see Genesis 15: 18 – 21).

### The Fourteenth Day of Nisan: The Passover Supper

These are the Lord's appointed feasts, the sacred assemblies you are to proclaim at their appointed times: The Lord's Passover begins at twilight on the fourteenth day of the first month. (Leviticus 23:4–5, NIV)

Passover always falls on a full moon, the first full moon of spring. All Jewish males were commanded by God to go to Jerusalem three times each year to commemorate the feasts of Passover, Pentecost, and the Feast of Tabernacles. Passover was the first of these feasts. The biblical calendar reckons the beginning of a new day from sunset, as God did at creation, "And the evening and the morning were the first day" (Genesis 1:5). The Passover begins at 6:00 p.m. "In the fourteenth day of the first month at even [at 6:00 p.m.] is the Lord's passover" (Leviticus 23:5).

The *Haggadah*, the Jewish liturgy, says: "In every generation, each person should feel as though she or he were personally redeemed from Egypt." In the sacred cycle of festivals, the

Passover Supper on the evening of the fourteenth of Nisan allows all Jews in every generation since the Exodus to participate personally in the miracle of God's redemption of the enslaved Israelites. The Passover holds forth the promise of that final redemption when the Messiah will redeem all those who look to Him for salvation.

Passover is probably the most significant of all the festivals that Israel celebrates. For almost thirty-five hundred years, Jewish families have gathered on the evening of Passover to commemorate what God did for them when He delivered them from centuries of slavery in Egypt.

Six times in their history on this day, the fourteenth day of Nisan, the evening Passover Supper has marked a milestone in the spiritual and national life of Israel (see figure 4).

---

**Theme: The Covenant Relationship with God**

1. God's Covenant with Abraham — the Promised Land

2. The Passover supper eaten in preparation for the Exodus

3. The first Passover in Canaan — the Covenant renewed

4. The Book of the Law found and reaffirmed under Josiah

5. The dedication of the Second Temple

6. The Last Supper — a new Covenant is offered by Christ

---

*THE FOURTEENTH DAY OF NISAN*
*THE PASSOVER SUPPER*
*Figure 4*

### 1. *God's Covenant with Abraham Regarding the Promised Land*

"In the same day the Lord made a covenant with Abram, saying, unto thy seed have I given this land, from the river of Egypt unto the great river, the river Euphrates" (Genesis 15:18).

Abraham, the father of the Chosen People, left his home and travelled to a strange land that God promised He would "deed" to Abraham's descendants forever. Aside from the obvious obstacle of the strong pagan nations occupying this territory, an even greater obstacle seemed to stand in the way of God's promise to give a land to Abraham's "descendants": Abraham and his wife were long past the normal age for childbearing. However, as God later asked Abraham, "Is anything too hard for the Lord?" (Genesis 18:14).

The Lord confirmed His covenant with Abraham during this first unofficial "passover." God instructed Abraham to bring a heifer, a goat, a ram, a dove, and a young pigeon and cut them in half (except for the birds). After Abraham obeyed God, he fell into a deep sleep.

Several verses in Genesis indicate that this crucial event took place on Passover, the fourteenth of Nisan. However, God confirmed this fact in Exodus 12:41, which clearly states that the Passover Exodus, on the fourteenth of Nisan, occurred on the exact anniversary of the giving of the Abrahamic Covenant, 430 years earlier.

Then the Lord said to him, "And he said unto Abram, Know of a surety that thy seed shall be a stranger in a land that is not theirs, and shall serve them; and they shall afflict them four hundred years. And also that nation, whom they shall serve, will I judge: and afterward shall they come out with great substance. . . . And it came to pass, that, when the sun went down, and it was dark, behold a smoking furnace, and a burning lamp that passed between those pieces" (Genesis 15:13–14, 17). Due to the spiritual death that results from sin, a physical death and the shedding of blood was necessary for this covenant to be ratified and made effective.

### 2. *The Exodus Passover Supper*

On this night God concluded the last and most terrible of the ten plagues against Egypt with the "destroyer angel" killing every firstborn of Egypt. The Jews were divinely protected during this terrible plague by the sacrifice of the passover lamb and the application of its blood to their door posts. When the angel saw the blood, he passed over that home to continue his judgment of the Egyptians.

The next morning, exactly 430 years from the day when God made His Covenant with Abraham, the Lord brought the children of Israel out of their slavery in Egypt. "And it came to pass at the end of the four hundred and thirty years, even the selfsame day it came to pass, that all the hosts of the Lord went out from the land of Egypt" (Exodus 12:41).

## 3. *The First Passover in Canaan*

God had told Abraham that "this is my covenant, which ye shall keep, between me and you and thy seed after thee; Every man child among you shall be circumcised. And ye shall circumcise the flesh of your foreskin; and it shall be a token of the covenant between me and you" (Genesis 17:10–11). This Abraham did "the selfsame day" (verse 23), when every male in his household was circumcised.

Then, when God gave Moses regulations for celebrating the Passover, He reconfirmed that no male could participate in the Passover Feast unless he had been circumcised. However, none of the male children born during the forty years of wandering in the wilderness were circumcised. Joshua, Moses' successor, knowing God's commandment to Moses concerning circumcision and the partaking of the Passover Feast, "made him sharp knives and circumcised the children of Israel at the hill of the foreskins. . . . And it came to pass, when they had done circumcising all the people, that they abode in their places in the camp, till they were whole" (Joshua 5: 3, 8).

On the evening of the fourteenth of Nisan, the Israelites celebrated their first Passover Feast in the Promised Land. The Bible tells us "And they did eat of the old corn of the land on the morrow after the passover, unleavened cakes, and parched corn in the selfsame day. And the manna ceased on the morrow after they had eaten of the old corn of the land; neither had the children of Israel manna any more; but they did eat of the fruit of the land of Canaan that year" (Joshua 5: 11–12). The people celebrated their great national deliverance from Egypt, which was only a foretaste of their ultimate deliverance when Messiah would set up the final kingdom of God.

## 4. *The Discovery of the Book of Law*

Of all the kings that reigned over the divided kingdom of Judah, King Josiah was one of the most righteous. He began to reign when he was only eight years old and "he did that which was right in the sight of the Lord, and walked in the ways of David his father, and declined neither to the right hand, nor to the left. . . . He began to seek after the God of David his father" (2 Chronicles 34:2–3). In the eighteenth year of his reign, he ordered the cleansing and repair of the Temple, which had been neglected over many years by his predecessors.

During the restoration, "Hilkiah the priest found a book of the law of the Lord given by Moses" (verse 14). When the book (scroll) was read to the king, he took it and read it to the people. He was captivated and convicted by the sacred words: "And the king stood in his place, and made a covenant before the Lord, to walk after the Lord, and to keep his commandments, and his testimonies, and his statutes, with all his heart, and with all his soul, to perform the words of the covenant which are written in this book" (verse 31). One of the first things that Josiah did in obedience to God was to immediately celebrate the Passover Feast on the fourteenth day of Nisan. This feast was one of the greatest Passover celebrations in history.

### 5. The Dedication of the Second Temple

When the Jewish captives returned to Jerusalem under the decree of the Persian King, Cyrus the Great, in 536 B.C., they found the Temple Mountain ruins. When Nebuchadnezzar's soldiers had invaded the city in 587 B.C., "They burnt the house of God, and brake down the wall of Jerusalem, and burnt all the palaces thereof with fire, and destroyed all the goodly vessels thereof" (2 Chronicles 36:19).

In 520 B.C., the Israelites began to rebuild the Temple, despite great opposition from the Samaritans who had moved into Israel as colonists from Babylon. Finally, after five years of hard work and God's blessing, the Temple was finished in the spring during the month of Adar. On the fourteenth day of Nisan, 515 B.C., the exiles celebrated the Passover by dedicating the rebuilt Temple under the leadership of Ezra and the high priest, Joshua (see Ezra 6:16–19).

### 6. The Last Supper

After Jesus' disciples had sacrificed their Passover Lamb in the Temple, they met in a large upper room, all furnished, to prepare for their private feast. However, this Passover Supper was like no other they had ever celebrated. "And he took bread, and gave thanks, and brake it, and gave unto them, saying, This is my body which is given for you: this do in remembrance of me. Likewise also the cup, after supper, saying, This cup is the new testament in my blood, which is shed for you" (Luke 22:19–20).

In response to the Lord's commandment to "do this in remembrance of me," Christians have been meeting in catacombs, homes, and churches for some two thousand years to celebrate His completed sacrifice on the cross: "Ye do shew the Lord's death till he come" (I Corinthians 11:26). It is interesting to note that, even in this most solemn remembering of His Cross, our faith is focused on the fact that we will commemorate this event only until our resurrected Lord comes to wear His rightful Crown of Glory.

### The Fifteenth Day of Nisan: The Feast of Unleavened Bread

> And on the fifteenth day of the same month is the feast of unleavened bread unto the Lord: seven days ye must eat unleavened bread. In the first day ye shall have an holy convocation: ye shall do no servile work therein. . . . When ye are come into the land which I give unto you, and shall reap the harvest thereof, then ye shall bring a sheaf of the firstfruits of your harvest unto the priest: And he shall wave the sheaf before the Lord, to be accepted for you: on the morrow after the sabbath the priest shall wave it.
>
> (Leviticus 23:6–7, 10–11)

Although the Feast of Unleavened Bread (Hag-HaMatzot) is quite distinct from the Passover Feast, it occurs at the same time and lasts seven days from the fifteenth day of Nisan through the twenty-first. During these seven days, Israel eats bread without leaven (leaven symbolizes sin) in remembrance of the day when, in their haste to escape Egypt, they baked unleavened bread.

During the night of Passover, while the Lord sent the "destroyer" to slay all the first born of Egypt, the children of Israel prepared to leave Egypt in great haste. There was no time for the leaven to cause the dough to rise, so they were forced to carry unleavened bread — matzoh — as their only food. This became a symbol of their slavery that was transformed into their freedom by the miraculous redemptive act of God, known forever as the Exodus.

The matzoh (unleavened bread) reminds Israel of that terrible but hopeful night when Jews ate the sacrificial lamb and unleavened bread in obedience to God's command. After 430 years in Egypt they were faced with either imminent disaster or salvation from the centuries of slavery and bondage in Egypt. The unleavened bread symbolized the purging out of the sins of pagan Egypt.

The apostle Paul was thinking of this unleavened bread when he told the church at Corinth to "purge out therefore the old leaven, that ye may be a new lump, as ye are unleavened. For even Christ our passover is sacrificed for us: Therefore let us keep the feast, not with old leaven, neither with the leaven of malice and wickedness; but with the unleavened bread of sincerity and truth" (1 Corinthians 5: 7–8).

---

**Theme: The Purging Out of the Leaven of Sin**

1. The Exodus journey from the bondage of Egypt began

2. The Crucifixion of Christ, "our Passover Lamb"

3. The final fall of the Jewish resistance at Massada

---

### THE FIFTEENTH DAY NISAN
### THE FEAST OF UNLEAVENED BREAD
*Figure 5*

The Jews in both the Old and New Testament usually treated the first day of Unleavened Bread and the Passover as one, due to their historical connection and proximity. There have been three notable anniversary events that have occurred on the Feast of Unleavened Bread (see figure 5).

*1. The Exodus from Egypt*

> And it came to pass at the end of the four hundred and thirty years, even the selfsame day it came to pass, that all the hosts of the Lord went out from the land of Egypt.
> (Exodus 12:41)

On this day, God brought the children of Israel out of the centuries of bondage in Egypt on the exact day their father Abraham had prophesied it would happen some 430 years earlier. After the conclusion of the ten plagues, the Egyptian Pharaoh finally let the Jewish people go. In Deuteronomy 16:3, the bread eaten during the Feast of Unleavened Bread is called "the bread of affliction; for thou camest forth out of the land of Egypt in haste: that thou mayest remember the day when thou camest forth out of the land of Egypt all the days of thy life."

This unpleasant tasting bread symbolized all the burden and affliction in Egypt. Once Israel was free, this bread served as a reminder of the leaven and sinfulness of pagan Egypt that they had left behind, as well as the freedom they now enjoyed. The transformation of a symbol of bondage into one of freedom is paralleled for Christians in the transformation of the Cross from a tragic symbol of death into the glorious reminder of Christ's victorious resurrection over death and the grave.

2. *The Crucifixion of Christ, "Our Passover Lamb"*

Jesus described Himself by saying, "I am the bread of life" (John 6:35). Much of His life and ministry centered around the image of bread. Even Bethlehem, where He was born, means the "house of bread" in Hebrew. One time, when Jesus was talking to His disciples, He said: "The hour is come, that the Son of man should be glorified. Verily, verily, I say unto you, Except a corn of wheat fall into the ground and die, it abideth alone: but if it die, it bringeth forth much fruit. . . . Now is my soul troubled, and what shall I say? Father, save me from this hour: but for this cause came I unto this hour. Father, glorify thy name. Then came there a voice from heaven, saying, I have both glorified it, and will glorify it again" (John 12: 23–24, 27–28).

Christ, the kernel of wheat (the basis for bread) did indeed have to die and be buried in a tomb on the Feast of Unleavened Bread, the fifteenth day of Nisan. He rose on the Feast of Firstfruits to become "the firstfruits" of our resurrection.

3. *The Final Fall of the Jewish Resistance at Massada*

For two years following the destruction of Jerusalem and the Temple in A.D. 70, the remaining Jewish resistance, under the command of Eleazar, retreated to the southern mountain fortress of Massada. This impregnable fortress, built by King Herod, sits on a mountain top overlooking the Dead Sea. It could only be approached by a narrow "snakepath" that wound its way up the steep cliffs. A small group of Jewish soldiers bravely held off the

Roman legions for almost two years. Finally, the Roman general Silva built a huge earthen ramp up the western side of the mountain to enable his battering rams to break through. When the ramp was completed, the Jewish defenders knew that the war was lost. By early morning the Roman soldiers would overcome the 960 men, women, and children — the last remnant of a free Israel. The Jewish defenders knew, from grim experience, that their fate at the hands of the Roman soldiers included rape, torture, and death for every last one of them. Rather then submit their wives and children to the cruelties of Roman victory, they decided to take their own lives and die as free men.

On my recent trip to Massada, I stood in the ruins of the actual room where the Jews had chosen by lot those who would mercifully end the lives of the men, after each man had ended the life of his family. Several years ago, archeologists discovered in the floor of this room the pottery shards upon which the names of the men were written for the lots to be drawn. When the Romans stormed through the gates in the morning, they were stunned to find that they had been robbed of their slaughter. The Jewish historian, Flavius Josephus, in his *War of the Jews,* (bk. 5, chap. 9, sec. 1), records, "They came within the palace, and so met with the multitude of the slain, . . . nor could they do other than wonder at the courage of their resolution, and at the immovable contempt of death which so great a number of them had shown, when they went through such an action as that was." He states, "This calamitous slaughter was made on the fifteenth day of the month Nisan" (the Feast of Unleavened Bread).

### The Seventeenth Day of Nisan: The Feast of Firstfruits

The third of the seven feasts is celebrated on the seventeenth day of Nisan, the Feast of Firstfruits. This was the time for the harvesting of the early crops of spring. The feast celebrated Israel's acknowledgement that not only the firstfruits were owed to God, but that all they had was from God, a daily gift from His gracious hand. Moses wrote: "The first of the firstfruits of thy land thou shalt bring into the house of the Lord thy God" (Exodus 23:19).

Four historically important anniversary events have happened on the Feast of Firstfruits, the seventeenth day of Nisan (see figure 6).

### 1. *Noah's Ark Rested on Mount Ararat*

After the Flood destroyed all of humanity except for Noah and his family, the ark floated above the endless waters until, by God's mercy, it finally came to rest on the seventeenth day of Nisan on Mount Ararat in modern-day Turkey. These eight survivors of Noah's family witnessed the total destruction of all land animals and mankind due to the enormous sin, perversion, and violence. The Scriptures record: "And God saw that the wickedness of man was great in the earth, and that every imagination of the thoughts of his heart was only evil continually" (Genesis 6:5).

For a year Noah and his family floated upon the flood waters, no doubt wondering if they would ever see land or vegetation again. Imagine their gratitude to God when they felt their great ship rest on solid rock after nearly a year of not knowing when they would walk again upon the earth. The book of Genesis records this date precisely as the seventeenth day of Nisan (Genesis 8:4). One can easily imagine the descendants of Noah celebrating for many generations on this day, the "firstfruits" of their ultimate safe landing on the hills of the earth.

Most ancient nations, including Israel, began their calendar year in the fall (Sept.– Oct.). However, God changed Israel's calendar by rotating it six months so that, from the time of the Exodus, their New Year's Day now began in the spring on the first day of the month of Nisan (Mar.–Apr.). In order to commemorate Israel's miraculous deliverance from the bondage of Egypt in the month of Nisan, God instructed Moses to change their New Year's Day from the former date in the fall of the year to this new date in the first month of the year, Nisan, the month of the Exodus (see Exodus 12:1–2).

Thus, when Genesis 8:4 describes Noah's ark resting on Mount Ararat on the seventeenth day of the ancient calendar's seventh month (Nisan/March), it actually occurred exactly on the same day as the seventeenth day of the post-Exodus calendar's first month (Nisan/March), which ultimately became the holy day of the Feast of Firstfruits.

---

**Theme: Resurrection**

1. Noah's Ark rests on Mount Ararat

2. Israel miraculously crosses over the Red Sea

3. Israel eats the firstfruits of the Promised Land

4. The resurrection of Jesus Christ

---

## THE SEVENTEENTH DAY OF NISAN
## THE FEAST OF FIRSTFRUITS
### Figure 6

### 2. Israel Miraculously Crossed Over the Red Sea

On the night of Passover, when the pharaoh of Egypt was finally forced by God to let Israel leave Egypt, some 600,000 refugee Jewish adults, together with their wives and children, started out toward freedom. When they arrived on the shores of the Red Sea, after camping in the desert, they looked back and saw the dust of the approaching Egyptian army. This fearful sight provoked the first of many complaints to Moses: "Because there were no graves in Egypt, hast thou taken us away to die in the wilderness? Wherefore hast thou dealt thus with us, to carry us forth out of Egypt? Is not this the word that we did tell thee in Egypt, saying, Let us alone, that we may serve the Egyptians? For it had been better for us to serve the Egyptians, than that we should die in the wilderness" (Exodus 14:11–12). Their situation appeared utterly hopeless — the enemy behind them and the seemingly impossible barrier of the Red Sea before them.

As it was for Israel, so it often is for us. After a tremendous struggle and a great victory, we move forward with the assurance that we are in the will of God. Then, just as soon as we think the road ahead will be smooth and straight, we run up against the biggest challenge of all. Yet, "our extremity is God's opportunity."

Ahead of them, to the east, was the impassable Red Sea (which extended much farther to the north at that time); behind them, to the west, was the enormous Egyptian army; and surrounding Moses was a frightened multitude. He turned to the only sure help that exists for any of us. "And Moses said unto the people, Fear ye not, stand still, and see the salvation of the Lord, which he will shew to you today: for the Egyptians whom ye have seen today, ye shall see them again no more for ever. The Lord shall fight for you, and ye shall hold your peace" (Exodus 14: 13–14). Then, before their eyes, God parted the waters of this sea of certain death. The multitude of Israelites crossed over into a new life as a resurrected nation on the Feast of Firstfruits, the seventeenth of Nisan, to become the "firstfruits" of a nation reborn from the bondage of Egypt.

3.  *Israel Eats the Firstfruits of the Promised Land*

> The children of Israel encamped in Gilgal, and kept the passover on the fourteenth day of the month at even in the plains of Jericho. And they did eat of the old corn of the land on the morrow after the passover, unleavened cakes, and parched corn in the selfsame day. And the manna ceased on the morrow after they had eaten of the old corn of the land; neither had the children of Israel manna any more; but they did eat of the fruit of the land of Canaan that year. (Joshua 5:10–12)

Throughout the forty years that Israel wandered in the desert, God provided supernatural food (manna) to feed the mighty growing nation. The Bible records that after forty years in the wilderness they crossed over the Jordan River and ate the Passover Supper on the fourteenth of Nisan. The next day, on the fifteenth day of Nisan, the day after eating the Passover Supper, the Jews ate of the old corn of the land. The next day, the sixteenth day of Nisan, was the last day in which God provided the supernatural manna as food.

Note that the manna ceased on the sixteenth of Nisan, the day after they ate of the old corn of the land. The day following was the seventeenth day of Nisan, the Feast of Firstfruits, and with no more manna available, the people began to eat of the fruit of the land of Canaan that year — the firstfruits of the Promised Land. One can easily imagine their joy at eating the first natural and varied fruits and vegetables after their forty years in the desert since the Exodus began. The Jews still celebrate this Feast of Firstfruits every year at this time.

4.  *Resurrection of Jesus Christ*

As Jesus hung on the cross, Satan, the Romans, the Pharisees, and those who called for His crucifixion only saw His death. Even

His followers who looked at Him saw only defeat and death — the death of a great vision. Yet, as Jesus Himself had said, "Except a corn of wheat fall into the ground and die, it abideth alone: but if it die, it bringeth forth much fruit" (John 12:24). However, when the kernel falls to the ground and takes root, it is soon transformed into new life. It was essential for Jesus to die in order to triumph over death, sin, and Satan.

By far the most significant event that took place on the seventeenth day of Nisan was the resurrection of Jesus Christ, the "firstfruits" of all future resurrections into eternal life. "But now is Christ risen from the dead, and become the firstfruits of them that slept" (1 Corinthians 15:20). Jesus celebrated this Feast of the Firstfruits by first conquering death Himself, then by offering the firstfruits of His resurrection from death when "the graves were opened; and many bodies of the saints which slept arose, and came out of the graves after his resurrection, and went into the holy city, and appeared unto many" (Matthew 27:52–53). Resurrecting many of the Old Testament saints on this Feast of Firstfruits, Christ proved that His power over death was not limited to Himself alone. Other ancient writers, including Clement of Alexandria in his *Stromata*, refer to this miraculous resurrection of the dead, an event which, together with more than five hundred eyewitnesses to the risen Christ, assisted in the rapid spread of the Christian faith (1 Corinthians 15:4–6).

What an impressive way to present to God the "firstfruits" of the harvest. Jesus Christ the firstfruits, then "they also which are fallen asleep in Christ" (verse 18), and finally all believers who are alive at His Second Advent at the Rapture, will be raised in their new resurrection body. "Death is swallowed up in victory" (1 Corinthians 15:54).

## The Sixth Day of Sivan: The Feast of Pentecost

And ye shall count unto you from the morrow after the sabbath, from the day that ye brought the sheaf of the wave offering; seven sabbaths shall be complete. Even unto the morrow after the seventh sabbath shall ye number fifty days; and ye shall offer a new meat offering unto the Lord. . . . And ye shall proclaim on the selfsame day, that it may be an holy convocation unto you: ye shall do no servile work therein: it shall be a statute for ever in all your dwellings throughout your generations.

(Leviticus 23:15–16, 21)

---

**Theme: A New Revelation of God's Will**

1. The giving of the Law to Moses on Mount Sinai

2. The giving of the Holy Spirit to the Church

---

## THE FEAST OF PENTECOST
## THE SIXTH DAY OF SIVAN
### *Figure 7*

The fourth of the seven required feasts of Israel took place exactly fifty days after the Feast of Firstfruits, hence the name Pentecost, "penta" meaning fifty. This feast is very significant to Christians as well as to Jews. Pentecost, or Shavuot to the Jews, celebrated the end of the grain harvest, the summer harvest. It is also known as the Zeman Matan Tortenu, the "giving of the Law" to Israel. The Feast of Pentecost is the second of the three great feasts that all Jewish males were required to celebrate at the Temple in Jerusalem every year.

Two major events took place on the sixth day of Sivan; each event introduced a special time of spiritual stewardship to a specific new revelation of God: the giving of the Ten Commandments and the giving of the Holy Spirit (see figure 7).

### 1. *The Giving of the Ten Commandments*

After leaving Egypt, the Jews journeyed fifty days from the storehouse city of Rameses into the wilderness of Sinai. On the third day of the third month, Sivan, the Israelites arrived at Mount Sinai. Israel waited for three days at the base of Mount Sinai for Moses to return from conversing with God. The Lord told the people, "Be ready against the third day: for the third day the Lord will come down in the sight of all the people upon Mount Sinai" (Exodus 19:11). Although God had chosen Israel by His grace through Abraham, the Lord reconfirmed His covenant 430 years later by the presentation of His Law on the Feast of Pentecost, the sixth of Sivan.

This entire era, from the giving of the Law on Pentecost until Christ, is known as the Dispensation of Law. This period transformed human moral law. It began a new era of spiritual stewardship to the revealed will of God. The Jewish rabbinical teachings confirm that it was on the sixth day of Sivan that Moses received the Ten Commandments on Mt. Sinai. Also, The *Jewish Almanac* records that "historically, it (the sixth day of Sivan, Pentecost) commemorates the revelation on Mount Sinai when God gave the Torah to the children of Israel."

The book, *The Jewish Holidays: A Guide and Commentary*, describes this Feast of Pentecost as follows: "Shavuot (Pentecost, Feast of Weeks) occurs on the sixth day of Sivan. It celebrates the giving of the Torah, God's gift to the Jewish people."[1]

After describing the offerings that the people were to present to God at Pentecost, God told Moses: "And when ye reap the harvest of your land, thou shalt not make clean riddance of the corners of thy field when thou reapest, neither shall thou gather any gleaning of thy harvest: thou shalt leave them unto the poor, and to the stranger: I am the Lord your God" (Leviticus 23:22).

The book of Ruth, which describes Boaz ordering his servants to leave the gleaning of the harvest for Ruth and her mother, is read in synagogues worldwide on the day of Pentecost. This harvest-time story records Ruth's conversion to Judaism: "And Ruth said, Entreat me not to leave thee, or to return from following after thee: for whither thou goest, I will go; and where thou lodgest, I will lodge: thy people shall be my people, and thy God my God" (Ruth 1:16). The book ends with the genealogy of Ruth, showing that King David and, therefore, Jesus Christ, "the son of David," are descended from Ruth and Boaz (see Matthew 1:5–6). An old Jewish tradition claims that King David was born and also died on the Feast of Pentecost.

## 2.  The Giving of the Holy Spirit

Precisely fifty days after the Feast of Firstfruits, the day the Lord Jesus Christ rose from the dead, 120 of His disciples gathered "together in one place" (the Upper Room) to await the promise of Christ. He prophesied that they would be baptized with the Holy Spirit, "But ye shall receive power, after that the Holy Ghost is come upon you: and ye shall be witnesses unto me both in

Jerusalem, and in all Judea, and in Samaria and unto the uttermost part of the earth" (Acts 1:8).

Luke recorded that "when the day of Pentecost was fully come, they were all with one accord in one place" (Acts 2:1). On the sixth day of Sivan the Holy Spirit manifested Himself and "they were all filled with the Holy Ghost, and began to speak with other tongues, as the Spirit gave them utterance" (verse 4). Those ordinary people, His disciples, were transformed on that day into men of extraordinary spiritual power who would challenge their world of abject paganism with a dynamic Christian movement that not even the might of Rome could stop.

Within a few days over three thousand Jews became believers. Reliable reports suggest that despite horrible persecutions, tortures, and massive executions, within seventy years over ten million believers had joined the underground Christian Church throughout the Roman Empire.

It is no coincidence that on the same day of Pentecost in which God appeared to Moses in the wilderness of Sinai and revealed to man a new relationship based upon His sacred Law, He again revealed to man a new relationship based on His gift of the Holy Spirit. The mystical union of God and Israel that occurred on the Feast of Pentecost at the foot of Mount Sinai is mirrored in the union of God's Holy Spirit with Christ's Bride, the Church, on Pentecost, fifty days after Christ rose from the dead.

Enoch, the first prophet and teacher of righteousness, lived in the seventh generation from Adam. He was the first to reveal the prophecy of the coming Messiah who would set up His Kingdom (Jude 14). The Jewish writer H. L. Ginzberg wrote in *The Legends of the Jews* that according to Israel's oral tradition, Enoch was raptured — taken into heaven — on this very day of Pentecost, the sixth day of Sivan. "And Enoch walked with God: and he was not; for God took him" (Genesis 5:24).

**Notes to Chapter 4**

1. Michael Strassfeld, *The Jewish Holidays — A Guide and Commentary* (New York: Harper and Row, 1985), p. 63.

# 5

# *The Fasts of Mourning*

In our ongoing study of biblical anniversaries, there is a series of fast days that also have tremendous significance and demonstrate God's sovereign control over the history of Israel.

> Thus saith the Lord of hosts; The fast of the fourth month, and the fast of the fifth, and the fast of the seventh, and the fast of the tenth, shall be to the house of Judah joy and gladness, and cheerful feasts.          (Zechariah 8:19)

Each of the four fasts mentioned by the prophet Zechariah commemorate some tragic event connected with the destruction of the Temple and the city of Jerusalem when the Babylonian army conquered Israel in successive invasions from 606 B.C. to 587 B.C. The prophet Zechariah promised that, once the Messiah comes to set up His Kingdom, these four tragic fasts will be transformed into feasts of joy and gladness to celebrate the eternal peace and blessings of the messianic age. The fast of the fourth month, Tammuz, occurs on the seventeenth day of Tammuz (July). The fast of the fifth month, Av, occurs on the ninth day of Av (August).

## The Seventeenth Day of Tammuz

The next historically important anniversary, the seventeenth day of Tammuz, occurs in the month of July on our calendar. It is not a feast day but rather a day of fasting and mourning; nevertheless, this day has been significant in God's dealing with Israel.

The seventeenth day of Tammuz begins a three-week period of national mourning leading up to the fast of Tisha Be-av, the ninth day of Av. Three spiritually significant events have happened on the seventeenth day of Tammuz. Each event involved the breaking of a spiritual symbol that signified that God's disfavor had been incurred as a result of national disobedience (see figure 1). A mourning period followed due to the Jewish people's consciousness of their sin and their recognition that God's punishment would follow.

---

**Theme: The Breaking of a Spiritual Symbol of God's Favor**

1. Moses breaks the Tablets of the Law when he sees the idolatry of the golden calf

2. The Babylonian army breaks through the walls of Jerusalem and causes the daily sacrifice to cease

3. The Roman armies' attack on the Temple Mount forces the priests to stop the daily sacrifice

---

*THE SEVENTEENTH DAY OF TAMMUZ*
*THE FAST OF MOURNING*
*(Begins the three weeks of mourning until 9th of Av)*
*Figure 1*

*1. Moses Breaks the Tablets of the Law*

As discussed earlier in this chapter, the Lord gave the Law to Israel on the Feast of Pentecost and revealed Himself to the Jewish people in a dramatic and awesome display of divine power on the sixth day of Sivan. The Bible recounts the event: "Mount Sinai was altogether on a smoke, because the Lord descended upon it in fire: and the smoke thereof ascended as the smoke of a furnace, and the whole mount quaked greatly" (Exodus 19:18). Instead of recognizing God's authority and power, the very opposite occurred.

On the seventh day of Sivan, Moses returned to Mount Sinai to receive the complete Law which he later recorded in the Torah, the first five books of the Bible. He was on the mountain for forty days, time enough for the memory of God's power to fade in the minds of the people and for them to begin to crave the false idols that they had worshiped in Egypt. In Moses' absence, the people rebelled against God and built a golden calf idol to worship, mindless of the profound events taking place on Mount Sinai. Moses had received the Ten Commandments chiseled on stone tablets from the hand of God and was now descending the mountain to bring his people the greatest advance in law and morality since the world began.

As Moses came down to the plain on the seventeenth of Tammuz, he saw the golden calf and the people's lewd pagan dancing. He was filled with righteous anger at their sinful rebellion and their contempt for the God who had miraculously saved them from slavery and death. His anger burned within him and he broke into pieces the sacred Tablets of the Law at the foot of the mountain (Exodus 32:19). This is discussed in great detail in the rabbinical writings, including *Ta'anit* 28b.

Moses called out, "Who is on the Lord's side?" (Exodus 32: 26), and the priestly tribe of Levites rallied to him. The Lord commanded the Levites to destroy the worst of the offenders. More than three thousand died as a result of their stubborn rebellion.

### 2. *The Babylonians Attack on Jerusalem Stopped the Daily Sacrifice*

The second important event to occur on the seventeenth of Tammuz was the ceasing of the daily morning and evening sacrifice (the Korban Tamid). The city of Jerusalem fell after a two-year siege as the army of King Nebuchadnezzar finally broke through the city walls. In an attempt to continue the daily sacrifice during the two-year siege, the Jewish priests lowered a basket of gold coins from the walls of the city each day, and the Babylonian soldiers then put sheep for the sacrifice in the basket as a profitable trade in exchange for the gold.

When the outer walls of Jerusalem fell to the invaders on the seventeenth of Tammuz, the Babylonian soldiers refused to continue the trade because they knew that the whole city would fall to them in a matter of days. Rabbi Yacov Culi records in his commentary, *Meam Lo'ez*, that the priests mourned in despair because, for the first time in more than four hundred years, they could no longer continue the daily sacrifice of lambs as required by God's Law.

This ceasing of the daily sacrifice on the seventeenth of Tammuz marked the beginning of the end for Jerusalem. It clearly symbolized that God's divine protection was being withdrawn from Israel as a result of their continued national sin and rebellion. This day, the seventeenth of Tammuz, became an annual fast of mourning for the Jews. This mourning period lasted twenty-one days and ended on the ninth of Av, the day of Remembrance of the loss of the Temple.

### 3. *The Roman Army's Attack Forced the Stopping of the Daily Sacrifice*

Almost forty years after the crucifixion of Christ, the Roman army besieged Jerusalem to terminate the Jewish War of Independence against the Roman Empire that had begun in A.D. 66. The Romans fought to destroy Israel because the potentially successful rebellion threatened the Roman Empire's hold upon all her captive peoples.

In A.D. 70 General Titus besieged Jerusalem successfully, and famine raged within the city. The Roman army catapults were able to move close enough to the Temple on the seventeenth of Tammuz to continuously catapult large boulders onto the Temple and kill enormous numbers of priests. The writings of Flavius Josephus, the Jewish historian who was an eyewitness to these tragic events, tell us that this cruel bombardment and the resulting internal chaos of the city forced the priests to discontinue the daily sacrifice on the seventeenth of Tammuz, the anniversary of the exact day on which the Babylonian army inflicted the same trauma 656 years earlier. This event totally demoralized the Jewish defenders and demonstrated to them that once more God's protection was departing from the city. The final destruction of Jerusalem and the Temple was imminent.

It is surely significant that on this day, the seventeenth of Tammuz, three important historical events should occur that were each characterized by God permitting the destruction of a religious covenant symbol to reveal that He had turned away from Israel because of their national disobedience. (See Flavius Josephus, *Wars of The Jews*, bk. 6, chap. 2, sec. 1)

*An Intriguing Historical Footnote: The American Declaration of Independence*

One additional anniversary event occurred on the seventeen of Tammuz, July 4, 1776, when the American Declaration of Independence was announced. This broke America's bonds to Britain and opened up a potential home for Jewish refugees who had been fleeing from thousands of years of oppressive religious and racial persecution in Europe and Russia. This day, the seventeenth of Tammuz, finally witnessed an event that portended great favor for both Jews as individuals and, ultimately, for the state of Israel reborn in 1948.

## The Ninth Day of Av: A Fast of Mourning

When ye fasted and mourned in the fifth [Av] and seventh month.                                              (Zechariah 7:5)

This day of fasting, known as Tisha Be-Av, was a day of mourning and remembrance of Israel's loss of their sacred Temple. It is one of the most historically significant anniversaries in the life of their nation and is commemorated by Jews throughout the world as the tragic day when God withdrew His Presence and Israel wept as their precious Temple burned to the ground.

Throughout Israel's history, the ninth of Av (August), has witnessed eight of the greatest disasters (see figure 2) in their nation's history. It has become a day when Jews not only mourn their loss but also look forward to that great day when their Messiah will finally appear to end their centuries of suffering.

This phenomenon of eight major events of the same nature, namely the greatest national disasters in the history of the Jews, all occurring on the very same anniversary date is unprecedented in the history of nations. Tisha Be Av, Israel's fast of mourning on the ninth day of Av, has seen more national disasters than any other date in history. The prophet Zechariah refers to this day, "when ye fasted and mourned in the fifth [Av] and seventh month" (Zechariah 7:5). He goes on to state that when the Messiah and the long-promised Kingdom comes, all of their fasts, including this one, "shall be to the house of Judah joy and gladness, and cheerful feasts" (Zechariah 8:19).

---

**Theme: A Fast of Mourning**

1. The twelve spies return with their report — Israel loses faith and is condemned to die in the wilderness

2. The destruction of Solomon's Temple by the Babylonians in 587 B.C.

3. The destruction of the Second Temple by the Romans in A.D. 70

4. The Roman army plowed Jerusalem with salt in A.D. 71

5. The destruction of Simeon Bar Cochba's army in A.D. 135

6. England expelled all of the Jews in 1290

7. Spain expelled all the Jews in 1492

8. World War I is declared on the ninth of Av, 1914; Russia mobilized for World War I and launched persecutions against the Jews in Eastern Russia

---

THE FAST OF TISHA BE-AV
THE NINTH DAY OF AV
Figure 2

### 1. The Twelve Spies Return with Their Report

Moses sent out the twelve tribal leaders to spy out the Promised Land for forty days prior to entering Canaan. However, due to their unbelief, ten of the twelve spies returned with pessimistic reports about how impossible it would be to conquer the land, even though God had promised them victory. The ancient Jewish commentary, the *Mishna*, records that the people believed the evil report and mourned all night in fear. They turned against Moses and the two faithful spies (Joshua and Caleb) on the ninth day of the month of Av *(Ta'anit* 29a). The mutiny, according to Numbers 14:1–10, led to an attempt to stone Moses and to return to the bondage of Egypt on the ninth of Av, 1490 B.C.

If this rebellion had been successful, this violation of God's covenant with Abraham would have led to the death and assimilation of the Jewish people in Egypt. God destroyed the rebel leaders and told Israel that this sinful rebellion would result in the death of that whole generation while wandering in the wilderness of Sinai for forty years, even as the spies had searched out the land for forty days. This awful rebellion and unbelief in God's promises caused the loss of the Promised Land for this entire generation, save for the two faithful spies, Joshua and Caleb. The Bible records that "Moses told these sayings unto all the children of Israel: and the people mourned greatly" (Numbers 14: 39).

Thus, from this night on, the ninth of Av became a fast of mourning as Israel wept over their lack of obedience to God and the tragedies that followed repeatedly during the next thirty-five centuries.

## 2. *The Destruction of Solomon's Temple by the Babylonians*

The Babylonian army under Nebuchadnezzar besieged Jerusalem in 589 B.C. After a two-year siege, they breached the walls on the seventeenth of Tammuz, as recounted earlier. Twenty-one days later, the Babylonian army broke through the city walls to directly attack the Jews' final defenses on the massive Temple Mount on the ninth of Av, 587 B.C.

According to the Jewish commentary, *Me'am Lo'ez*, by Rabbi Yakov Culi and Rabbi Aguiti, and other historical sources, including *Ta'anit* 29a from the Jerusalem *Talmud*, the Babylonian army fought their way into the Temple on the seventh day of Av. "His men ate, drank and caroused there until the ninth of Av. Toward evening, they set the Temple on fire. It burned all night and through the next day, the tenth day of Av." Jeremiah, who was an eyewitness to the terrible destruction of Jerusalem, records that the Babylonian captain of the guard, Nebuzaradan, conquered the city, captured King Zedekiah, and burned the Temple. With no one attempting to fight the enormous fire, the huge Temple complex burned throughout the next day, the tenth of Av (Jeremiah 52: 5–14).

This tragedy has been commemorated by the Jews ever since the solemn fast, on the ninth of Av, known as Tisha Be Av. For more than two thousand years, on this day, the Jews have read the book of Lamentations in which Jeremiah laments the Babylonian destruction of Jerusalem and the great Temple of Solomon. "The Lord hath cast off His altar, He hath abhorred His sanctuary, He hath given up into the hand of the enemy the walls of the palaces; they have made a noise in the House of the Lord, as in the day of a solemn feast" (Lamentations 2:7; Zechariah 8:9).

## 3. *The Destruction of the Second Temple by the Romans in* A.D. *70*

As mentioned earlier, the Romans had been at war with the Jews since A.D. 66, and finally were about to crush the revolt by destroying their capital, Jerusalem, in A.D. 70. Over 1,250,000 people were surrounded inside the city by the encircling Roman legions. The original attack had occurred on the Feast of Passover when a huge number of pilgrims came to Jerusalem to celebrate the Passover and were thereby trapped.

The daily sacrifice in the Temple had ceased on the seventeenth of Tammuz and now, twenty-one days later, on the ninth day of the month of Av, the Roman army reached the edge of the Temple compound. The Roman general, Titus, gave strict orders that the beautiful Temple, the greatest building in the Roman Empire, should not be destroyed. He implored the Jewish defenders to surrender on terms that would have preserved their city and their beloved Temple. However, the judgment of God had been delivered almost forty years earlier by Jesus Christ, and this terrible appointment with destiny could not be avoided (Luke 19:41–44). The Jewish rebel leaders rejected the offers of General Titus, and the final pitched battle for the Temple Mount began.

Despite his firm orders to the Roman centurions, the enraged soldiers threw torches into the Temple and, within minutes, the Holy Place became an inferno. An eyewitness, Flavius Josephus, reported that General Titus stood in the great entrance to the Holy Place and beat back his soldiers with his sword in a vain attempt to save at least the Inner Temple from their act of destruction. It is also reported that when Titus saw that the flames had reached the inner sanctuary, he fell to his knees and cried out, "As God is my witness, this was not done by my order."

Neither General Titus nor his soldiers realized that they were unconsciously fulfilling two very specific scriptural prophecies. First, the prophet Daniel, more than six hundred years earlier, had predicted in his great prophecy of the Seventy Weeks, that "after threescore and two weeks shall Messiah be cut off, but not for himself: and the people of the prince that shall come shall destroy the city and the sanctuary; and the end thereof shall be with a flood, and unto the end of the war desolations are determined" (Daniel 9:26).

This strange phrase reveals two facts: (1) the people (the

Roman soldiers), would be responsible for the destruction, not their leader, "the prince"; and (2) "the prince that shall come" refers to the "prince" of the Roman Empire. When General Titus initially began the Jewish War, he was not of royal blood. However, his father, the General Vespasian (once a commoner), became emperor in A.D. 69. When the final siege was undertaken in A.D. 70, Titus, Vespasian's son, had become the "prince" and thus perfectly fulfilled the ancient prophecy.

A future and final fulfillment of this prophecy will see the Antichrist and his revived Roman Empire again attack the city of Jerusalem and the rebuilt Temple during the last days.

The second major prophecy regarding the destruction of the Temple was given by Jesus Christ in Luke 19:41–44. After the Pharisees had told Jesus to restrain His disciples from their joyful praise of God, "He answered and said unto them, I tell you that, if these should hold their peace, the stones would immediately cry out" (Luke 19:40). As the crowd drew near to Jerusalem, Jesus looked at the city and its Temple and wept over it.

He said, "For the days shall come upon thee, that shine enemies shall cast a trench about thee, and compass thee round, and keep thee in on every side, and shall lay thee even with the ground, and thy children within thee; and they shall not leave in thee one stone upon another; because thou knewest not the time of thy visitation" (verses 43–44).

This prophecy was fulfilled to the smallest detail in A.D. 70. As the Romans burned the Temple, the tremendous heat of the fire melted the sheets of gold that covered much of the Temple building. The molten gold ran down into every crack between the foundation stones. When the fire finally died down, the Roman soldiers used wedges and crowbars to overturn every stone to search for this gold, thus fulfilling Christ's words.

### 4. The Romans Plowed Jerusalem and the Temple A.D. 71

In A.D. 71, one year after the destruction of the city of Jerusalem and the burning of the Temple, on the ninth of Av, the Roman army plowed the Temple Mount and the city. This was a complete fulfillment of the prophecy of Micah: "Therefore shall Zion for your sakes be plowed as a field, and Jerusalem shall become heaps, and the mountain of the house as the high places of the forest" (Micah 3:12). A rabbinical source, *Ta'anit* 26b, records that this was done to turn the city into a Roman colony.

### 5.   *The Destruction of Bar Kochba's Army* A.D. 135

After the fall of Jerusalem in A.D. 70, there was a period of enforced peace. In Matthew 24, Jesus spoke about Daniel's prophecy of the destruction of the Temple. Then He said, "If any man shall say unto you, Lo, here is Christ, or there; believe it not. For there shall arise false Christs, and false prophets, and shall shew great signs and wonders; insomuch that, if it were possible, they shall deceive the very elect" (Matthew 24: 23–24).

Among those false prophets was a dynamic Jewish leader named Simon Bar Kochba. As Jesus had predicted, many people, including the famous Jewish scholar Rabbi Akiba, proclaimed Simon Bar Kochba as the Messiah. Jesus prophesied before His rejection, "I am come in my Father's name, and ye receive me not; if another shall come in his own name, him ye will receive" (John 5:43). How sad that after rejecting the true Messiah they would now accept a counterfeit.

For two years Simon Bar Kochba and his followers succeeded in defeating the Romans. Finally, Emperor Hadrian and his enormous Roman army attacked and destroyed the Jewish rebels at Beitar, southwest of Jerusalem. On that tragic ninth of Av, A.D. 135, the last great army of an independent Israel was slaughtered without mercy.

Dio Cassius, the Roman historian, says that 580,000 Jewish soldiers fell by the sword alone, not counting those who fell by fire and famine. The horses of the Romans, he says, were wading in blood up to their girths in the mud and mire of the valley battleground. Sixty-five years to the day after the city of Jerusalem and the Temple were destroyed, in A.D. 70 this final rebellion against Rome ended in tragedy for the Jews with the destruction of Israel's army in A.D. 135.

The prophet Isaiah may have referred to this event when he prophesied, "Within sixty-five years Ephraim [Israel] will be too shattered to be a people" (Isaiah 7:8 NIV). In 721 B.C., sixty-five years after Isaiah spoke these words, the Assyrian exile of the northern tribes of Israel fulfilled Isaiah's prophecy. However, it would appear that Isaiah may also have been alluding to the final shattering of the people of Israel in 135 A.D., which also occurred on the sixty-fifth anniversary of the burning of the Temple, the ninth of Av.

### 6. England Expelled All Jews in 1290

On July 18, 1290, the ninth of Av, King Edward I ordered the expulsion of all Jews from England. Almost four hundred years later, Oliver Cromwell, Lord Protector of England, granted the Jews the legal right of settlement in 1657. It is interesting to note that the British Empire's prosperity and world power can be traced to the reign of Lord Cromwell. The Jews returned and prospered in England and all her colonies. The history of England's rise and fall can be traced to this ancient prophecy in the book of Genesis. "And I will bless them that bless thee, and curse him that curseth thee: and in thee shall all the families of the earth be blessed" (Genesis 12:3).

On November 2, 1917, Lord Balfour gave his historic declaration endorsing the setting up of a national homeland for the Jews. This was partly in response to the tremendous scientific contribution in producing explosives to aid England's war effort made by Chaim Weizmann, who later became Israel's first president. At the end of World War I, a victorious England held power through its British Empire over one-quarter of the world. Tragically, at the same time, Lawrence of Arabia was promising the Arabs that England would give them the lands that were occupied by the Turkish Empire in return for their help in defeating Germany and Turkey in the war. However, in these intense negotiations, the territory of Israel itself was never demanded by the Arabs. The reason for this lack of interest is that few Arabs lived in this barren and empty land. Ultimately, the Arabs received five hundred times as much territory as Israel, over five million square miles of land which now comprise twenty-one countries. Meanwhile the Jews received only eight thousand square miles of land in a strip alone the Mediterranean Sea (less than one-fifth of 1 percent of what the Arabs received).

In the 1920s and throughout the period until 1948, England repeatedly reversed its promises to the League of Nations and failed to provide a national homeland for the Jews. Israel ultimately received only 17.5 percent of the territory promised her by the Balfour Declaration and the League of Nations British Mandate. Britain stopped Jewish immigration to Palestine throughout the period, a factor that contributed tragically to the magnitude of the Holocaust because the Jews of Europe had no homeland to flee to when the savage persecution of Adolf Hitler began. The six million who died in the death camps may have been able to flee to Palestine had the British not broken their word and stopped Jewish immigration to Palestine.

It is not improbable that the decline of Britain from its exalted status as the preeminent superpower that "ruled the seas" to its diminished position as a second-level power is connected to her abandonment of the Jews and their national homeland. In this same period, 1917–1948, England lost her vast empire, one-quarter of the globe, and even lost the southern part of Ireland. Over four thousand years ago, God gave us insight into the history of the rise and fall of nations and His intervention in history: "I will bless them that bless thee, and curse him that curseth thee." (Genesis 12:3)

### 7. Spain Expelled All Jews in 1492

On August 2, 1492, the ninth of Av, the Spanish government ordered the expulsion of some 800,000 Jews. This event marked a watershed in the rise of the Spanish Empire. From this point on, the empire's fortunes began to decrease, possibly another fulfillment of God's promise to Abraham that "I will bless them that bless thee, and curse him that curseth thee" (Genesis 12:3).

It is interesting to note that the ninth of Av, 1492, was the very same day that Christopher Columbus left Spain to discover the New World. This pivotal event was of tremendous importance to the Jews because America ultimately provided a place of refuge for the Jewish people. In addition, there is some evidence to suggest that Columbus may have been of Jewish ancestry and that the ninth of Av, 1492, was therefore a propitious day for him to leave Spain. When the new nation of Israel was reborn in 1948, the United States of America became Israel's strongest protector and supporter.

### 8. Russia Mobilized for WW I and Launched Persecutions against the Jews

On the ninth of Av, August 1, 1914, as the Jews fasted and mourned, World War I was declared by Russia and Germany. This war involved the greatest military struggle in history to this point as "nation shall rise against nation and kingdom against kingdom" (Matthew 24:7). The mobilization of Russia's army triggered persecutions and attacks against the Jews in eastern Russia, killing tens of thousands and forcing many to emigrate to the Holy Land. These Russian and eastern European Jewish immigrants joined the native-born Jewish "Sabras" in building the agricultural settlements and infrastructure of the embryonic state. This immigration helped set the stage for the dramatic events leading to the creation of Israel in 1948.

As mentioned earlier, the phenomenon of eight major historical disasters affecting one nation over thirty-five centuries happening on the same anniversary day is totally unprecedented in human history. As a student of history for the last twenty years, I can assure you that no other nation has experienced any such pattern of historical anniversaries or "coincidences."

In fact, if any of my readers are mathematically inclined, I would suggest that they check the probability that these eight historical tragedies could have occurred by chance rather than by God's foreknowledge and sovereignty (see figure 2). Because there are 365 days in a year, the chance that even a second significant historical tragedy could occur by chance alone on the anniversary date of a previous tragedy on a given day, say, the ninth day of Av (August), is one chance in 365. The odds against a third similar event occurring on the exact same day, the ninth day of Av, is $1 \times 365 \times 365 = 133{,}225$.

In other words, the odds against even three of these national disasters occurring by chance alone on a particular anniversary day, such as the ninth day of Av, is only

one chance in 133,225.

This is why the historical records of the nations throughout human history do not reveal any other nation, except for Israel, that has sustained repeated victories or defeats on particular anniversary dates of the calendar.

The odds that all eight disastrous events for Israel would occur by chance alone on the ninth day of Av, rather than by God's design, can be calculated as follows:

$$1 \times 365 \times 365 \times 365 \times 365 \times 365 \times 365 \times 365 \times 365 =$$
one chance in 863,078,009,300,000,000

or

1 chance in 863 million times a billion!

It is important to remember that the above probability analysis only considers eight of Israel's anniversary events, only those which occurred on the ninth day of the biblical month of Av.

In all, there are more than forty major anniversary events which have occurred throughout Israel's history that we are examining in this book. If we were to add these additional dates to our probability figures, the numbers would be so astronomically high that no rational person could conclude that these events have happened on their respective dates by chance alone.

The consideration of these facts will lead many to believe, along with this author, that the only rational explanation for this phenomenon is that God has had His hand upon the Jews and Israel. Furthermore, this evidence provides strong proof that the Bible, which reveals these staggering, historically verified events, is truly the inspired Word of God.

# 6

# *Feast of Trumpets, Day of Atonement, and Feast of Tabernacles*

And the Lord spake unto Moses, saying, Speak unto the children of Israel, saying, In the seventh month, in the first day of the month, shall ye have a sabbath, a memorial of blowing of trumpets, an holy convocation.

(Leviticus 23:23–24)

Of the seven "holy convocations" or appointed "Feasts of the Lord" mentioned in Leviticus 23, it is fascinating to note that four of them have had a prophetic fulfillment in the major events in the life of Jesus Christ:

1. The Passover Supper, the fourteenth of Nisan — the Last Supper
2. The Feast of Unleavened Bread, the fifteenth of Nisan — the Crucifixion
3. The Feast of Firstfruits, the seventeenth of Nisan — the Resurrection
4. The Feast of Pentecost, the sixth of Sivan — the giving of the Holy Spirit

There are still three appointed feasts to consider. Some scholars believe that the final three festivals — the Feast of Trumpets, the Day of Atonement, and the Feast of Tabernacles — will be fulfilled at the climactic Battle of Armageddon and the ushering in of the Millennium.

## The Feast of Trumpets (The First Day of Tishri)

The Feast of Trumpets occurs on the first of Tishri, in the fall (Sept.–Oct.). As soon as the new moon was sighted in eastern Israel, the watchers would trumpet the signal from hill to hill until the signal finally reached the Temple. Then the high priest would blow the ram's horn (the shofar) and announce the beginning of the new year.

Rosh Ha'Shanah, the ancient New Year's Day for Israel as well as for most middle eastern cultures, is celebrated on the first day of Tishri. Jewish tradition reveals its fourfold meaning: (1) New Year's Day, (2) the Day of Remembrance, (3) the Day of Judgment, (4) the day of blowing the shofar (the ram's horn).

On this day the synagogue lesson of Isaiah 60–61 teaches of that long-awaited day when the Lord will be revealed as King and accepted as the ruler of the world. Two spiritually important events have already occurred on the anniversary of the Feast of Trumpets. One remains to be fulfilled in our future (see figure 1).

---

**Theme: A Day of New Beginnings**

1. Joshua brought the first offering to the rebuilt altar

2. Ezra read the Law to the returned exiles to affirm the Covenant

3. The possible anniversary date for the Battle of Armageddon

---

*THE FEAST OF TRUMPETS*
*THE FIRST DAY OF TISHRI*
*ROSH HA'SHANAH — THE ANCIENT NEW YEAR'S DAY*
*Figure 1*

1. *Joshua Brought the First Offering to the New Altar*

When King Cyrus of Persia decreed in 536 B.C. that the Jewish exiles could return to Jerusalem to rebuild the Temple, he sent with them fifty-four hundred articles of gold and silver that had been taken from the Temple when the Jews were captured and exiled. More than forty-two thousand people settled in towns around Jerusalem. The first thing the leaders of the people did was rebuild the altar of God (Ezra 3:1–6).

Even before the foundation of the Temple was built, the priests began to offer burnt offerings to the Lord on the first day of Tishri. The high priest, Joshua (*Jeshua* in Hebrew), presented this offering on the rebuilt altar. The name Joshua is "Jesus" in the Greek language. Therefore, Joshua has been seen as a type of Christ, our great High Priest.

## 2. Ezra Read the Law to the Returned Exiles

The rebuilding of the Temple was completed, before the people were able to rebuild the walls of the city to keep out invaders.

> And Ezra the priest brought the law before the congregation both of men and women, and all that could hear with understanding, upon the first day of the seventh month. And he read therein before the street that was before the water gate from the morning until midday, before the men and the women, and those that could understand; and the ears of all the people were attentive unto the book of the law. (Nehemiah 8: 2–3)

This day, the Feast of Trumpets, marked a new beginning for Israel as they accepted God's Covenant once again.

## 3. The Possible Day for the Battle of Armageddon

The prophet Joel seems to connect the great Day of the Lord — the Battle of Armageddon — with this day, the Feast of Trumpets. Consider the prophecy of Joel:

> Sanctify ye a fast, call a solemn assembly, gather the elders and all the inhabitants of the land into the house of the Lord your God, and cry unto the Lord, Alas for the day! for the day of the Lord is at hand, and as a destruction from the Almighty shall it come. (Joel 1:14–15)

> Blow ye the trumpet in Zion, and sound an alarm in my holy mountain: let all the inhabitants of the land tremble: for the day of the Lord cometh, for it is nigh at hand. (Joel 2:1–2)

The prophet Jeremiah may also be referring to Armageddon and the Feast of Trumpets when he says,

> Declare ye in Judah, and publish in Jerusalem; and say, Blow ye the trumpet in the land: cry, gather together, and say, Assemble yourselves, and let us go into the defenced cities, Set up the standard toward Zion: retire, stay not: for I will bring evil from the north, and a great destruction.
>
> (Jeremiah 4:5–6)

Time alone will prove whether this interpretation is correct and whether or not the Battle of Armageddon will begin on Rosh Ha'Shanah, the Feast of Trumpets. However, one additional fact supports this interpretation. Both Daniel (9:27) and the book of Revelation (12:6) confirm that the period of the Great Tribulation commences with the Antichrist profaning the rebuilt Temple and concludes exactly 1260 days later with the destruction of Antichrist at the Battle of Armageddon by Jesus Christ, at His Second Coming.

In his attempt to deceive Israel about his messiahship, it is possible that the Antichrist will enter the Temple and be killed and raised from the dead by Satan on Passover in order to "fulfill" the prophecies and prove his claims (Revelation 13:2–8,14). It is remarkable that there are exactly 1260 days between Passover and the Feast of Trumpets, three and a half years later.

The ancient oral tradition of Israel suggests several other notable events that occurred on the first day of Tishri (Rosh Ha'Shanah): Adam and Eve were created (see *Sanhedrin* 38b); Adam and Eve were expelled from the Garden of Eden; the waters from the flood were dried up and Noah removed the covering from the ark (see Genesis 8:13); Sarah, Rachel, and Hannah all prayed and had their prayers answered on the first day of Tishri (*Yevamot* 64b); and Joseph was released after spending sixteen years in an Egyptian prison (*Rosh Ha'Shanah* 10b).

Two more "appointed feasts" are yet to be fulfilled: The Day of Atonement and the Feast of Tabernacles.

### The Day of Atonement (The Tenth Day of Tishri)

> And the Lord spake unto Moses, saying, Also on the tenth day of this seventh month there shall be a day of atonement: it shall be an holy convocation unto you; and ye shall afflict your souls, and offer an offering made by fire

unto the Lord. And we shall do no work in that same day: for it is a day of atonement, to make an atonement for you before the Lord your God. (Leviticus 23:26–32)

The prophetic fulfillment of the final two "appointed feasts," the Day of Atonement and the Feast of Tabernacles, may also occur during the events leading up to the Millennium when Christ returns in glory to set up His Kingdom.

## The Day of Atonement — Yom Kippur

Yom Kippur, the Day of Atonement, is the holiest day in the Jewish calendar. It is the day when all Israel mourns for their sins. On this day, the tenth day of Tishri, and only on this day (see Hebrews 9:7), the high priest entered the Most Holy of Holies in the Temple, the place where the Shekinah glory dwelt. He dressed in special clothing, a "sacred linen tunic," entered the Holy of Holies with the blood from the sacrificial animals, and sprinkled the blood before the mercy seat. For twenty-four hours the people ceased their work and spent the entire time confessing the sins that they had committed during the past year.

The writer of the book of Hebrews describes Christ as our great High Priest who "neither by the blood of goats and calves, but by his own blood he entered in once into the holy place, having obtained eternal redemption for us. . . . How much more shall the blood of Christ, who through the eternal Spirit offered himself without spot to God, purge your conscience from dead works to serve the living God?" (Hebrews 9:12,14).

The Day of Atonement was to be observed every year. However, every fiftieth year this day commenced the Year of Jubilee. Leviticus 25 describes this celebration: "Then shalt thou cause the trumpet of the jubilee to sound on the tenth day of the seventh month, in the day of atonement shall ye make the trumpet sound throughout all your land. And ye shall hallow the fiftieth year, and proclaim liberty throughout all the land unto all the inhabitants thereof: it shall be a jubilee unto you; and ye shall return every man unto his possession, and ye shall return every man unto his family" (Leviticus 25:9–10).

In this Year of Jubilee, on the Day of Atonement, all debts were cancelled, slaves were set free, and family lands that had been sold would be returned to their original owners. This was a year of celebration and renewal. Modern Jews refer to the Day of Atonement as Yom Kippur. The word "Kippur" comes from the Hebrew word *kapper*, which means "to cover over." God covers over the sins of His people through the blood of the sacrifice. When Christ was crucified, His blood "covered over" our sins so that now when God looks at a repentant sinner, He no longer sees the sin; rather, He sees the blood of His righteous Son. We have miraculously become righteous before our God because of the price that Jesus Christ paid when He died upon the cross. "For he hath made him to be sin for us, who knew no sin; that we might be made the righteousness of God in him" (2 Corinthians 5:21).

The blood sprinkled in the Holy of Holies on the Day of Atonement prefigured the ultimate sacrifice, God's only begotten Son, whose death paid to atone for your sins and mine forever.

The Talmud of the Jews states, "There is no atonement except with blood" (*Yoma* 5a). Hebrews 9:22 says, "Without shedding of blood is no remission." As the first and only sinless man, Jesus was the only person in history who did not deserve the judgment of eternal separation from God that the Bible calls hell. Thus, as a perfect sacrifice, He could stand in our place and pay the price of physical and spiritual death that each one of us deserves for our sinful rebellion. Then, by His triumph over death and hell, He won for us that righteousness that allows us to enter heaven.

Two historically important events have already occurred on the tenth day of Tishri, and one future event will possibly transpire on this date (see figure 2).

1. *Aaron, the High Priest, Made the First Atonement in the Wilderness*

On the tenth day of Tishri, in the wilderness, Aaron sacrificed for the sins of his people. This, of course, was the first time God commanded the sacrifice. This first Day of Atonement is recorded during the Exodus in Leviticus 16:1–28.

2. *Israel Saved from Annihilation in the 1973 Yom Kippur War*

On Yom Kippur, the tenth day of Tishri, the holiest day of the Jewish year, Arab armies attacked Israel without warning. More than one hundred thousand Egyptian soldiers invaded Sinai against some three thousand Jewish defenders of the Bar Lev line of defense on the Suez Canal. In a miracle as great as any in Bible times, the enemies of Israel paused to regroup at a point when they could easily have overrun the Jewish state. God intervened in this war of Yom Kippur, and Israel turned the tide of battle to win against Syria and Egypt.

---

**Theme: Mourning and Atonement for Sin**

1. Aaron, the first high priest, made atonement for Israel

2. Israel was saved from annihilation when the Arabs overran their defenses in the Yom Kippur War, October 1973

3. The possible date when Israel will mourn as they see their Messiah, whom they have pierced

---

### THE TENTH DAY OF TISHRI
### THE DAY OF ATONEMENT
### Figure 2

3. *Israel Will Mourn When They See Their Messiah, Whom They Have Pierced*

The prophet Zechariah, after describing the Battle of Armageddon, goes on to describe a supernatural outflowing of grace to the Jewish remnant several days after their Messiah defends them at the Battle of Armageddon (which will occur possibly on the first of Tishri):

> And I will pour upon the house of David, and upon the inhabitants of Jerusalem, the spirit of grace and of supplications: and they shall look upon me whom they have pierced, and they shall mourn for him, as one mourneth for his only son, and shall be in bitterness for him, as one that is in bitterness for his firstborn. In that day shall there be a great mourning in Jerusalem, as the mourning of Hadadrimmon in the valley of Megiddon.
> (Zechariah 12:10–11)

> In that day there shall be a fountain opened to the house of David and to the inhabitants of Jerusalem for sin and for uncleanness. (Zechariah 13:1)

It is probable that this final reconciliation will take place on the tenth day of Tishri, the appointed Day of Atonement. On this day,

Israel's rejected Messiah will finally be accepted by the nation He chose.

The prophet Ezekiel tells of a great day of restoration for Israel: "A new heart also will I give you, and a new spirit will I put within you: and I will take away the stony heart out of your flesh, and I will give you an heart of flesh. . . . Thus saith the Lord God; In the day that I shall have cleansed you from all your iniquities I will also cause you to dwell in the cities, and the wastes shall be builded" (Ezekiel 36:26, 33).

Paul prophesied of Israel's greatest Day of Atonement when he declared, "And it shall come to pass, that in the place where it was said unto them, Ye are not my people; there shall they be called the children of the living God" (Romans 9:26).

### The Feast of Tabernacles (The Fifteenth Day of Tishri)

And the Lord spake unto Moses, saying, Speak unto the children of Israel, saying, The fifteenth day of this seventh month shall be the feast of tabernacles for seven days unto the lord. . . . Ye shall dwell in booths seven days; all that are Israelites born shall dwell in booths: that your generations may know that I made the children of Israel to dwell in booths, when I brought them out of the land of Egypt: I am the Lord your God.　　　　(Leviticus 23:33–34, 42–43)

The Feast of Tabernacles was the third of the three annual feasts that all Jewish men were required to attend in Jerusalem each year. This feast, known as Sukkot, was instituted by God in the wilderness of Sinai. It begins on the fifteenth day of Tishri, five days after the solemn Day of Atonement. It is sometimes referred to as the great "Harvest Home" because it occurred at the end of the fruit harvest (Sept.–Oct.).

During this feast of seven days, the people were to live in booths — temporary dwellings made of branches — to commemorate their dwelling in tents for forty years in the wilderness. It is noteworthy that on each of the seven days, they were to offer fourteen lambs without blemish (Numbers 29:15, 32). There is an interesting parallel in the Gospel of Matthew where Matthew lists the genealogy of Jesus, the Lamb of God. The generations from Abraham to David are fourteen, from David to the Babylonian captivity are fourteen, and from the captivity to Christ are fourteen.

Although there is no clear, scriptural proof of the exact date of the birth of Christ, John's gospel uses the unusual word "tabernacled" to describe the birth of Christ, suggesting, perhaps, that the day He was born was in fact the Feast of Tabernacles: "The Word was made flesh, and dwelt [*tabernacled* in the Greek] among us" (John 1:14).

Christ's age of thirty-three and one-half years at His death on the Feast of Passover, as evidenced by the historical data in appendix B, would correspond precisely to this birth date of the fifteenth day of Tishri, the Feast of Tabernacles. Considering the phenomenon that over forty major events in Israel's spiritual history have occurred on the anniversary dates of biblical feast days or fast days, it is more than probable that the birth of our Lord Jesus Christ also followed this pattern and occurred on the anniversary of the Feast of Tabernacles. If this supposition is correct, then each major event in the life of our Lord followed one of the three main feast days when it was required that all male Jews go to the Jerusalem Temple to worship the Lord. Jesus would have been born on the Feast of Tabernacles (the fifteenth of Tishri), would have been crucified on the Feast of Passover (the fifteenth of Nisan), and would have sent forth His promised Comforter, the Holy Spirit, to baptize His church with power on the Feast of Pentecost (the sixth of Sivan).

It is a well-attested phenomenon reported by many Christian scholars, including Donald Guthrie in his *New Testament Introduction* (p. 282), that the gospel of John is arranged to illustrate the life of Christ in the sequence of the Jewish liturgical seasons and feast days. The *Introduction to Saint John* in the authoritative *Jerusalem Bible* (p. 141) states, "Moreover, this gospel is far more interested than the Synoptics [Matthew, Mark, and Luke] in worship and sacraments. It relates the life of Jesus to the Jewish liturgical year, and associates his miracles with the principal feasts: the Temple is often given as the setting both for them and for Christ's discourses." Regarding the analysis and division of John it states, "In the first place there is no doubt that he attaches special importance to the Jewish liturgical feasts which he uses to punctuate his narrative. These are: three feasts of Passover, 2:13, 6:4, 11:55, etc. . . . Secondly, the evangelist on several occasions very deliberately calculates the number of days with a view to divide the life of Christ into set periods." Finally it states, "This division suggests that Christ not only fulfilled the Jewish liturgy but by doing so brought it to an end" (p. 142).

R. H. Lightfoot in his *St. John's Gospel: A Commentary* also describes this gospel's focus on this phenomenon: "Finally, each of the sections is connected, more or less closely, with a festival of the Jewish sacred year. From the first it was a recognized part of the tradition that the Lord's death had taken place at Passover time, and in thus spreading the incidents of the Jewish feasts throughout the ministry, St. John . . . Invites the reader to see the Lord's whole work in close connection with the Jewish festival, especially the Passover. . . . In St. John's view all these festivals in different ways have pointed forward to the coming of the Lord, and in that coming they have now been fulfilled" (p. 20).

There are two notable historical anniversary events connected with the Feast of Tabernacles and one possible future fulfillment (see figure 3).

### 1.   *The Dedication of Solomon's Temple on the Feast of Tabernacles*

The dedication took place on the fifteenth day of Tishri, the Feast of Tabernacles, 1005 B.C. Second Chronicles records that, on this day, "Solomon assembled the elders of Israel, and all the heads of the tribes, the chief of the fathers of the children of Israel, unto Jerusalem, to bring up the ark of the covenant of the Lord out of the city of David which is Zion. Wherefore all the men of Israel assembled themselves unto the king in the feast which was in the seventh month" (2 Chronicles 5:2–3).

As they begin to praise God, "having cymbals and psalteries and harps, stood at the east end of the altar, and with them an hundred and twenty priests sounding with trumpets: . . . For He is good; for his mercy endureth for ever: that then the house was filled with a cloud, even the house of the Lord; So that the priests could not stand to minister by reason of the cloud: for the glory of the Lord had filled the house of God" (2 Chronicles 5:12-14).

"Then Solomon assembled the elders of Israel . . . that they might bring up the Ark of the Covenant of the Lord out of the city of David, which is Zion. And all the men of Israel assembled themselves unto king Solomon at the feast in the month Ethanim [Tishri], which is the seventh month" (I Kings 8:1–2).

## 2. *The Possible Birthday of Jesus Christ*

As described previously, the evidence from John 1:14 indicates that Jesus was born on the Feast of Tabernacles in the fall of the year, rather than the traditional date of December 25th. If this is correct, then the normal period of pregnancy would mean that Mary conceived Jesus forty weeks earlier, precisely on December 25th. This curious fact may account for the early Church's acceptance of the date of December 25th and the transformation of the existing Roman holiday into a Christmas celebration of Christ's incarnation.

---

**Theme: The Coming of the Presence of God**

1. The dedication of Solomon's Temple

2. The possible birthday of Jesus Christ

3. The possible ushering in of the kingdom age and the long-awaited Messiah

---

### THE FIFTEENTH DAY OF TISHRI
### THE FEAST OF TABERNACLES
### Figure 3

## 3. *The Beginning of the Kingdom Age — The Millennium*

It is possible that this great Feast of Tabernacles will see its prophetic fulfillment in that glorious day when the Lord of hosts will usher in the long-awaited Millennium of peace.

> And the Lord shall be king over all the earth: in that day shall there be one Lord, and his name one. . . . And it shall come to pass, that every one that is left of all the nations which came against Jerusalem shall even go up from year to year to worship the King, the Lord of hosts, and to keep the feast of tabernacles. (Zechariah 14:9, 16)

The Lord says that His command for all nations and people to commemorate this Feast of Tabernacles forever is so important that if they disobey, God will punish them (Zechariah 14:16–21). What is the possible significance of this Feast of Tabernacles to Gentile nations? Today, most non-Jews are totally unaware of this feast day and its meaning. What event could happen on the Feast of Tabernacles that would be of such worldwide significance that all nations will commemorate its anniversary forever in Jerusalem? The defeat of Satan's plan to destroy man, the judgment of the wicked nations, and the commencement of the Millennium would surely be celebrated forever with thanksgiving on this anniversary date by all nations saved from the final holocaust by Christ's Second Coming.

On the Feast of Tabernacles, leaders in Jewish synagogues throughout the world read this passage in Zechariah 14:1–21 which promises in detail the Jews' final messianic deliverance from their persecutors and the beginning of the prophesied Kingdom.

### The Twenty-Fourth Day of Chisleu

Chisleu, the ninth month in the Jewish calendar, corresponds to our months of November–December. On the twenty-fifth day of the month, the Jews celebrate the Feast of Hanukkah. Although not one of the "appointed feasts," Hanukkah commemorates the cleansing and rededication of the Second Temple in 165 B.C.

On the day before the Feast of Hanukkah, on the twenty-fourth day of Chisleu, Israel has witnessed four major historical events. It is quite possible that we will also see the defeat of Gog and Magog (the Russian-Arab armies) when they attack Israel on this anniversary date (see figure 4).

---

**Theme: Cleansing and Rededication**

1. The foundation of the Second Temple was laid in 520 B.C.

2. The abolition of the Temple sacrifice by Antiochus in 168 B.C.

3. The recapture of the Temple and the cleansing of the Temple Sanctuary in 165 B.C.

4. Jerusalem was freed from Turkish rule in 1917

5. The possible date for the miraculous defeat of the Russian invasion of Israel — War of Gog and Magog

---

THE TWENTY-FOURTH DAY OF CHISLEU
*Figure 4*

1. *The Foundation of the Second Temple (520 B.C.)*

The Jewish exiles returned from Babylon in 536 B.C. After sixteen years of tedious rebuilding of their farms and homes, the

Jews received the word of the Lord through the prophet Haggai in 520 B.C. The Lord said that He would bless their endeavors only if they would change their priorities and first rebuild the Temple which lay in ruins. Haggai 1:15 records that they began to clear the rubble that had accumulated during the seventy years of desolation. After three months of preliminary work, the prophet declares that "from the four and twentieth day of the ninth month, even from the day that the foundation of the Lord's Temple was laid, consider it. . . . From this day I will bless you." (Haggai 2:18–19)

This day, the twenty-fourth day of Chisleu, ended the prophesied seventy years of "desolations" to the exact day, seventy biblical years (70 years × 360 days = 25200 days) after the Babylonians began the "desolations" of the land with the besieging of Jerusalem on the tenth day of the month of Tebeth, 589 B.C. (2 Kings 25:1).

2.  *The Abolition of the Temple Sacrifice (168 B.C.)*

After the Jews rebuilt the Temple in 520 B.C., as decreed by Cyrus and Darius, they continued the observance of all the feasts even after Alexander the Great conquered Persia and made Israel into a province of his Greek Empire in 332 B.C. His successors, the Greek Seleucid kings, allowed the Jews to practice their religion until 168 B.C., when the Greek-Syrian king, Antiochus IV, known as "Epiphanes," entered the Temple and "took away the golden altar and the candlestick of light" and other Temple furnishings. He broke the sacred objects into pieces and carried them off to his own country.

Later, he proclaimed that all the people should follow pagan gods and leave their own laws. He forbade the Jews to offer "sacrifices and atonements" in the Temple of God, and also commanded that they "should prohibit the sabbath and festival days to be celebrated" (1 Maccabees 1). The last true daily sacrifice took place on the twenty-fourth of Chisleu. The pagan sacrifices began the next day on the "five and twentieth day of the ninth month (Chisleu)" (1 Maccabees 4:54).

3.  *The Recapture of the Temple and Cleansing of the Sanctuary (165 B.C.)*

The abominations demanded by Antiochus IV provoked a revolution by those Jews who resisted his pretensions to be worshiped as a "god." A Jewish rebellion, led by an old man named Mattathias and his five sons, resulted in a spectacular war of religious independence. The sons, led by Judas Maccabaeus ("the Hammer"), fought the Syrian army occupying Jerusalem and defeated them against impossible odds in 165 B.C. The Jews reconquered the Temple site on the twenty-fourth day of the ninth month, exactly three years to the day after the evil King Antiochus IV had forced the ending of the daily sacrifice.

The next day, after conquering the Temple Mount on the twenty-fourth day of Chisleu, the anniversary of the last true daily sacrifice, "Early in the morning on the twenty-fifth day of the ninth month of Chisleu . . . they rose and offered sacrifice, as the law directs, on the altar of burnt offering which they had built. At the very season and on the very day that the Gentiles had profaned it, it was dedicated with songs and harps" (1 Maccabees 4:52–54). Although a nearby Syrian fortress held out for some time, the Jews immediately cleansed the Temple precisely three years to the day after it was defiled.

Jewish legend, as recounted in the Talmud, says that a priest found a one-day's supply of the sacred oil hidden in a wall of the Temple. When the oil was used to light the lamp, it miraculously lasted for the full eight days of the celebration, until new oil could be made.

Today, this Feast of Dedication is commemorated by the Hanukkah celebration, or the "Feast of Lights," for eight days, commencing on the twenty-fifth day of Chisleu. This festival, representing the inextinguishable nature of the Jewish faith in God, was celebrated also by Jesus Christ (John 10:22–23).

### 4. *Jerusalem Freed from Turkish Rule (A.D. 1917)*

For almost two thousand years the land of Israel was occupied by one empire after another. The Turkish rule lasted for almost four hundred years until World War I demolished the Ottoman Empire. The Allied Expeditionary Force, under the command of General Allenby, approached Jerusalem on December 9, 1917, the twenty-fourth day of Chisleu. General Allenby, a Christian, was concerned that the city of Jerusalem would be destroyed by his artillery unless the Turks first surrendered. Its huge walls could have held out for a considerable period. Miraculously, the Turks "gave up the city without a shot being fired."

Allenby accomplished this feat by the use of propaganda. He flew planes over Jerusalem and dropped thousands of leaflets to the Turkish defenders. Isaiah 31:5 may well have foreseen this unusual event: "As birds flying, so will the Lord of Hosts defend Jerusalem: defending also he will deliver it; and passing over he will preserve it." The leaflets, telling the Turks to flee Jerusalem, were signed by Lord Allenby. Interestingly, the Turks had an old prophecy that they would never lose the Holy City until "a man of Allah" came to deliver it. This name, Allenby, reminded the Turks of this prophecy, (Allen, *Allah*; Beh, *man*) and this encouraged them to flee the city. Victorious in saving Jerusalem, General Allenby chose to enter the city humbly on foot, grounded by his conviction that only Christ had the right to enter Jerusalem as a conquering King. Israel was now governed by the British mandate under the Balfour Declaration, which promised them a Jewish homeland. Thus the foundation of modern Israel was laid on this anniversary, the twenty-fourth day of Chisleu, 1917.

These are the four major events that have already occurred on this date. God's words to Haggai — "Consider now from this day and upward, from the four and twentieth day of the ninth month, even from the day that the foundation of the Lord's temple was laid, consider it . . . from this day will I bless you" (Haggai 2:18–19) — certainly has been fulfilled in the history of the Jewish people so far. Is it unreasonable to expect that God will fulfill yet another prophetically significant event on this day?

5. *The Russian Invasion of Israel (Possible Date of the War of Gog and Magog)*

The prophet Ezekiel (38:19–39:8) describes the awesome destruction God will inflict on those nations that Russia will lead in attacking Israel. If you carefully compare Ezekiel 38:19–22 with Haggai 2:18–22, you will see the strong probability that the twenty-fourth day of Chisleu — the day before Hanukkah, in our month of December — is probably the day for this prophetic fulfillment. The Bible does not reveal the year of this battle, but recent events indicate it may be fairly soon.

Ezekiel 38:19–20 and Haggai 2:6–7 state that an earthquake will occur and will be so catastrophic that the whole world will be affected.

> Yet once, it is a little while, and I will shake the heavens and the earth, and the sea and the dry land; and I will shake all nations, and the desire of all nations shall come: and I will fill this house with glory, saith the Lord of hosts.
> (Haggai 2:6–7)

> And I will call for a sword against him throughout all my mountains, saith the Lord God: every man's sword shall be against his brother. And I will plead against him with pestilence and with blood; and I will rain upon him, and upon his bands, and upon the many people that are with him, an overflowing rain, and great hailstones, fire, and brimstone. Thus will I magnify myself, and sanctify myself; and I will be known in the eyes of many nations, and they shall know that I am the Lord.     (Ezekiel 38:21–23)

Notice the similarity in the wording of the prophecy of Haggai to the words of Ezekiel's prophecy:

> Consider now from this day and upward, from the four and twentieth day of the ninth month, even from the day that the foundations of the Lord's Temple was laid, consider it. . . . From this day I will bless you. And again the word of the Lord came unto Haggai in the four and twentieth day of the month [ninth], saying, . . . I will shake the heavens and the earth; and I will overthrow the throne of kingdoms, and I will destroy the strength of the kingdoms of the heathen, and I will overthrow the chariots, and those that ride in them; and the horses and their riders shall come down, every one by the sword of his brother.
> (Haggai 2:18–22)

There are awesome days ahead for Israel and the nations as the Lord of hosts once more intervenes in history to reveal His sovereignty and power. Only time will reveal whether "the day whereof I have spoken" will occur on this anniversary of so many of Israel's past deliverances.

> Behold, it is come, and it is done, saith the Lord God; this is the day whereof I have spoken.          (Ezekiel 39:8)

# 7

# *Russia's Day of Destruction in Israel*

And the word of the Lord came unto me, saying, Son of man, set thy face against Gog, the land of Magog, the chief prince of Meshech and Tubal and prophesy against him, and say, Thus saith the Lord God: Behold I am against thee, O Gog, the chief prince of Meshech and Tubal: and I will turn thee back, and put hooks into thy jaws, and I will bring thee forth, and all thine army, horses and horsemen, all of them clothed with all sorts of armor, even a great company with bucklers and shields, all of them handling swords: Persia, Ethiopia, and Libya with them; all of them with shield and helmet: Gomer, and all his bands; the house of Togarmah of the north quarters, and all his bands: and many people with thee.    (Ezekiel 38:1–6)

God is in control of history. As the earlier chapters of this book demonstrate, some of God's appointments with destiny for Israel and the nations have already occurred. Several additional appointments remain to be fulfilled in the future. Russia and her allies (the former republics of the USSR, Eastern Europe, and the Arabs) still await their appointment with destiny.

The Lord gave the prophet Ezekiel a prophetic warning

directed to the nations of the "far north." Ezekiel was raised near the Temple in Jerusalem and had studied to be a priest. He was among those Jewish captives from Jerusalem who were taken to Babylon when Nebuchadnezzar conquered Israel. It was he who wrote "among the captives by the river of Chebar, . . . the heavens were opened, and I saw visions of God" (Ezekiel 1:1). These prophecies written in Babylon from about 593 B.C. to 570 B.C. were directed to Ezekiel's fellow captives and to those Jews still living in Jerusalem, as well as to the generations that would follow.

Ezekiel was given an astonishingly accurate prophetic vision about the rebirth of the nation of Israel that would occur in the spring of 1948, as detailed in chapter 3. He foretold that Israel would arise miraculously from the graveyard of the nations, where she was buried with the ruins of Jerusalem in A.D. 70 by the Roman army led by Titus. Incredibly, God promised that the Jews, after almost two thousand years of exile, would return to the Promised Land. The ancient prophets also foretold that the Jewish exiles would become "a mighty army" in her ancient homeland. In 1948, Israel triumphed against an invasion by six well-armed Arab armies. Israel's military forces consisted of a small, voluntary citizen army composed of unskilled farmers and scholars who were equipped with inadequate weapons, a few jeeps, and two small airplanes. Israel's armored force consisted of several vehicles captured from her enemies, including trucks with improvised steel plates. Yet, like David's miraculous victory over Goliath, God supernaturally intervened to allow a weak Israel to survive and prosper, defeating her Arab enemies against incredible odds.

Ezekiel's amazing vision depicted the Jewish people as a "valley which was full of dry bones." This certainly described the fate of Israel after it's destruction by Rome in 70 A.D. and the centuries of persecution that followed. Israel was buried in the graveyard of the ancient nations. Anyone who has seen the sickening scenes of the huge pits full of emaciated, skeletal remains of victims from Nazi death camps can imagine that this might have formed part of the vision that the prophet saw twenty-five centuries ago. The Lord asked him, "'Can these bones live?' and I answered, 'O Lord God, thou knowest'" (Ezekiel 37:3). Yet God told Ezekiel to watch a miraculous resurrection of these "dry bones." "So I prophesied as He commanded me, and the breath came into them, and they lived, and stood up upon their feet, an exceeding great army" (Ezekiel 37:10). Today, Israel has the world's third most powerful air force and possesses more tanks than any other nation except the United States and Russia. The Israeli Defense Forces have rewritten the military manuals of the world with their audacious and brilliant tactics. Today (according to many military analysts), the small nation of Israel has the fourth most powerful armed forces on earth after America, Russia, and China.

Geographically, Israel occupies an area of land smaller than the state of New Jersey — only one-half the size of tiny Switzerland. Yet, despite its insignificant size and a population of only five million, Israel has attained a position of prime importance in the global struggle between nations. For the last several years, almost half of all of the resolutions of the General Assembly of the United Nations have concerned Israel. Newspapers throughout the world carry front-page stories about Israel several times a week. This astonishing fact can be explained only by prophecy and the deep hatred for Israel expressed by Russia, the former republics of the USSR, Iran, the Arab nations, and many Third World nations.

The prophet Zechariah prophesied twenty-five hundred years ago, "Behold, I will make Jerusalem a cup of trembling unto all the people round about, when they shall be in the siege both against Judah and against Jerusalem. And in that day will I make Jerusalem a burdensome stone for all people: all that burden themselves with it shall be cut in pieces, though all the people of the earth be gathered together against it" (Zechariah 12:2–3). Ironically, the first nation to formally recognize the state of Israel was Russia. In 1948, Joseph Stalin hoped that Israel would become a socialist nation and help offset the growing influence that the Western powers exercised in the Middle East. However, as Stalin soon came to realize, Israel would not become a Russian pawn, so Russia quickly turned to the Arabs and encouraged their hatred toward the Jewish state.

More than twenty-five hundred years ago, Ezekiel prophesied about an invasion by Russia (called "Magog") and her allies that would occur during the last days, "after many days." He said that after Israel was reborn as a nation, Russia and her allies would attack her in a violent attempt to completely annihilate the Jewish state. Naturally, Ezekiel did not describe the present nations of

Russia, Germany, Syria, and Iraq by their modern names. Rather, he referred to them by the names of the ancient tribes that occupied the geographical territories of the present nations at the time of his writing. The prophecies found in Ezekiel, chapter 38 and 39, describe this massive, future Russian-Arab invasion of Israel and the spectacular defeat of the enemies of the Jews by the supernatural act of God.

The Lord warned the leader of Russia in these words addressed to Gog, the ruler of Magog (Russia):

> Be thou prepared, and prepare for thyself, thou, and all thy company that are assembled unto thee, and be thou a guard unto them. After many days thou shalt be visited: in the latter years thou shalt come into the land that is brought back from the sword, and is gathered out of many people, against the mountains of Israel, which have been always waste: but it is brought forth out of the nations, and they shall dwell safely all of them. Thou shalt ascend and come like a storm, thou shalt be like a cloud to cover the land, thou, and all thy bands, and many people with thee.
> (Ezekiel 38:7–9)

Many of the tribal names in Ezekiel 38 are recorded in the book of Genesis. Following the Flood, Noah's sons and grandsons dispersed to various parts of Asia, Europe, and Africa. Genesis 10 records the ancient genealogy of the nations, naming the tribes descended from Noah's children, later referred to by Ezekiel. Ancient historians, including Herodotus and Flavius Josephus in his *Antiquities of the Jews*, tell us where most of these tribes ultimately settled. Many Jewish and Christians scholars conclude that the tribes referred to by Ezekiel are those listed in figure 1 and figure 2, which show the ancient name of each tribe and the modern nation that now occupies that particular territory.

### THE NATIONS OF EZEKIEL 38: 1–6

| The Ancient Nations | The Modern Nations |
| --- | --- |
| The land of Magog | Russia |
| Meshech and Tubal | Somewhere in Russia |
| Persia | Iran, Iraq, Afghanistan |
| Ethiopia | Ethiopia and Sudan |
| Libya | Libya |

| | |
|---|---|
| Ashkenaz | Austria and Germany |
| Gomer | Eastern Europe |
| Togarmah | Southeastern Europe — Turkey |
| "Many peoples with thee" | Various other nations allied to Russia |

*Figure 1*

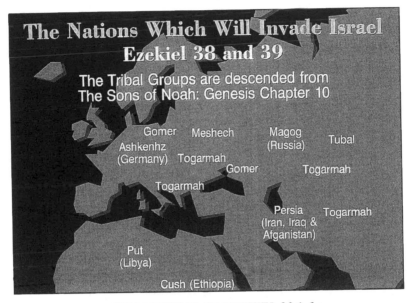

THE NATIONS OF EZEKIEL 38:1-6
THE WARS OF GOG AND MAGOG
*Figure 2*

## The Identification of "Gog and Magog" as Russia

The names "Gog and Magog" are famous in biblical prophetic literature and in Jewish rabbinical writings because of their future role in the great War of Gog and Magog predicted by the prophet Ezekiel (chap. 38 and 39). The book of Revelation (chap. 20) also records that an army of millions will once again join with the nations represented by "Gog and Magog" in a final attack, led by Satan, against the "beloved city" and the "camp of the saints" at the end of the Millennium. This final war will be the last battle in human history. Biblical prophecies indicate that three enormous wars will convulse the planet during the apocalyptic period known as "the last days."

The first war, as described by Ezekiel, is the War of Gog and Magog (a Russian-Arab invasion against Israel), the subject of this chapter. The second war, known as the Battle of Armageddon, will occur a minimum of seven years later. Armageddon is described in the prophecies of Joel, Zechariah, and especially the book of Revelation (16:16). This cataclysmic conflict will involve nations across the entire world as the significant armies of the East battle against the armies of the West under the Antichrist. These titanic armies will be pitted against each other and Israel. During the conclusion of this struggle, Jesus Christ will descend from heaven with His army of angels and heavenly saints (the resurrected Church). Both armies will then turn their fury against Jesus and His saints. The returning King of Kings will utterly defeat them and inaugurate the Millennium of peace under the Kingdom of God. Finally, Revelation 20:8 tells us about a third war, the final battle in human history. This will occur one thousand years after Armageddon, at the end of the Millennium. Millions of people born during the Millennium to those who survive the tribulation period will choose to join Satan in his attack against the future City of God. The prophet John foretold that his army would include the nations of "Gog and Magog," referring to Russia and other nations to the extreme north of the Holy Land.

The question of the proper identification of the nation of "Magog" is of great interest to serious Bible students who wish to clearly understand these great biblical prophecies. "Magog" is a real nation occupying a territory that was known to Ezekiel and his Jewish readers in the fifth century before Christ. I believe the evidence supports the conclusion that Magog refers to the territory that is currently occupied by the present nation of Russia, including several of the southern republics of the Commonwealth of Independent States (formerly the USSR). The majority of prophecy teachers agree with this conclusion. However, a number of biblical scholars have challenged this identification of Magog with the Russian nation. Some scholars suggest that Magog was connected with some small tribal groups in ancient Mesopotamia in the area presently occupied by Iran. Others suggest Magog is connected with the tribes led by an ancient king known as Gyges in the area of ancient Lydia (present-day Turkey) to the south of

Russia. The ancient historian Pliny claimed the Syrians thought the name Gog was the same as Gyges, a king of Lydia whose country was named from him — Gygea, or Gog's land. King Gyges was the grandfather of King Croesus (*Natural History* 1. 5.c.23).

In 1986 my wife, Kaye, and I were standing with our guide on the Great Wall of China. He told us that enemy armies from Mongolia and Siberia have attacked China at that very spot numerous times throughout Chinese history. The Chinese guide pointed out that due to the geography of this rugged terrain, this location would be the logical place for the next Russian-Mongol attack on China. Arab writers confirm that in the Arabic language their name for the Great Wall of China is called "the wall of Al Magog" because the Great Wall was built to keep out the invading armies from Magog (Russia).

Many liberal scholars reject Ezekiel's literal interpretation of prophecy, including the identification of Russia. These academics often interpret his prophecy merely as a symbol of the apocalyptic war between good and evil. However, precise descriptions in this prophecy of specific nations, weapons, places, and actions during the war strongly suggest that this is not a symbolic war. If we want to understand this prophetic message of Ezekiel, we must examine its literal implications and determine the correct identification of Gog and Magog. A summary of the research material I have collected on the identification of Magog follows.

## Jewish Scholarship and Magog

The passages in Ezekiel 38 and 39 were studied in minute detail for thousands of years by Jewish sages. Consequently, the conclusions drawn by these scholars should illuminate the true meaning of the Hebrew words "Gog and Magog." Genesis 10 lists Magog as a literal grandson of Noah who ultimately gave birth to a nation. This name, "Magog," was well known to every Jew who studied this Genesis passage every year as part of the annual Sabbath reading of the Torah. In his prophecy about the future war, the prophet Ezekiel named "Magog," along with other specific nations such as Libya, Persia, and Ethiopia. This strongly suggests that Ezekiel expected the name "Magog" would be understood by his Jewish readers as a real nation, not as an abstract symbol of evil.

A recent commentary on Genesis, *Bereishis Genesis: A New Translation With a Commentary Anthologized from Talmudic, Midrashic, and Rabbinic Sources,* includes this commentary on Genesis 10:2. "Magog is mentioned several times in Scripture, e.g. Ezekiel 38:2; 39:6 as the name of the land of Gog. *Kesses HaSofer* identified them with the Mongols who lived near China, for in fact the very name Mongol is a corruption of Magog." The commentary also cites Arab writers who refer to the Great Wall of China as the wall of Al Magog. A 1961 biblical commentary by Dr. J. H. Hertz, the late chief rabbi of the British Empire, called *The Pentateuch and Haftorahs* identifies the Magog of the famous Genesis 10 passage: "Magog — The Scythians, whose territory lay on the borders of the Caucasus." The Jewish-Christian scholar Dr. Alfred Edersheim in his book, *Bible History, Old Testament,* also identifies Magog as the Scythians.

A fascinating 1980 Jewish commentary, *Daniel,* published by The ArtScroll Tanach Series, makes the following comments on the identity of Magog:

> The various traditions concerning the identity of Magog, who in Genesis 10:2 is listed among the sons of Noah's son Japheth, tend to place the land of Magog in what today is southwest Russia–The Caucasian region, which lies between the Black and Caspian Seas . . . This is in agreement with *Yerushalmi Megillah* 3:9 which renders Magog as "the Goths," a group of nomadic tribes who destroyed the Scythians and made their homes in Scythian territory. . . . Our identification of Magog as Caucasia, which was at one time inhabited by the Goths, is based on the assumption that the land of Magog is named after Japheth's son. . . .
>
> Rabbi Chisdai Ibn Shaprut wrote to the king of Khazaria (a Caucasian kingdom in southern Russia which converted to Judaism in the eighth century after Christ) in which he addresses the king as 'prince, leader of Meshech and Tubal.' This salutation, drawn from our verse, indicates that the Gaonim had a tradition that these countries were indeed located in Russia.

This acclaimed commentary concludes this section with a fascinating comment:

> In this light one may understand an oral tradition passed down from the Vilna Gaon (see *Chevlei Mashaiach BiZemaneinu*, p. 134), that when the Russian navy passes through the Bosporus it will be time to put on Sabbath clothes (in anticipation of the coming Mashiach.)

The Bosporus is the narrow strait in Turkey that links the Black Sea to the Mediterranean Sea through the Dardanelles strait. The Jewish sages warned that the generation who witnessed the Russian preparation to invade Israel should prepare their hearts because the coming of the Messiah was at hand. The famous Jewish historian Flavius Josephus, who lived at the time of Saint Paul, wrote a definitive history of the Jewish people called the *Antiquities of the Jews.* Josephus identified Magog as follows. "Magog founded those that from him were named Magogites, but who are by the Greeks called Scythians" (pp. 30–31).

### Christian Scholarship Identifying Magog as Russia

The section of Dr. R. Young's book, *Young's Analytical Concordance of the Holy Bible*, dealing with Magog speaks of ancient Scythia or Tartary, a name used to describe southern Russia in past centuries. Professor Young said that the name "Gog" was derived from a phrase that meant a "high mountain" and that the name "Gog" in Ezekiel 38 referred to "A prince of Rosh, Mesheck, Tubal, and Tiras, in ancient Scythia or Tartary." Young also refers to "the descendents of Magog and their land, called Scythia, in the N. of Asia and Europe." The authoritative 1973 reference work, *Eerdman's Handbook to the Bible*, came to the same conclusion, "Magog, Meshech, Tubal and Gomer were all sons of Japheth (Noah's son). They gave their names to Indo-European peoples living in the Black Sea/Caucasus region, on the northern fringe of the then-known world."

*The Comprehensive Commentary of the Holy Bible*, edited by Dr. William Jenks, provides some fascinating information regarding the identity of Magog.

> Magog was the son of Japheth (Genesis 10:2), from whence the Scythians are generally supposed to be

derived. The Mogul Tartars, a people of the Scythian race, are still called so by the Arabian writers . . . the Jews of his day thought 'Magog to be the Scythian nations, vast and innumerable, who are beyond Mount Caucasus and the Palus Mæotis, and near the Caspian Sea, stretching even to India.

The same commentary, quoting Professor William Bochart, gives the following information.

The Koran, and a Christian poet of Syria (Ephraem the Syrian - see chapter 9) before the Koran was published, both allude to a fable of Alexander's shutting up the barbarous and troublesome nations, Gog and Magog, near the N. Pole by an iron and brasen wall. The mountain Scythians extended hence (from the river Araxes) to the Caucasus, and those of the plain to the Don, the sea of Azof, and the N. Ocean. It is credible, that from the Rosh and Meshech nations dwelling about the Araxes, are descended the Russians and Moscovites.

Dr. Dwight C. Pentecost is the author of an excellent study of the major themes of Bible prophecy entitled *Things to Come*. During the last few years I have discussed a number of prophetic issues with him and have a great appreciation for his superb book. Dr. Pentecost quotes Professor Bauman on the identification of Magog as follows:

Magog's land was located in, what is called today, the Caucasus and the adjoining steppes. And the three, Rosh, Meshech and Tubal were called by the ancients, Scythians. They roamed as nomads in the country around and north of the Black and the Caspian Seas, and were known as the wildest barbarians.

One of the most important scholarly tools employed in the exegesis of Scripture is *Gesenius' Hebrew and Chaldee Lexicon*. Numerous scholars utilize this book as an authority on the precise meaning of Hebrew and Chaldee words found in the original languages of the Old Testament. In the section of his definitive work dealing with this identification, Gesenius wrote the following:

Magog - PR. N. of a son of Japheth, Genesis 10:2; also of a region, and a great and powerful people of the same name, inhabiting the recesses of the north, who are at some time to invade the Holy Land Ezekiel 38, 39. We are to understand just the same nations as the Greeks comprised, under the name of Scythian (Josephus *Antiquites of the Jews* 1.6.1.)

It is important to note that Professor Gesenius referred to "Magog" as a real nation that will invade the Holy Land in the future. Gesenius' concluded that "Gog" was a

prince of the land of Magog . . . also of Rossi, Moschi, and Tibareni, who are to come with great forces from the extreme north (38:15; 39:2), after the Exile (38:8,12) to invade the holy land, and to perish there, as prophesied by Ezekiel.

In addition, Gesenius described the Revelation 20:8 passage as a reference to a final war involving "Gog and Magog" at the end of the Millennium. However, he correctly concludes this final war will be a totally separate event: "Gog and Magog in the Apocalypse belong to a different time to those spoken of in Ezekiel, so it is in vain to point out a discrepancy."

The literal interpretation of "Magog" by Gesenius and other biblical scholars stands in marked contrast to the allegorical interpretation of many modern scholars who treat Ezekiel 38–39 as "apocalyptic literature" (referring only to a symbolic war between good and evil). Gesenius identified Magog as a real country, which exists to the extreme north of the Holy Land that will invade Israel in the future. He also identified Magog with the "same nations as the Greeks comprised under the name of Scythians." In light of the many scholastic sources that identify Magog with Scythia, we must answer a critical question: Who were the Scythians and what geographical area did they occupy?

## The Scythians

Professor G. Rawlinson wrote a definitive study of the ancient tribes and empires that ruled the Middle East called *Five Great Monarchies*. Chapter 9 of that work, dealing with Assyria, includes the following footnote: "The Scythians proper of Herodotus and

Hippocrates extended from the Danube and the Carpathians on the one side, to the Tanais or Don upon the other." The geographic territories described by Professor G. Rawlinson that were ruled by the Scythians are clearly located in the south of Russia and include the Ukraine, Georgia, and Armenia (see figure 3 for the location of the Scythians).

*MAGOG AND THE SCYTHIANS*
*Figure 3*

In Ezekiel 38:7 the prophet foretells that in this future conflict Russia (Magog) will also be the arm's supplier for all of these nations. God says, "Be thou a guard unto them." It is fascinating to observe that the armories of these nations (as listed by Ezekiel), without exception, are filled with Russian AK-47 assault rifles, SAM missiles, RPG7 anti-tank weapons and various other Russian-manufactured arms, exactly as the Bible foretold thousands of years ago. The prophet described an invasion that would come without warning in which the enemy invaded like a "storm" or "cloud to cover the land." It is possible that the prophet saw in vision an airborne invasion force, like D day, and used the best language he had available to describe such an event.

## The Coming Russian-Arab Invasion of Israel

Bible prophecy also provides some insight into the ongoing peace negotiations between Israel and its Arab neighbours. Thousands of years ago the prophet Ezekiel (chaps. 38–39) predicted that a huge confederacy of Arab nations under Russian leadership would join together to attack Israel in the generation after the Jewish exiles returned to their homeland. Despite massive changes in Russia, the hard-liners in the KGB, the army, and military-industrial complex maintain their solid grip on the levers of power. A recent study of the role of the military in Russia revealed that President Boris Yeltsin secretly appointed over 14,000 senior military generals to assume command of every single department of the Russian government in the spring of 1996. These departments included the health, agricultural, transportation, and mining ministries. Until the recent political changes in Russia, no men could rise above the rank of major in Russia's army unless they were an approved member of the Russian Communist Party. Therefore, the military officers controlling the "democratic" government of Russia are virtually all Communists. By this action Yeltsin has allowed the Communist Party and their military allies to secretly assume control over all major decisions in his government. Although Yeltsin won the June 1996 elections, the Communists hold a clear majority in the Duma (Parliament). Despite all the media hype about Russian democracy, the real leadership of Russia remains firmly in the hands of the resurrected Communist Party, the renamed KGB (now called the Foreign Intelligence Service), and the powerful army generals.

Twenty-six centuries ago the prophet Ezekiel prophesied that a military leader would arise in the land of Magog to lead a Russian-Arab alliance of nations to attack Israel. Ezekiel predicted that this leader would say, "I will go up against a land of unwalled villages; I will go to a peaceful people, who dwell safely, all of them dwelling without walls, and having neither bars nor gates" (Ezekiel 38:11). It is interesting to note that, during the lifetime of Ezekiel and throughout history up until 1900, virtually all of the villages and cities in the Middle East had strong walls for defense. Ezekiel had never seen a village or city without defensive walls. Yet, in our day, Israel is truly a "land of unwalled villages" for the simple reason that modern techniques of warfare (bombs, tanks, and missiles) make city walls irrelevant for defense. This is one more indication that his prophecy refers to our modern generation.

THE RUSSIAN INVASION OF ISRAEL
THE WAR OF GOG AND MAGOG
*Figure 4*

Since 1948 Israel has been forced to live as an armed camp while surrounded by twenty-one nations with two hundred million Arabs that are publicly committed to her destruction. The Jewish state has not been able to "dwell safely." This threatening situation compels Israel to spend more of its budget on defense than any other country in the world. However, the present peace negotiations between the PLO and Israel may create a false sense of security during the next few years. The Jewish state will relax its defenses as a result of the misconception that she can "dwell safely." This present peace process may set the stage for the fulfillment of the great War of Gog and Magog prophesied by the prophet Ezekiel.

When this Russian-Arab alliance attacks Israel, the prophet declared that God will intervene with supernatural earthquakes, hail, and pestilence to defeat the combined forces of Russian and Arab armies. This miraculous deliverance by the hand of God may set the stage for Israel to build the Third Temple as described in

Daniel 9:24–27. These awesome prophetic events concerning the defeat of Russia will prepare the way for the fulfillment of the prophecies of the rise of Antichrist to rule the earth and his seven-year treaty with Israel. This treaty with the Antichrist will commence a seven-year countdown to the return of the Messiah at the Battle of Armageddon to establish His eternal Kingdom on earth.

These critical developments in the Middle East encourage believers to live in constant expectation of the glorious return of our Messiah. Jesus said, "When these things begin to come to pass, then look up, and lift up your heads; for your redemption draweth nigh"(Luke 21:28). Yet we, as Christians, must live in a spiritual balance during these last days. Although our Messiah may return soon, He may also delay His return for a generation or more because our Lord "is long-suffering to us-ward, not willing that any should perish, but that all should come to repentance"(2 Peter 3:9). We must live each day watching for His return. We must faithfully witness to those around us as though His return will occur immediately. Yet we must also plan and work as though we still have a hundred years. Our Lord commanded, "Occupy till I come"(Luke 19:13).

## The Strategic Importance of the West Bank and the Golan Heights

If Israel's present government under Prime Minister Netanyahu continues the disastrous policies of former prime ministers Rabin and Peres and surrenders the vital strategic territory in the West Bank and the Golan Heights in its "Land for Peace" negotiations with the PLO and its Arab neighbours, Israel will face military disaster in the next war. The tragic four-thousand-year history of the Middle East indicates clearly that another Arab-Israeli war will occur. It is only a question of timing. Israel requires military control of the land on the Golan Heights, Gaza, and the West Bank in order to provide the strategic depth to defend itself against the overwhelming military force of twenty-one enemy Arab nations. The Arab nations possess territory that is five hundred times the size of tiny Israel. Why do the Arabs need the small strategic territory of the Golan Heights and the West Bank? The real reason that the Arabs need this territory is so they can destroy the Jewish state of Israel. Every single European or American military study in the last thirty years has concluded that

Israel cannot be defended by conventional weapons if it surrenders military control over these vital strategic territories. The 1992 study by the U.S. Joint Chiefs of Staff confirmed that Israel can not surrender the Golan, Gaza, or the West Bank and expect to survive the next Arab invasion.

History shows that victorious nations have never returned land captured from their enemies following a defensive war in which they were forced to defend themselves against their attackers. The Golan Heights represents less than 1 percent of the territory of the large nation of Syria. The Golan Heights was only controlled by Syria for a few decades after World War I. They lost it to Israel in the Six-Day War in 1967. The only reason Syria needs this small territory is to use it to attack Israel. However, Israel desperately needs the Golan Heights to resist Syria's tanks. Moreover, 30 percent of Israel's water comes from the Golan Heights. If they surrender control of the West Bank territory, Israel will be less than nine miles wide at its center near Tel Aviv, where almost 80 percent of its population lives. In a future conflict Arab armies could easily cut Israel in two by attacking from the PLO-controlled high ground of Judea and Samaria (West Bank). The Jewish state could then be overrun in a matter of days. Unlike other conflicts in which defeat leads to a loss of territory and political freedom, an Arab conquest of Israel would lead to a massive slaughter of the Jewish population.

In a future war Israel may be quickly forced to resort to nuclear weapons when they find their small diminished territory about to be overcome by Arab armies. The Israeli army describes this desperate scenario as "the Samson Option" because it would lead to the destruction of the whole Middle East; Samson, too, brought down the temple on his enemies and on himself. Despite this grim reality, the Israeli government has agreed to relinquish much of the strategic area of the West Bank and all of Gaza while continuing negotiations with Syria about the Golan Heights. Military and intelligence sources have informed me that if this "Oslo II" peace process continues, for the first time since its creation in 1948, Israel's conventional army and air force will soon be unable to successfully defend its vital territory and population from an overwhelming Arab armed invasion.

The Lord commands all believers to "pray for the peace of Jerusalem: they shall prosper that love thee" (Psalms 122:6). However, the current peace process between the PLO and Israel

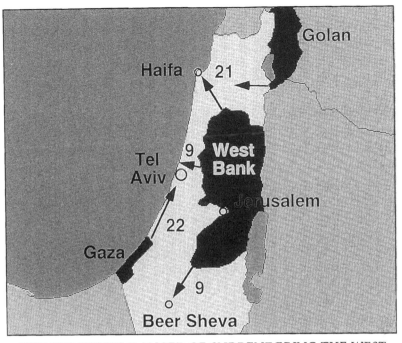

*THE STRATEGIC DANGER OF SURRENDERING THE WEST*
*BANK AND THE GOLAN HEIGHTS*
*Figure 5*

may set the stage for the fulfillment of these tremendous prophecies about the War of Gog and Magog and how they lead to the Messiah's return in our generation. While we long for true peace in the Middle East, we must recognize that the ancient prophets warned that a false peace in the last days would precede the final conflict that would conclude with the Battle of Armageddon. The prophet Jeremiah warned that in the last days men would say, "Peace, peace! When there is no peace" (Jeremiah 6:14). Our world will not know true peace until Jesus the Messiah, the Prince of Peace returns. Scriptures reveal that real peace will only come to the Middle East when the Arabs and the Jews finally dwell as brothers in true peace under the rule of their Messiah, who alone can heal the ancient hatred between them.

### The Proposal That Israel Surrender Land for Peace

For fifty years, the United Nations and the Arab states have continually demanded that the tiny nation of Israel surrender its vital land to "buy" peace with its Arab neighbours. However, we should consider some questions. How large is Israel compared to her Islamic neighbours? The state of Israel is less than one-tenth of 1 percent as large as the thirty-five Islamic states surrounding her throughout the Middle East. These thirty-five Islamic states possess 8,879,548 square miles of territory and a combined population of 804,500,000. To put this in perspective, the tiny nation of Israel is only 8,020 square miles in size with a population of less than five million people. This means that the surrounding Islamic nations are 1,107 times larger than the Jewish state of Israel. The state of Texas alone is over thirty-two times the size of Israel. The Islamic state of Saudi Arabia is over one hundred and seven times the size of Israel. Islam is the major religion in thirty-five nations, or 22 percent of the 159 member-states of the United Nations. Judaism is the major religion in only one nation on earth, the state of Israel.

In addition, these Arab and Islamic nations are incredibly wealthy as a result of their oil resources. They are also naturally related to the Arab Palestinians by both race and religion. In addition, most of the Palestinian Arabs were born in Arab states surrounding Israel. Why should Israel surrender its incredibly small and strategically vital territory to her Arab enemies when the Islamic states have more than a thousand times the land and their vast oil wealth that can be utilized to absorb the Palestinian Arabs?

## Israel's Covenant with Death

The world was astonished to witness the leader of Israel and its deadly enemy, the Arab PLO, sign an agreement on September 13, 1993, promising to end the brutal warfare that has characterized the Middle East for the last fifty years. PLO leader Yasser Arafat and the late Prime Minister Yitzchak Rabin took the first tentative steps towards a possible peace treaty in the Middle East. Does this mean true peace is at hand? Or, will a false peace set the stage for the War of Gog and Magog prophesied by the ancient prophets of Israel?

The Arab governments and the PLO now claim that they are offering Israel "peace for land." But what kind of "peace" are they offering? There are two concepts or terms for "peace" in the Arab language. One represents true peace such as the peace between Canada and the United States, where we genuinely wish our neighbours well. The other refers to something more like "an armed truce." During the Crusades, the leader of the defeated Muslim armies, Saladin, offered the English general, Richard the Lion Heart, a peace treaty. However, two years later, after rebuilding his Arab armies, Saladin suddenly broke his agreement and defeated the English armies in Israel. In Yasser Arafat's speeches to Arab audiences, he boasts that he will offer Israel "the peace of Saladin." This proves that he is offering Israel "an armed truce" rather than "true peace." The PLO have not relinquished their commitment to conquer all of the land of Israel, or to destroy the Jewish population. All Arab Palestinian groups use emblems, flags, letterhead symbols, and maps that deny acknowledgement of the existence of the Jewish state.

The PLO have repeatedly declared to Arab audiences that their long-term strategy is to eliminate Israel in a plan called "Liberation in Phases." Since 1974 Yasser Arafat decreed that during the first phase of his "Liberation in Phases" plan, the PLO would seek to establish a beachhead in Gaza and the West Bank. In the second phase their armies will take over Jerusalem. In the final phase, they will build up their strength in Gaza and the West Bank to join their Arab-nation allies in an invasion to finally conquer all of Israel. On September 1, 1993, Arafat confirmed to an Arab audience that his peace accord was part of his previous "Phases" plan. During interviews, many Arab leaders, as well as individual Palestinians, have declared that they would never be content until they recovered the entire land of Israel from the Jews. In 1980 Yasser Arafat clearly stated, "Peace for us means the destruction of Israel." One of the problems for Israel is that the Koran teaches that if a land was ever occupied in the past by Muslims, then it must be recovered by Jihad, or holy war. Although Yasser Arafat has pledged to eliminate the references in the PLO Charter of the Palestine Liberation Organization that call for the destruction of Israel and the Jews, he has consistently refused to fulfill this pledge. Furthermore, most of his Arab allies refuse to relinquish their goals to destroy the Jewish state. The Arab states continue to arm for war against Israel.

### The PLO Charter

Excerpts from the PLO Charter, including the revisions made in 1968 and 1974, still include the following language calling for the destruction of Israel. Article 1 declares that "Palestine is the homeland of the Palestinian Arab people and an integral part of the great Arab homeland, and the people of Palestine is a part of the Arab Nation." Significantly Article 2 of the Charter affirms that "Palestine with its boundaries that existed at the time of the British Mandate is an integral regional unit." This means that the PLO not only claims the West Bank and Gaza plus Jerusalem, but they still demand that the Jews surrender every single inch of Israel also. Article 3 declares, "The Palestinian Arab people possesses the legal right to its homeland, and when the liberation of its homeland is completed it will exercise self-determination solely according to its own will and choice." This means that the Jews will have no rights, no will, and no choice if the Palestinians succeed. Articles 7, 8, and 9 confirm that "armed struggle is the only way to liberate Palestine." Lest anyone misunderstand their intent regarding the Jews who have lived in Israel all their lives, the PLO Charter declares the following in Article 15: "The liberation of Palestine, from an Arab viewpoint, is a national duty to repulse the Zionist, imperialist invasion from the great Arab homeland and to purge the Zionist presence from Palestine . . . until the liberation of its homeland." Finally, the Charter's articles reflect the Arabs' fundamental rejection of any truly peaceful cooperation with the Jewish people to share any portion of the Holy Land. Article 19 states, "The establishment of Israel is fundamentally null and void . . ." In case any reader still wonders if the PLO intends to live in peace with the Jews they should carefully consider the words of Article 22: "The liberation of Palestine will liquidate the Zionist and imperialist presence. . . ."

The prospects for lasting peace in the Middle East are remote. Even if Israel recklessly surrenders military control of the West Bank, Gaza, and the Golan Heights, this will still not satisfy the ultimate goals of the Arab nations nor the PLO. Since the Arab's true stated goal as revealed in countless speeches and the PLO Charter is the annihilation of Israel, this preliminary surrender of land simply alters the strategic balance massively and irreversibly in favor of the Arabs. However, the implacable hatred of the Arabs is the true cause of the last four wars against Israel. The Arab nations tried to annihilate the Jewish state in three wars (1948, 1956, and 1967) long before the Jews had occupied the West Bank, Gaza, and the Golan Heights. Obviously, Arab hatred against the

Jews will never be satisfied by simply surrendering these territories to the PLO and Syria. These surrenders will simply allow the Arabs to be in a much improved strategic position to launch a final annihilating war against Israel. Despite the current euphoria, Israel's Arab neighbors will continue to harbor thoughts and plans of launching a future war against the Jewish people. Far from leading to a real peace, if Israel does surrender these vital territories, it will make a future war more certain.

## Setting the Stage for a Seven-Year Treaty with Antichrist

The United Nations and the Arab states continue to demand the elimination of Israel's nuclear weapons. The introduction of Iranian nuclear weapons and the growing possibility of Libya, Syria, and Iraq joining the nuclear club has seriously altered the strategic balance of the Middle East. It is difficult to see how a balance of nuclear terror could continue for very long between Israel and the Islamic states who remain dedicated to Israel's destruction. United Nations' resolutions to ban nuclear weapons from the Middle East may tempt a future Israeli government to recklessly agree to relinquish their nuclear option. The present leaders of Israel realize that an unstable Arab regime, such as Iraq or Libya, might be tempted to use their nuclear, biological, or chemical warheads even though they know it would result in mutual destruction. In Islamic religious philosophy Muslims believe they will gain paradise if they die in a devastating war to cleanse the "infidels" from Jerusalem. In a few years following the War of Gog and Magog, the defeat of the Arab armies will pave the way for a European superpower to come forward to guarantee Israel's security and borders. Several prophecies describe the revival of the Roman Empire in the end times to dominate Europe and the rest of the world, as it did thousands of years ago in the days of Christ. The rise of the European Union is creating an economic and political superpower that is increasing its involvement in the Middle East peace process. The prophet Daniel wrote that a future Antichrist would arise in the last days to take over the revived Roman Empire (Daniel 7). Daniel predicted that "He shall confirm a covenant with many for one week." The word "many" means the Jews, and the word "week" is commonly used symbolically in Hebrew to refer to a period of seven years. This verse indicates that this future European dictator would confirm a treaty to defend Israel for seven years. The signing of this future treaty will start the final seven-year countdown to Armageddon, the climactic battle when Jesus Christ will defeat the armies of the world and establish His kingdom forever. This interim peace agreement between the PLO and Israel may set the stage for the fulfillment of these tremendous prophecies that lead to Christ's return in our generation.

The prophet Isaiah also spoke of this final seven-year peace treaty based on Israel's false confidence in the Antichrist: "You have said, 'We have made a covenant with death, and with Sheol we are in agreement. When the overflowing scourge passes through, it will not come to us, for we have made lies our refuge, and under falsehood we have hidden ourselves'" (Isaiah 28:15). The leaders of Israel will cynically make this seven-year treaty with the powerful dictator of the European superstate believing that he will protect Israel from the overwhelming military force of her enemies during that terrible time. However, the treaty will fail to protect them. In Isaiah 28:18 the prophet reveals God's judgment on Israel's treaty with the Antichrist: "Your covenant with death will be annulled, and your agreement with Sheol will not stand; when the overflowing scourge passes through, then you will be trampled down by it." After three and one half years the Antichrist will betray Israel and break the treaty. He will enter the rebuilt Temple in Jerusalem and claim to be god. When he demands that Israel worships him, most of the Jews will rebel against him. The book of Revelation describes the righteous Jews fleeing into the wilderness for 1260 days (three and one half years) after this betrayal.

When the "Gog and Magog" invasion occurs (see figure 4), it appears that the only response from the Western democracies will be a diplomatic protest. Ezekiel 38:13 says that "Sheba and Dedan and the merchants of Tarshish" and "the young lions thereof, [probably the United Kingdom, the United States, and the Commonwealth nations] shall say unto thee, "Art thou come to take a spoil?" Tarshish, Sheba, and Dedan were ancient trading nations and are believed by many Bible scholars to refer to Spain or Britain and their former colonies ("the young lions thereof"). It will not be the Western democracies that respond to this attack. The superpower who intervenes to save Israel in its greatest hour of need will be their great defender, the God of Abraham.

God declares through His prophet Ezekiel that He will defeat Russia and its Arab allies in the greatest military disaster in history. According to Ezekiel 39:2, five-sixth's of the Russian-Arab armies (85 percent) will be annihilated by God upon the mountains of Israel. The Lord will trigger the greatest earthquake experienced thus far in history, centered in the mountains of Israel, but affecting the cities around the globe. In addition, the supernatural destruction will be accompanied by God's additional judgments, including "pestilence, overflowing rain, great hailstones, fire, brimstone" (38:22). The Lord will send such confusion and chaos upon the enemy that "every man's sword shall be against his brother" (verse 21). The devastation and loss of human life will be so great that "seven months shall the house of Israel be burying of them" (Ezekiel 39:12). The captured weapons and fuel supplies will provide fuel for the towns and villages of Israel for seven years following the supernatural victory (verse 9).

In my research, I have found that some new Russian weapons have been produced. These weapons are manufactured using a new material known as lignostone. Prepared from compressed wood-product, this material was developed in Holland to be used as fuel. However, the Soviet weapons laboratories discovered that this unique substance, called lignostone, is as strong as steel, light, pliable, and almost invisible to radar. These unique characteristics encouraged the Russian military to utilize this material in many military vehicles and weapons. One of the characteristics of lignostone is that it burns at very high temperatures and can be readily used as an alternative fuel. The use of lignostone, and the fact that mobile Russian military units can carry large amounts of fuel (in containers 100 yards across) for their tanks and helicopters, may explain the prophecy that the defeat of this army will provide ample fuel for Israel for a period of seven years.

The prophecy recorded in Ezekiel 38:21 and 39:21–22 indicates that God's purpose in this extraordinary intervention in history is to glorify and sanctify His Holy Name in the sight of Israel and the Gentile nations. The awesome destruction associated with this victory over the Russian-Arab armies will not be confined solely to the invading armies. God declared, "And I will send a fire on Magog, and among them that dwell carelessly in the isles: and they shall know that I am the Lord" (Ezekiel 39:6). Russia (Magog) will be devastated by the wrath of God, as well as those nations "dwelling carelessly in the isles" which may refer to Europe and America.

Russia has prepositioned enormous military supplies in Lebanon, Iraq, Syria, Libya, and Egypt in preparation for the coming Russian-Arab invasion of Israel. It is both easier and more efficient for Russia to airlift huge numbers of lightly armed men into Syria, Egypt, and Lebanon to pick up previously positioned weapons, than to airlift the military supplies for them. Military equipment often weighs five to ten times the weight of the soldier who will use that equipment. The same logic motivates the United States military to preposition enormous amounts of military supplies in Europe to be available for American and Canadian troops who would be flown into France and Germany in the event of a Russian invasion of Western Europe. The PLO, Iraq, Jordan, Lybia, and Syria are themselves already so heavily armed that they have little practical use for this additional equipment.

God set an appointment more than twenty-five hundred years ago to destroy Gog and Magog on the mountains of Israel: "Thus saith the Lord God; Art thou he of whom I have spoken in old time by my servants the prophets of Israel, which prophesied in those days many years that I would bring thee against them?" (Ezekiel 38:17). As I mentioned earlier, it is fascinating to read the Jewish commentaries on Ezekiel 38 and 39 that describe an oral tradition recorded from the Vilna Gaon that advises Jews to observe carefully when the Russian fleet (Magog) passes from the Black Sea through the Bosporus to the Mediterranean. "It is now the time to put on your Sabbath clothes because the Messiah is coming." For the first time in history, the Russian Navy has surpassed all other navies in the world in size. Russia has moved many of its ships from the Black Sea into the Mediterranean Sea opposite Israel to challenge the former U.S. naval supremacy in that strategic area.

Although Scripture does not indicate the year in which this future invasion and defeat of Russia will occur, the prophet Haggai gives us a strong indication of what the actual day may be. Haggai reveals that on the twenty-fourth day of the ninth month (Chisleu) of the Jewish calendar, the day before Hanukkah, God will deliver Israel as He did twice before on this day: (1) the defeat of the Syrian army and recapture of the Temple in 165 B.C. and (2) the British capture of Jerusalem from the Turks in 1917 during the closing battles of WWI.

The prophet Haggai declares: "The Word of the Lord came unto Haggai in the four and twentieth day of the month [Chisleu], saying, Speak to Zerubbabel, governor of Judah, saying, I will shake the heavens and the earth; and I will overthrow the throne of kingdoms and I will destroy the strength of the kingdoms of the heathen; and I will overthrow the chariots, and those that ride in them; and the horses and their riders shall come down, every one by the sword of his brother" (Haggai 2:20–22).

This description by Haggai, and the exact language of his prophecy, is uncannily like the language of Ezekiel 38 and 39 that describes Russia's defeat. The interesting point is that Haggai names the exact day of the year on which this will occur. Since so many other prophecies have been so precisely fulfilled to the day, there is a strong probability that this prophetic event will also occur on its appointed anniversary date of the biblical calendar. "Behold, it is come, and it is done, saith the Lord God; this is the day whereof I have spoken" (Ezekiel 39:8). God's appointment with Russia is set; it will not be postponed.

# 8

# The Rebuilding of the Temple

*May it be Thy will that the Temple be speedily rebuilt in our days.*
The ancient Jewish prayer for the rebuilding of the Temple

During the centuries of exile from the Promised Land, generations of righteous Jews have prayed this prayer: "May the Temple
be rebuilt speedily in our days!" For almost two millennia it was
impossible for most Jews to even visit the ruins of their beloved
Temple, so those who longed for God's Sanctuary had to content
themselves with the study of its features and their prayers.

For two thousand years, devoted Jews have turned toward
Jerusalem, the Holy City, three times a day to pray that God would
return the Divine Shekinah Presence to their rebuilt Temple. After
many centuries of dreaming of the prospect of rebuilding the
Temple in the last days, the Jewish people in this final generation
have been given the momentous task of turning these dreams into
reality.

The great Rabbi Moses Maimonides, affectionately called
Rambam, stated that the study of the Temple was of eternal significance because it revealed the nature of God and His relationship to Israel. He noted that the 613 mitzvot or commandments of
the Torah contain God's direct command to build the Temple. The

Lord gave this command to Israel: "And let them build me a sanctuary; that I may dwell among them. According to all that I show thee, after the pattern of the tabernacle, and the pattern of all the instruments thereof, even so shall you make it" (Exodus 25:8).

In this passage the Lord revealed to Moses not only the direct command to build the Sanctuary, but He also showed him the blueprints (the pattern) of the Tabernacle so that the earthly Sanctuary would duplicate as far as humanly possible the heavenly Sanctuary. It is fascinating to observe that both the Tabernacle in the Wilderness and the magnificent Temple built by King Solomon are patterned after the eternal Sanctuary in the heavens — even to the details of the instruments and vessels of the Temple, including the Ark of the Covenant.

The Temple had two distinct purposes for Israel. First, the Temple's fundamental purpose was to reveal the Divine Presence, the Shechinah glory of God to mankind. Its second purpose was to be the prescribed place, chosen by God, for the offering of divine sacrifices as outlined in the book of Exodus. The Lord commanded Moses to "speak unto the children of Israel, that they bring me an offering: of every man that gives it willingly with his heart ye shall take my offering." (Exodus 25:2)

Maimonides concludes his brilliant fourteen-volume Mishneh Torah with a final volume called *Hilchos Bais HaBechirah: The Laws of God's Chosen House*. This book contains six mitzvot or commandments that summarize God's laws given to Israel regarding the Temple:

1. They are to build a sanctuary.
2. They are to build the altar with stone which is not hewn.
3. They are not to ascend the altar with steps — must use a ramp.
4. They must fear and reverence the Temple.
5. They must guard the Temple completely.
6. They must never cease watching over the Temple.

For two thousand years the Jews have mourned the loss of their Temple on the ninth day of the month of Av (August) in 587 B.C. On this solemn day every year since the destruction of Solomon's Temple, the Jews have read the book of Lamentations, written by the prophet Jeremiah, in which the Babylonian destruction of the Temple is described. They mourn for the loss of their holy Sanctuary where God had communed with them for centuries. After the Roman army burned the Second Temple on the very same day, the 9th of Av, A.D. 70, the sacred Temple was lost, seemingly forever, as the center for Israel's spiritual life. For centuries thereafter, the religious leadership of Israel was left with only the synagogue, the Torah, and rabbinical writings in the *Talmud* for expression of their love for God's holy name. However, the Lord prophesied that the Jewish exiles would someday return to the Promised Land to rebuild the Temple in the last days.

Some of the most interesting prophecies yet to be fulfilled describe the rebuilding of the Temple in Jerusalem in the last days.

> But in the last days it shall come to pass, that the mountain of the house of the Lord shall be established in the top of the mountains, and it shall be exalted above the hills; and people shall bow unto it. (Micah 4:1)

> In that day will I raise up the tabernacle of David that is fallen, and close up the breaches thereof; and I will raise up his ruins, and I will build it as in the days of old. (Amos 9:11)

> The glory of this latter Temple shall be greater than the former, says the Lord of Hosts. (Haggai 2:9)

Now, after twenty centuries of exile among the nations, the Jewish people once again possess the sacred soil of the Holy Land. In addition, the Jews are also in possession of the Holy City, Jerusalem. The tragedy of the Middle East is that both the Arabs and the Jews claim the right to the land, the Holy City, and the Temple Mount.

Despite the fact that Israel is smaller than the state of Massachusetts, the nations of the world are vitally interested in this Promised Land and in the ensuing struggle between the Arabs and the Jews. The land of Israel and the strategic control of the Middle East are of immense military importance to America, Russia, China, and the European powers. In a few years we will witness the climactic struggle between these powers in the valley that lies below the mount of Megiddo — the final Battle of Armageddon.

Israel, especially the city of Jerusalem, stands at the center of the world's spiritual, political, and military conflicts. The Bible prophesies that the battle for the soul of mankind will reach its conclusion in Jerusalem. The current political, military, and religious developments in the Middle East are laying the foundation for the coming messianic kingdom. Research projects conducted by the Temple Institute in Jerusalem and the religious leadership in Israel are rapidly preparing the way for the rebuilding of the Third Temple.

Numerous prophecies indicate that the Third Temple will be built before Satan's world dictator, the Antichrist, takes worldwide control. He will finally be destroyed by Jesus Christ at the Battle of Armageddon, when Christ returns to set up His Kingdom.

The prophet Daniel foresaw in his vision of the Seventy Weeks (see Daniel 9:24–27) that this last great world dictator would make a "covenant" (peace treaty) with Israel for seven years. After three and one half years he would break the treaty and enter their rebuilt Temple in Jerusalem and "he shall cause the sacrifice and the oblation to cease" (Daniel 9:27). Obviously, the Antichrist cannot stop the daily sacrifice unless, prior to this, the Levitical sacrificial system has been reinstated. No Jewish Temple sacrifices have occurred since A.D. 70, when the Romans burned the Second Temple. Therefore, at some point in the future, the Jews will have to reinstate the Levitical sacrifice system on the Temple Mount.

In talking to His disciples about the last days and the Great Tribulation, Jesus Christ warned the Jews that "when ye therefore shall see the abomination of desolation, spoken of by Daniel the prophet, stand in the holy place, (who so readeth, let him understand:) then let them which be in Judea flee into the mountains" (Matthew 24:15–16). The "abomination of desolation" is the ultimate defiling of the Holy Place in the last days when Satan will demand that the Antichrist be worshiped as "God" in the Temple. This prophecy has not yet been fulfilled. Christ's prophecy clearly indicates that the Temple must be rebuilt in the future in order for this prediction to be fulfilled.

In his second letter to the church at Thessalonica, the apostle Paul advised that the Lord would not return in glory to set up His Kingdom until "that man of sin," the Antichrist, is revealed — "the son of perdition; who opposeth and exalteth himself above all that is called God, or that is worshipped; so that he as God sitteth in the temple of God, showing himself that he is God" (2 Thessalonians 2:3–4).

Obviously, in order for these events to occur, the Third

Temple must be rebuilt by the Jews as a legitimate Temple of God. For almost two thousand years, religious Jews have dreamed of rebuilding the Temple. Since the stunningly victorious Six-Day War in June 1967, Israel has possessed the whole of the city of Jerusalem. Despite the United Nations' attempts to "internationalize" Jerusalem, the attitude of Israel is best expressed in the words of General Moshe Dayan who said at the time, "No power on earth will remove us from this spot again." It should be noted that Israel still allows the Arab Moslems to control and police the Temple Mount with its Muslim shrine, the Dome of the Rock. Religious Jews, of course, will not worship there, thereby fulfilling the prophecy of Luke 21:24 that "Jerusalem shall be trodden down of the Gentiles, until the times of the Gentiles be fulfilled."

"Should the Temple be Rebuilt?" was the headline of an article in *TIME* magazine on June 20, 1967, following the recapture of the Temple Mount. The writer said, "Assuming that Israel keeps the Western Wall, which is one of the few remaining ruins of Judaism's Second Temple, has the time now come for the erection of the third Temple?" The article continues with this theme: "Such is Israel's euphoria today that some Jews see plausible theological grounds for discussing reconstruction. They base their argument on the contention that Israel has already entered its "Messianic Era."

In 1948, Israel's chief rabbi ruled that, with the establishment of the Jewish state and the ingathering of the exiles, "the age of redemption" had begun. Today many of Israel's religious leaders are convinced that the Jews' victory over the Arabs in the Six-Day War in 1967 has taken Judaism well beyond that point. Says historian Israel Eldad: "We are at the stage where David was when he liberated Jerusalem; from that time until the construction of the Temple of Solomon, only one generation passed, so will it be with us."

For two thousand years Jews have longed for the day when they could return to the Promised Land and finally rebuild their beloved Temple on the Temple Mount. During the years since 1948, a number of Israelis have begun to transform this longing into reality with a series of practical steps that are necessary if Israel is to ever see a Temple in its future.

The television show *60 Minutes* reported in March 1985 that rabbinical students in Jerusalem are now studying the reintroduction of the ancient Jewish rites of sacrifice on the Temple Mount. The show was called "One Step in Heaven." Within five hundred yards to the northwest of the Western Wall of the ancient Temple, I took a photograph of this yeshiva (a theological college), led by the late Rabbi Goren, the former chief rabbi of the Israel Defense Forces. This same rabbi blew the shofar, the ram's horn, immediately after the recapture of the Western Wall of the Temple in June 1967. This conquest returned the Temple site to Jewish control for the first time in almost two thousand years. In a *Newsweek* interview in November 1981, Rabbi Goren declared that "the secret of the location of the Ark will be revealed just prior to building the Third Temple."

God gave King David a detailed blueprint of the Temple that contained a place for the Court of the Gentiles in both Solomon's Temple and the Second Temple. In addition, the prophet Zechariah prophesied about the future millennial kingdom: "And it shall come to pass, that every one that is left of all the nations which came against Jerusalem shall even go up from year to year to worship the King, the Lord of Hosts, and to keep the Feast of Tabernacles" (Zechariah 14:16). These passages reveal that the Temple is to be a place of worship for both the Jews and the Gentiles.

In Jerusalem today, religious Jews are forbidden by the chief rabbi to walk on many areas of the Temple Mount, lest they inadvertently approach the place of the Holy of Holies. In the near future a dramatic change must occur to allow the rebuilding of the Temple. Do the prophecies of the Bible give us a hint as to what this motivation will be? In my estimation, they do. The answer to the question regarding the Jews' motivation to rebuild the Temple may involve the recovery of the lost Ark of the Covenant.

The question of the rebuilding of the Temple inevitably brings up the question as to how Israel could build its Temple without destroying the existing structure known as the Dome of the Rock. This beautiful Moslem building was erected by Caliph Abdel Malik on the Temple Mount in A.D. 691. For almost thirteen centuries people have believed that this building was built directly over the site of the original Temple and Holy of Holies. If this were the case, it would be difficult to envision a situation in which Israel would be able to rebuild the Temple. Israel has been extremely protective of the religious and holy sites of both the Muslims and the Christians, despite the fact that both religions have previously destroyed Jewish holy buildings. This sensitivity to Islamic veneration for the sacred Dome of the Rock led Moshe Dayan, as Israel's defense minister, to allow the Muslims to retain a guardianship role over the Temple Mount site, even after Israel had conquered Arab East Jerusalem in 1967.

This act of generous toleration and sensitivity to Moslem feelings for the Dome of the Rock is seen by many Israelis today to have been a tremendous error in political judgment. However, even this decision was the fulfillment of a two-thousand-year-old prophecy made by the prophet John in the book of Revelation, chapter 11. In a vision of the final Tribulation period of three and one-half years leading up to the Battle of Armageddon, John was told by the angel to "rise and measure the temple of God, and the altar, and them that worship therein, But the court which is without the temple, leave out, and measure it not, for it is given unto the Gentiles: and the holy city shall they tread under foot forty and two months." (Revelation 11:1-2).

In other words, the prophet saw in his vision that there would be a period after the rebuilding of the Temple and the sacrificial altar in which a part of the Temple Mount known as the Court of the Gentiles would still be given over to the Gentiles (the Arab Muslims) for forty-two months (three and one-half years) until Christ returns to set up His Kingdom.

The solution to this problem of the rebuilding of the Temple has awaited the completion of recent archeological research on the Temple Mount. In the last few years, archeological discoveries have enabled Jewish authorities to determine that the original site of Solomon's Temple — and hence, the location for the rebuilding of the Temple — is in the open area of the Temple Mount directly north of the existing Dome of the Rock.

In the months following the recapture of the Temple in June 1967, Israeli archeologists began to carefully dig a nine-hundred-yard-long tunnel in a northerly direction along the Western Wall from the area known as Wilson's Arch to the northwest corner of the ancient Temple Mount. This tunnel is almost sixty-five yards below the level of the present-day streets of Jerusalem. It has become known as the Rabbi's Tunnel because, after 1967, the rabbis used it to privately approach the ancient site of the Holy of Holies.

As I walked through the underground area where the orthodox Jews keep their sacred Torah Scrolls I was able to see where
the scientists had dug deep down to expose the original massive
Herodian foundation stones. Some of these gigantic carved limestone foundation blocks were 46 feet by 10 feet by 10 feet. These
massive stones can weigh up to a thousand tons and are fitted so
perfectly together that it is impossible to place even a razor blade
between them (see figure 3). Many scholars believe that these
ancient stones were placed into this Western Wall under the direction of King Solomon almost three thousand years ago. It is fascinating to note that modern machinery, including cranes and helicopters, would be unable to move these one-thousand-ton stones
one mile from the quarry where they were excavated to their
location on the Temple Mount.

Further along the tunnel they have discovered something that
archeologists only dream of finding. Several hundred feet north of
Wilson's Arch they uncovered an ancient gate that led into the
subterranean passages beneath the Temple Mount which had
been built by King Herod the Great in the time of the Second
Temple. This Herodian gate was almost directly opposite the Eastern (Golden) Gate. The *Mishna* records that these Temple gates
were precisely opposite each other and that the Eastern Gate led
directly, in a line, into the Beautiful Gate of the Second Temple.
Now, after almost two thousand years, the Western Gate has been
discovered. This proves beyond a shadow of a doubt that the
location of the Temple, which lay precisely between these two
gates, is north of the Dome of the Rock. An interesting photo I took
from the Garden of Gethsemane, directly opposite the Eastern
(Golden) Gate, shows clearly that the Dome of the Rock is built
over one hundred and fifty feet to the south of the true site,
directly west of the Eastern Gate (see the first photo in the center
photo section).

The Western Gate was filled with rocks and debris from the
brutal destruction of the Temple by the Roman army of Titus on
the ninth of Av, A.D. 70. As the debris was cleared away, it was
discovered that this gate led into a complex subterranean network
of tunnels, some of which led directly eastward under the former
site of the Second Temple; others led in different directions. This
confirmed the Jewish legends that the whole area underneath the
Temple Mount is honeycombed with secret passages and huge

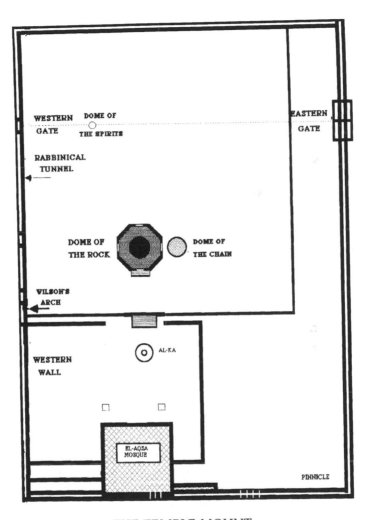

## THE TEMPLE MOUNT
### Figure 1

cisterns, as reported by the Jewish historian Flavius Josephus. The Muslim authorities furiously demanded that this newly discovered Western Gate be immediately sealed, and the Israeli government agreed to limit the archeological digging for the moment. Several of the individuals who entered this tunnel, including Rabbi Getz, the rabbi of the Western Wall, declared later that they had seen, at a distance, some of the golden Temple objects. However, they were not able to closely examine these objects.

One of the underground cisterns that I saw, beneath the Temple Mount, could hold hundreds of thousands of gallons of water. These thirty-four cisterns, cut out of the natural limestone underlying the Temple Mount, can hold over twelve million gallons of water. Water storage was essential for cleansing the sanctuary, as well as for water reserves in the case of a siege.

Another confirmation of the true site of the ancient Temple and the Holy of Holies is the location of a small Arabic cupola. It lies over a hundred and fifty feet to the north of the Dome of the Rock and is exactly on a line drawn between the Eastern Gate and the newly discovered Western Gate in the archeologist's tunnel. This small Arab building, known as *Qubbat el-Arwah*, the Dome of the Spirits (or Winds), stands isolated on the site of a flat foundation stone composed of the original bedrock of Mount Moriah. The Arabs also call this site *Qubbat el-Alouah*, the Dome of the Tablets. These two names may well reveal the ancient Muslim knowledge that this stone is, in fact, the ancient foundation stone that supported the Ark of the Covenant with the tablets in the Holy of Holies. The *Mishna* records that there was a foundation stone in the Temple known as "Even Shetyah" and that the Ark of the Covenant rested upon this foundation stone in Solomon's Temple. The *Mishna* records that the foundation stone stood alone in the Holy of Holies in the Second Temple because the Ark of the Covenant was missing.

In 1896, a short distance southeast of the Dome of the Spirits, British archeologists located a cistern that conforms exactly to its description in the *Mishna*. It was positioned between the Temple porch and the altar of sacrifice. This pit was apparently designed to contain the libation offerings connected with the Temple services. The discovery of this cistern may also confirm the location of the Holy of Holies as being north of the Dome of the Rock.

As the diagrams of the Temple Mount illustrate (see figures 3 and 4), the Third Temple can now be rebuilt on the exact location of Solomon's Temple, with the Holy of Holies built around the ancient foundation stone, now covered by the Dome of the Spirits. This means that Israel could rebuild the Temple without disturbing the Muslim's Dome of the Rock. In addition, the pictures of the model of the Second Temple clearly show that the Third Temple could be rebuilt on the original Temple site. The Dome of the Rock could then remain undisturbed in the ancient area of the Court of

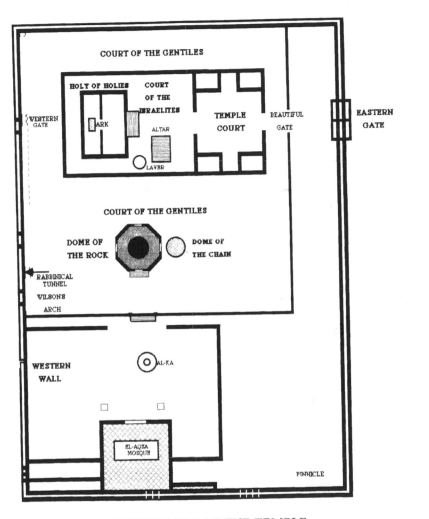

**REBUILDING OF THE TEMPLE**
*Figure 2*

the Gentiles over one hundred and fifty feet to the south of the rebuilt Temple.

Within Israel a group calling itself Netemanei Har Habayit, the Faithful of the Temple Mount, has built a detailed model of the Temple, and a fund has already been set up for donations to rebuild the Temple. Sources in Israel have told me that millions of dollars have been set aside by many Jews, in wills and trusts, to aid in the financing of the reconstruction.

The Temple Mount is in Israeli hands, and the exact site for rebuilding is known and available. A fund has been created, and a Temple priesthood of Jews from the tribe of Levi is in training by Rabbi Goren's Yeshivat Torat Kohanim and other groups. In light of the evidence provided in the following chapter that the Ark of the Covenant may have been returned from Ethiopia, it seems that the path has been cleared for the momentous events described by the ancient prophets of the Bible. Truly the approaching footsteps of the Messiah can be heard in these exciting events.

# 9

# *The Prophetic Role of the Ark of the Covenant*

According to all that I show you, that is, the pattern of the tabernacle and the pattern of all its furnishings, just so you shall make it. And they shall make an ark of acacia wood. (Exodus 25:9–10)

During the first year of Israel's wandering in the wilderness, God gave specific directions to Moses to create the Tabernacle and a number of sacred objects, patterned after the worship objects in the heavenly Temple. The completion of these objects would provide an expression of His eternal covenant with His chosen people. Israel carried several sacred objects through the wilderness for forty years until they reached the Promised Land and could place them in the Ark of the Covenant, and in a Sanctuary befitting their importance. The first of these sacred objects was the rod. The High Priest Aaron used this rod to perform miracles before the pharaoh of Egypt. Also included was the manna, the daily bread from heaven that God provided for forty years in the Sinai wilderness. The third item was the two tablets of stone on which God had written the Ten Commandments. Aaron's rod symbolized God's sovereign choice and the supernatural deliverance of Israel from Egypt. The bowl of manna symbolized God's daily provision for His people. The tablets represented God's concern for His people, as He gave them His divine law. All of these objects represented God's presence in the life of Israel and prophetically pointed to our salvation in Jesus Christ.

God gave explicit instructions to Moses regarding the building of the sacred Ark of the Covenant. The word "ark" comes from the Hebrew word which means a chest, box, or coffin. The Ark was built of acacia wood covered with gold within and without, and its dimensions were 45 by 27 by 27 inches. It was covered by a lid of pure gold (called the mercy seat). Two gold cherubim facing each other from the two ends of the lid represented the angelic cherubim who surround the throne of God in heaven. The Lord said that His Divine Presence would dwell with the Ark forever. This "Shekinah" glory filled the tribes of Israel with awe and reverence.

When it was finished, the Ark of the Covenant was placed in the Tabernacle of worship that was moved from place to place at God's discretion as Israel wandered forty years in the wilderness. Finally, the priests carried the Ark through the miraculously dried-up river bed of the Jordan River into the Promised Land on the tenth day of the month Nisan. "And the priests that bare the ark of the covenant of the Lord stood firm on dry ground in the midst of Jordan, and all the Israelites passed over on dry ground, until all the people were passed clean over Jordan" (Joshua 3:17). When the priests stepped into the river with the Ark, the waters miraculously stopped flowing, allowing the tribes of Israel to cross the river bed into Canaan on dry land. In the famous battle of Jericho, the priests carried the Ark around the city seven times. The walls miraculously fell, and the Israelites marched over the collapsed walls into the city. As documented in my book *The Signature of God*, archeologists in 1930–1936 discovered that the walls of Jericho had actually collapsed just as the book of Joshua records. For centuries the Israelites victoriously carried the Ark into battle against the pagan armies that opposed them.

God gave instructions to Moses regarding the proper handling and care of the Ark by the Levites and priests (see Exodus 25:10-22). The holiness and Divine Presence of God surrounding the Ark of the Covenant was so overpowering that improper handling resulted in instant death. The Lord commanded that only the Levites were to carry the Ark, and then only by resting the poles which extended from the ends of the Ark on their shoulders. One time King David violated God's instructions and ordered the priests to carry the Ark in an ox cart instead of using the method God had commanded Moses. The oxen stumbled and the cart began to tip over. Uzzah reached out to keep the Ark from falling and died because of his violation of the laws of God regarding transportation and handling of the Ark. Perhaps the many years of storing the Ark in Abinadab's house caused his son, Uzzah, to lose his sense of reverence for the holiness of God's Presence which surrounded the Ark. On another occasion, after the Ark was recaptured from the Philistines, the Jewish men of Bethshemesh, out of curiosity, violated its sanctity by opening the Ark. This caused more than fifty thousand people to die of the plague.

When the first Temple was completed under King Solomon, the Ark was placed in the Holy of Holies. The Bible describes this dramatic event:

> Then the priests brought in the ark of the covenant of the Lord to its place, into the inner sanctuary of the temple, to the Most Holy Place, under the wings of the cherubim. Nothing was in the ark [at this time] except the two tablets of stone which Moses put there at Horeb, when the Lord made a covenant with the children of Israel, when they came out of the land of Egypt. And it came to pass, when the priests came out of the holy place that the cloud filled the house of the Lord, so that the priests could not continue ministering because of the cloud; for the glory of the Lord filled the house of the Lord. Then Solomon spoke: 'The Lord said He would dwell in the dark cloud. I have surely built You an exalted house, and a place for You to dwell in forever. (1 Kings 8:6, 9–13)

God's special Shekinah glory dwelt above the mercy seat upon the Ark of the Covenant and guided and protected Israel. It symbolized the person of Christ, the Messiah, who would come to fulfill God's covenant with His people. Jesus later explained to Israel His role as their Messiah-King: "I and My Father are one" (John 10:30). He explained that he did not come to "destroy the Law or the Prophets . . . but to fulfill" it (Matthew 5:17).

*THE ARK OF THE COVENANT*
*Figure 1*

The Ark remained in the Temple until the final years of King Solomon's reign when, according to many scholars, it was taken to Ethiopia. From the time of Solomon till the present, the Bible is strangely silent about the location of the Ark. We know it was not present in the Second Temple after the Jewish captives returned from the Babylonian captivity in 536 B.C. Yet according to the prophet Jeremiah, the Ark of the Covenant will play a pivotal role in our future. He prophesies in Jeremiah 3:15–17 that, just before the return of the Messiah, Israel will once again visit and discuss the Ark of the Covenant. When the Messiah comes, the Ark will no longer be the central focus of Israel's worship; they will then worship Christ directly. This prophecy implies that this sacred object must play a crucial role in the prophetic events leading up to the rebuilding of the Temple and the coming of the Messiah.

Several biblical commentators, including Dr. David Lewis and Arthur Bloomfield, have written about scriptural indications that the lost Ark will return to the Temple Mount in the last days. They believe the Ark will become the subject of newspaper headlines in the near future. The prophecies of the Bible indicate that, after being hidden for almost three thousand years, the Ark is once again about to take its place on the forefront of human history. If the Ark of the Covenant is brought forth publicly, I believe that the Jewish leadership of Israel would be compelled to rebuild the Temple with the Holy of Holies to provide a proper home for it. The religious leaders of Israel would also have to prepare for animal sacrifices to fulfill Daniel's prophecy (Daniel 9:27). Is this possible? What happened to the holy Ark in the first place? Where is it now?

In his detailed prophecy describing the coming Russian-Arab invasion of Israel (the War of Gog and Magog), the prophet Ezekiel declared: "I will set my glory among the heathen, and all the heathen shall see my judgment that I have executed; and my hand that I have laid upon them. So the house of Israel shall know that I am the Lord their God from that day and forward" (Ezekiel 39:21-22). These words, "I will set my glory among the heathen" may refer to the actual presence of the Shekinah glory of God above the mercy seat of the Ark. Throughout the Scriptures the phrase "My glory" is used exclusively in reference to either Christ Himself or to the Shekinah glory surrounding the Ark of the Covenant. The context of Ezekiel 39:21 strongly suggests that the Ark is in view in Ezekiel's prophecy.

To discover the truth about the Ark of the Covenant we will need to examine evidence from two different sources: (1) the secular history of ancient Ethiopia and (2) the prophecies and historical records of the Bible. These records will enable us to come to a determination on the Ark's probable location and its possible role in our prophetic future. The last time the Ark of the Covenant was unquestionably in the hands of Israel is reported in 2 Chronicles 8:11, in which Solomon asked his wife, the pagan daughter of the Egyptian pharaoh, to leave the area where the Ark of the Covenant was stored because she was not a believer. Shortly after this event, the Ark of the Covenant, the most important and powerful religious object in history, disappeared from Israel's national life. In all of the Bible's subsequent accounts of battles, rebellions, invasions, and the looting of the Temple by various pagan empires, the Scriptures are silent about the location of this most sacred and powerful object.

What happened to the Ark of the Covenant? There is one brief mention of an "ark" in 2 Chronicles 35:3, where King Josiah orders the priests to return the ark to the Temple. It had been removed earlier by a wicked king to make room for his pagan idols. However, it is unlikely that this "ark" object referred to in 2 Chronicles 35:3 is the true Ark of the Covenant because the biblical writer does not call it "the Ark of the Covenant." Also, in light of the devastating divine punishment given to past defilers of the true Ark, such as Uzzah, it is difficult to believe that an evil king could have simply removed the true Ark of the Covenant and substituted false idols in the Temple without divine retribution. However, if Ethiopian history is correct, then the "ark" object referred to in 2 Chronicles 35:3 was only a replica of the true Ark of the Covenant. This would explain how they could have removed this replica "ark" with impunity.

### The Ethiopian Historical Records from the Royal Chronicles

During the reign of King Solomon, the famous Queen of Sheba visited Solomon in Jerusalem several years after Solomon placed the Ark of the Covenant in the Holy of Holies of the newly completed Temple. Second Chronicles 9:12 tells us, "And King Solomon gave to the Queen of Sheba all her desire, whatsoever she asked, beside that which she had brought unto the king. So she turned, and went away to her own land, she and her servants." We know from the Bible that Solomon was not adverse to marrying foreign women and having children by them. According to Ethiopian history, the Queen of Sheba married King Solomon and they produced a son.

The Ethiopian royal chronicles record that Prince Menelik I of Ethiopia was this son. He grew up in the palace in Jerusalem with his father, King Solomon. While being educated by the priests of the Temple, he became a strong believer in Jehovah.

In a September 1935 article in *National Geographic*, Leo Roberts recorded his interviews with various priests in different parts of Ethiopia, all of whom consistently told the following story. They recounted that the Queen of Sheba had visited King Solomon and had a child, Menelik I.

> Solomon educated the lad in Jerusalem until he was nine-teen years old. The boy then returned to Ethiopia with a large group of Jews, taking with him the true Ark of the

Covenant. Many people believe that this Ark is now in some church along the northern boundary of present-day Ethiopia, near Aduwa (Adua) or Aksum; but, if it is here, it is so well guarded by the priests that no student from the Western world has been able to confirm or deny the legend. (see photo section)

An *Encyclopedia Britannica* article confirms this tradition also.

It [Aksum-Aduwa] contains the ancient church where, according to tradition, the Tabot, or Ark of the Covenant, brought from Jerusalem by the son of Solomon and the Queen of Sheba, was deposited and is still supposed to rest.

Menelik I, as a royal son of Solomon, was the founder of the longest-lived monarchy in history. His royal dynasty extended to the late Emperor Haile Selassie (he called himself the "Lion of Judah"), who claimed direct descent from King Solomon. During the 1974 takeover of Ethiopia by a communist military coup, Emperor Haile Selassie was imprisoned and died in jail the following year under mysterious circumstances. The Marxist Ethiopian government buried him secretly in an unknown grave. However, a number of Emperor Haile Selassie's descendants escaped and are now living in the West. The current emperor is living in England.

Prince Stephen Mengesha, the great-grandson of Emperor Haile Selassie, who now lives in Canada, was kind enough to agree to several interviews in connection with this book. He confirmed my research about the importance of the Ark of the Covenant in Ethiopian history. Prince Mengesha's father, Prince Mengesha Sevoum, was the governor-general of Ethiopia governing the province of Tigre, which contains the ancient city of Aksum, where the Ark was secretly hidden away by the custodians of the religious relics thousands of years ago. Prince Mengesha Sevoum is the director of an Ethiopian relief operation in the Sudan. He appeared in an interview on a national television program in the United States and verified that the Ark of the Covenant was protected in Ethiopia. He showed photos of Queen Elizabeth II, Prince Philip, and Emperor Haile Selassie during the royal trip to Aksum, where the Queen and Prince visited the repository of this ancient Ark of the Covenant.

Prince Stephen Mengesha spent several summers as a teenager exploring the region of Aksum (located in northern Ethiopia) and visited many of the ancient and almost inaccessible cave churches where early Ethiopian Jewish Christians held their services. He confirmed that the historic Church of Zion of Mary in Aksum was the repository of the Ark of the Covenant. A picture of Aksum and this Church of Zion of Mary is included in the photo section of this book. The original ancient building was burnt during the sixteenth century. The present church was rebuilt several hundred years ago over the original foundations and subbasements of the ancient repository. This area of Aksum is in the northern Tigre province of Ethiopia. The Tigre province joined forces with the Eritreans in the successful 1991 civil war to defeat the Ethiopian Marxist army leaders who killed Emperor Haile Selassie in 1975.

The Ethiopian official historical records, known as the *Glory of the Kings* (*Kebra-Nagast*), contain an explanation of what happened to the Ark of the Covenant. In addition, there are several detailed Ethiopian murals (see photo section) that tell how the Ark and the Tablets of the Law were taken to Ethiopia for safekeeping by Prince Menelik I thousands of years ago. The records indicate that when the Queen of Sheba died, her nineteen-year-old son Prince Menelik I prepared to leave Jerusalem to return twenty-five hundred miles to his native country to become its king. Before he left, King Solomon (to whom the prince bore an uncanny resemblance in beauty and regal bearing) ordered his craftsmen to create a perfect replica of the Ark for his son to take with him to Ethiopia. The great distance between the two royal cities would prevent the prince from ever again worshiping at the Temple in Jerusalem. However, the Ethiopian records suggest that Prince Menelik was concerned with the growing apostasy of Israel and the fact that his father, Solomon, was now allowing idols to be placed in the Temple to please his pagan wives. King Solomon gave the prince a going-away banquet and, after the priests were filled with wine, Menelik and his loyal associates switched the replica ark with the true Ark. He then took the true Ark of the Covenant home to Ethiopia to Aksum, the ancient capital of the kingdom of the

Queen of Sheba. The Ethiopian royal chronicles claim he left the perfect replica of the Ark in the Holy of Holies.

The Ethiopian royal archives record that a group of holy Jewish priests, along with some representatives from several of the tribes of Israel, reverently took the true Ark of the Covenant to Ethiopia for safekeeping until Israel repented their pagan idol worship and returned to the pure worship of God. Unfortunately, throughout the last three thousand years, Israel never repented as a nation or returned to the laws of the Scriptures to follow God exclusively. As a result of their lack of repentance, Israel suffered a succession of mostly evil kings until both Israel and Judah were finally conquered by the Assyrians and Babylonians four hundred years later. Thus, the Jewish descendants of Menelik I of Ethiopia, the royal son of Solomon, never returned the Ark of the Covenant to Jerusalem. The descendants of Menelik I and his Jewish priests, advisors, and servants from the various tribes of Israel called themselves Beta-Israel and ultimately grew to become a considerable portion of their country's population. Today they are called "Falasha" Jews (see figure 2).

These Ethiopian descendants of Israel formed the ruling class during thousands of years of Ethiopian history. The royal dynasty from Solomon and the Queen of Sheba ruled continuously until the twelfth century. The Abyssinian royal chronicles record that the Jewish Ethiopian kingdom was ruled by Queen Judith about A.D. 950 and the dynasty continued for another two centuries. For several hundred years following a Muslim invasion in the twelfth century, the Muslims ruled most of Ethiopia until the original Solomonic dynasty was reestablished in 1558 by a Jewish king. This Ethiopian-Jewish dynasty continued until the communist coup and death of Emperor Haile Selassie in 1975.

## The Church of Zion of Mary

Deep within a complex of underground passages far beneath the ancient Church of Zion of Mary, in Aksum of northern Ethiopia, is a secret passage that leads to a highly guarded hiding place for the most sacred object in human history. For three thousand years, from the time of King Solomon, this passage to the Holy of Holies was protected by royal priestly guards of the ancient Ethiopian Jewish monarchy.

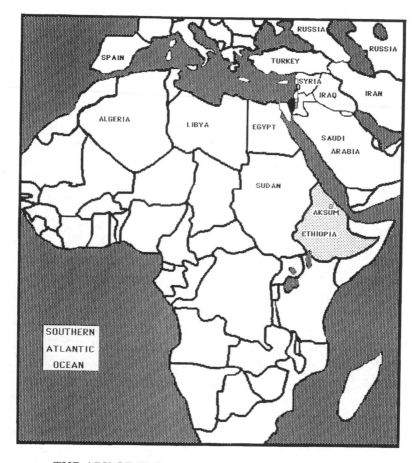

*THE ARK OF THE COVENANT TAKEN TO ETHIOPIA*
*Figure 2*

Within this underground temple are seven concentric rings of interior circular walls. An ordinary Ethiopian Coptic priest can worship within the areas of the first to the fourth outermost rings. Only the highest priests and the Emperor can enter the fifth and sixth innermost rings. The final, innermost seventh ring forms a walled circular room. It is the secret Holy of Holies. The Ethiopians claim that the holy Ark of the Covenant with the mercy seat and the Shekinah glory of God has been protected in this sacred room of their temple for three thousand years. Only one person is allowed to enter this room; he is called the Guardian of the Ark. This Ethiopian priest-guard is chosen at the age of seven, the age of understanding, from the main priestly family. He is trained as a child, in his age of innocence, and agrees to guard the Ark for the rest of his life. This individual gives up the freedom of a normal life. As Guardian, he fasts for 225 days every year according to the Ethiopian Jewish sacred festival calendar. He prays, meditates, and guards the sacred Ark with his life. He never leaves this Holy of Holies until the day of his death, when he is replaced by another chosen Guardian. Each day the High Priest enters the sixth innermost ring to bring the Guardian food.

Some have asked how the Ark could exist in Ethiopia when Revelation 11:19 refers to the prophet John as seeing the Ark of the Testimony in his vision of heaven. However, the Scriptures record that the Ark of the Covenant was built by Moses after the pattern of the Ark in heaven (Exodus 25). Therefore, there is no contradiction between John's vision of an Ark of the Covenant existing in heaven and the earthly Ark of the Covenant being located in Ethiopia.

It is interesting to note also that Ethiopia has had a large Christian community since the beginning of the Church Age. In Acts 8:26–39 we read that Philip, one of the early Church's first evangelists, was led by God to Gaza, where he met the Ethiopian eunuch who was treasurer to Candace, Queen of Ethiopia. This high government official of Ethiopia, as a member of the royal Jewish tribe, had travelled 1500 miles to Jerusalem to worship (probably at one of the three great annual feasts, i.e., Passover). On his return he was riding along a desert road, reading from the scroll of Isaiah where the prophet describes Jesus as the suffering Messiah (Isaiah 53:7–8), when he came upon Philip. Philip led him to accept Jesus Christ as his personal Savior and baptized him. The conversion of this Ethiopian Jewish royal officer led to the beginning of the Ethiopian Coptic Church, one of the oldest Christian communities in history. It has persevered despite two thousand years of persecution.

Prince Mengesha reported that an amazing explosion of Christian evangelism has occurred during the last decade, even among the revolutionary youth that formed the majority of the armies in the civil war that ended in 1997. Apparently the years of war, political repression, and famine have caused many Ethiopians to turn to Christ despite the efforts of the former communist government to suppress the Christian church.

Visitors to Ethiopia have reported that the altars and communion tables of both ancient and modern Christian churches contain a wooden carving of the Ark of the Covenant, called the Tabot (the Holy Ark-Ge'ez), which symbolizes that the ancient Ark is still in their midst. Several news articles also have referred to the location of the Ark. The Jewish magazine, *B'nai B'rith Messenger*, reported the following in 1935:

> The Tablets of the Law received by Moses on Mount Sinai and the Ark of the Covenant, both said to have been brought to Ethiopia from Jerusalem by Menelik, the son of King Solomon and the Queen of Sheba, who was the founder of the present Abyssinian dynasty, have been removed to the mountain strongholds of Abyssinia for safekeeping because of the impending Italian invasion, according to word received here from Addis Ababa, the capital of Ethiopia.

Canada's largest newspaper, the Toronto *Star*, dated July 19, 1981, included the following information:

> In July 1936, a news service reported from Paris that a Semitic syndicate had approached French underwriters about insuring the Ark — said by the dispatch to be in Ethiopia — against war damage. The report explained that 'the oblong, coffin-like chest of acacia wood, overlaid with gold within and without, was carried in ancient times as a protection against the enemy. It was believed that the Ethiopians, with their Semitic tradition and ancestry, might again bring it forth. This time it would be in the midst of tanks, airplanes, and machine guns instead of spear-bearing bowman as recorded in the Old Testament.

The Ethiopian language, Ambaric, is of Semitic origin. The name "Falashas," which means "exiles," was applied to Ethiopians descended from this group of Ethiopian Jews who still embraced the Jewish faith. In May 1948 word spread among the Jews of Ethiopia that Israel had declared itself an independent nation. Many of the "Falashas" began converging to the capital to discuss plans to return to Israel and help with the rebuilding of the Temple. Over the last fifty years, thousands of Ethiopian Jews trickled back to Israel. However, Israel officially admitted the

"Falashas" into Israel under their "Law of Return" as legitimate Jews beginning in 1989.

From the rebirth of Israel in 1948, the Jewish government enjoyed very close relations with Emperor Haile Selassie and supplied considerable technical support and financial aid to Ethiopia. Members of the royal family have told me that Israeli government representatives helped Ethiopia on many occasions and that Israeli agents repeatedly asked the Emperor about the Ark of the Covenant in Aksum. These diplomatic agents suggested that, since Israel had returned from captivity to become a strong nation and had recaptured the Temple Mount in 1967, the time had come for the Ethiopians to return the Ark to its ancient resting place in a rebuilt Temple in Jerusalem. The Emperor is reported to have replied, "In principle, I agree that the Ark should be returned to the Temple, but the correct time has not yet come." He felt that God would reveal the right time to return the Ark to Jerusalem. Tragically, the marxist army coup killed the emperor in 1975, devastated the nation economically, and led Ethiopia into a brutal civil war that finally ended in 1991.

In 1988, as the rebel armies advance from the north, Israel made an agreement with the leaders of the corrupt, marxist Ethiopian government to begin a partial rescue of the thousands of endangered Ethiopian Jews from the northern provinces of the country. In return Israel would supply desperately needed technical and financial aid. In 1991 Israel launched an extraordinary rescue operation, known as Operation Solomon, during the chaotic final days of the Ethiopian civil war. This rescue mission flew over 85,000 of the Ethiopian Jews to the ancient homeland that their forefathers had left three thousand years earlier. The corrupt military leaders of Ethiopia's communist government demanded and received millions of dollars in bribes from Israel during the final months of the war for permitting the Israelis to rescue these persecuted Ethiopian Jews. Israel flew numerous military cargo flights into the Ethiopian capital, Addis Ababa, to gather these destitute people who had fled to the capital to escape the growing persecution in their traditional homeland in the northern province of Gonder. After a great deal of research, debate, and counsel, the two Chief Rabbis of Israel accepted the "Falasha — Ethiopian Jews" as legitimate Jews who were separated from the twelve tribes in the ancient past.

## A Secret Mission: Return The Ark of the Covenant to Israel

In the years following this Israeli rescue, I interviewed three individuals who were knowledgeable about the details of a secret mission carried out at the end of the civil war. Two of my sources, one Ethiopian and one Israeli, personally knew participants of the rescue mission to bring the Ark home to Jerusalem. The third source was the Honorable Robert N. Thompson, a former Canadian diplomat and former member of Canada's Parliament. He traveled to Ethiopia during the final days of the civil war in a successful attempt to rescue the surviving princes and princesses of the Ethiopian royal family who had endured imprisonment for fourteen years under the communist dictator. I have known Robert Thompson since I was a young boy and have admired his incredible career as a military officer, a missionary, a member of Parliament, a leader of a conservative political party in Canada, and a diplomat serving as Canada's ambassador to NATO. In the years following World War II, Robert Thompson served as an advisor to Emperor Haile Selassie, assisting in the creation of Ethiopia's educational and health-care systems. During his visit to my parent's home when I was a young boy, he told me that the true Ark of the Covenant was held in Aksum, Ethiopia. Following his return from the rescue of the remaining members of the royal family in Ethiopia, I had the opportunity to discuss these events with Mr. Thompson. He revealed to me that his Ethiopian sources had disclosed to him other details that confirmed the story I now relate.

All three of my sources confirmed essentially the same account. During the final days of the civil war, negotiations about the Ark of the Covenant in Aksum took place between Israel's agents and the Ethiopian generals. The Ethiopian military leaders demanded a bribe of several million dollars to allow the Ark to be taken home to Israel. A number of wealthy Jewish people donated the necessary funds. Large suitcases containing the ransom money were delivered to the corrupt officials, who promptly deserted Ethiopia to fly with their loot to Switzerland. However, unknown to the departing officials, the suitcases contained counterfeit U.S. dollars. The Israeli agents phoned the banks in Switzerland to inform them of the worthless value of the counterfeit currency these Ethiopian officials were trying to deposit. Israel then took the real money raised by their Jewish donors and gave it to the Eritrean rebels who had just conquered the Ethiopian capital of Addas Ababa. Since the outgoing corrupt officials had looted the country's treasury, these millions of dollars from Israel were desperately needed by the new, struggling democratic government as they attempted to reconstruct their country after years of mismanagement by the communists.

I was then informed, by these same sources, that a special team of young Israeli soldiers flew an unmarked Israeli military cargo plane into the northern province of Gonder and secretly entered the sacred city of Aksum at night during the closing days of the civil war. Each of these Israelis were handpicked soldiers, descendants from the tribe of Levi. It is fascinating that Israeli genetic scientists have recently found a special variation of the Y chromosome that is shared by Jews descended from the priestly sub-tribe (Kohanim) who are descended directly from Aaron, the High Priest, from the tribe of Levi. This research by Professor Karl Skorecki proves that these Kohanim priests are all descended from one ancient patriarch — Aaron. According to the law of Moses, only trained Levites were to carry the Ark of the Covenant (Numbers 4:15). Jews who have the surname Levi are the only Jews who can be sure of their tribal identity as Levites. According to my sources, these specially trained men, accompanied by Israeli elite special troops, secretly removed the Ark from the underground treasury in the deep complex tunnels beneath the Church of Zion of Mary in Aksum. These Levites carried the Ark, with its special covering, into the military cargo plane using staves to hoist it on their shoulders, in the biblically prescribed manner. After arriving in Israel, the Ark was taken to a secure place in Jerusalem where it will be held until the time comes to place it in its appointed place within the Holy of Holies of a rebuilt Temple sometime in the future. Obviously, such reports are impossible to document or prove. However, the three people who gave me this information are credible, and the facts related are consistent with other details that I have discovered.

## Other Suggested Locations of the Ark

Some Christian and Jewish scholars believe that the true Ark of the Covenant will be found in a location other than Ethiopia. For example, there are Jewish traditional legends from the books of the Apocrypha that relate that Jeremiah secretly hid the Ark and the altar of incense in a cave in Mount Pisgah in Jordan before the Babylonians burned Solomon's Temple (2 Maccabees 2:4–8). However, the story includes many elements which appear unlikely, including the fact that it contradicts the Bible's account of the Babylonian army capturing thousands of Temple artifacts and removing them to Babylon. Others have suggested the Ark was taken to Massada by Jewish rebels in A.D. 70. This is contradicted by the fact that the Jewish *Mishna* commentary states clearly that the Ark was not in the Second Temple. Recently, Ron Wyatt has declared that he discovered the Ark under Golgotha, the place of Christ's crucifixion. He has produced a video that claims to prove that he has found the true Ark. After interviews with Wyatt and with several volunteers who assisted him, I have concluded that his claim is unfounded. The people in charge of the site of the Empty Tomb in Jerusalem dismiss his claims. Jesus was crucified at Golgotha, the place of execution in the capital of Israel. This site of death and execution of criminals was the most spiritually defiled place in Jerusalem for religious Jews. The suggestion that the righteous Jews would choose to hide their most sacred possession, the true Ark of the Covenant, under the place of execution of criminals is not credible.

Some writers have suggested that the Ark is located in one of the secret tunnels underneath the Temple Mount. One source told me in confidence that Jewish archeologists and rabbis believed they had seen an object, possibly the Ark, at a distance in one of these tunnels but were prevented from approaching it because the Muslim authorities immediately sealed up the tunnel entrance. If this report is correct, then I would presume that in the light of the historical evidence and prophetic Scriptures already quoted, the object seen in the tunnel under the Temple Mount is either the replica that was made for Prince Menelik I by his father, King Solomon, or possibly some of the other Temple objects of worship such as the Altar of Incense.

Whether the true Ark of the Covenant was returned from Ethiopia or is found in a secret passage under the Temple, the Bible indicates that the Ark has a significant role to play in the final events of this age.

## The Role of the Ark of the Covenant in Future Prophetic Events

Do Bible prophecies reveal anything about the location and the future of the Ark?

As mentioned earlier, the last time Scripture definitively mentions the authentic Ark of the Covenant is in 2 Chronicles 8:11, during the reign of King Solomon three thousand years ago. There is another reference to an "ark" in the historical records of the Kingdom of Judah in 2 Chronicles 35:3 when, several hundred years later during the reign of King Josiah, a "holy ark" was returned to the Temple. A wicked king had removed this "ark" years earlier. If the Ethiopian history is correct, then the true Ark of the Covenant was in Ethiopia at this time. Therefore, the "ark" in 2 Chronicles 35:3 that was returned by King Josiah was actually the replica that had been prepared in the time of King Solomon for his son Menelik.

When we turn to the Old Testament prophets to discover any references to the Ark, we find several intriguing references to a sacred object that may be the "lost" Ark of the Covenant. In the verses that follow, the original word in each case is the Hebrew *nes*, but it has been translated in each verse by a different English word to fit the context as interpreted by the Bible translators. The Hebrew word *nes* refers to an important object of respect, an object to awaken hope, such as a nation's flag. For example, the altar raised by Moses to celebrate God's defeat of the Amalekite forces was called "Jehovah Nissi" (Jehovah my Banner). The word "Nissi" is derived from the root *nes*. It is possible that the word *nes* refers to the Ark of the Covenant.

If the above suggestion is correct, then prophecy seems to indicate that at the time Israel is invaded by Russia and her allies, God will bring forth the ancient Ark of the Covenant and miraculously defeat the enemies of Israel once again. The prophet Jeremiah (4:6) states, "Set up the standard [*nes*] toward Zion: retire [strengthen], stay not: for I will bring evil from the north, and a great destruction." In the great prophecy of Ezekiel (chap. 38–39) about the coming War of Gog and Magog, he describes the supernatural defeat of the armies of the Russian and the Arab nations. The prophet then reports that God will set up an object of worship ("my Glory") that both the Gentile nations and Israel will recognize as proof that God has once again intervened in history to save His chosen people.

The prophet Ezekiel declared, "And I will set my glory among the heathen, and all the heathen shall see my judgment that I have executed, and my hand that I have laid upon them. So the house of Israel shall know that I am the Lord their God from that day and forward" (Ezekiel 39: 21–22). In Isaiah 18 we find the clearest indication that the Ark of the Covenant will be brought from Ethiopia at the time of the end. God addresses the people of Ethiopia in the first two verses and tells them of the role they will play in the unfolding events of the last days. Isaiah's prophecy reads, "Woe to the land shadowing with wings, which is beyond the rivers of Ethiopia: . . . All ye inhabitants of the world and dwellers on the earth, see ye, when he lifteth up an ensign [*nes*, ark] on the mountains: and when he bloweth a trumpet, hear ye." The closing verse declares, "In that time shall the present [*nes*, ark] be brought unto the Lord of hosts . . . [from Ethiopia] . . . to the place of the name of the Lord of hosts, the Mount Zion "(Isaiah 18: 1, 3, 7). This prophecy of Isaiah may refer to the return of the Ark from Ethiopia in this decade.

Another fascinating prophecy states that Israel will miraculously have its ancient, pure language, Hebrew, restored to it when God once again brings the Jews back into their land. Even in the time of Christ, Hebrew was a "dying" language. It was used only by the scribes and priests for official religious purposes in the Temple. Everyone else used the Greek language, which had become the international "English" of its day. The revival of the ancient language of Hebrew in modern Israel is another miraculous fulfillment of prophecy in our day. This recovery of a "dead" language and its revival after some two thousand years is a phenomenon without precedent in human history. It is interesting that God calls Hebrew a "pure" language.

> For then will I turn to the people a pure language, that they may all call upon the name of the Lord, to serve him with one consent. From beyond the rivers of Ethiopia my suppliants, even the daughter of my dispersed shall bring mine offering                         (Zephaniah 3:9–10)

Notice that this prophecy connects the return of the "offering" from the dispersed of Ethiopia to the rebirth of Israel and the time of the revival of the pure Hebrew language. This "offering" could very well be the returning to Israel of the long lost Ark of the Covenant.

One final prophecy provides, perhaps, the strongest evidence that the Ark will be recovered and play an important role in our future. The prophet Jeremiah describes a time after the Battle of Armageddon has been won and Israel is enjoying its messianic kingdom.

> And it shall come to pass, when ye be multiplied and increased in the land, in those days, saith the Lord, they shall say no more, the Ark of the Covenant of the Lord: neither shall it come to mind; neither shall they remember it; neither shall they visit it; neither shall that be done any more. At that time they shall call Jerusalem the throne of the Lord; and all the nations shall be gathered unto it, to the name of the Lord, to Jerusalem:       (Jeremiah 3: 16-17)

In other words, Jeremiah prophesied that once the Battle of Armageddon is over and the millennial kingdom has commenced Israel will stop talking about the Ark, they will stop thinking about the Ark, and they will stop visiting the Ark. The reason the Ark of the Covenant will no longer be important to Israel is that Jesus Christ will be present to be worshiped directly as their Messiah-King.

However, consider the fact that Jews have not publicly talked about, thought about, or visited the Ark of the Covenant for almost three thousand years since it disappeared during the days of King Solomon, approximately 980 B.C. This prophecy of Jeremiah 3:16–17 does not make sense unless the lost Ark of the Covenant will be rediscovered and unless, in the years leading up to Israel's final great crisis, the Ark will play a pivotal role in the spiritual life of the nation.

If the tentative suggestions of this chapter are correct, the recovery of the lost Ark and its subsequent role in Israel's miraculous victory in the War of Gog and Magog would encourage the Jews to begin the rebuilding of their Temple. The return of the Ark of the Covenant to the Holy of Holies of a rebuilt Temple would signal for Israel the final ushering in of the long-awaited messianic era.

# 10

# *The Second Exodus, from Russia*

Behold, I will bring them from the north country, and gather them from the coasts of the earth, and with them the blind and the lame, the woman with child and her that travaileth with child together: a great company shall return thither. (Jeremiah 31:8)

One of the most exciting events in both prophecy and human history that has occurred in this generation is the miraculous release of Jews from Russia. In 1991, when the Union of Soviet Socialist Republics disintegrated due to internal corruption, hatred, and loss of faith in Marxist communism, hundreds of ethnic minorities and the fourteen former USSR republics declared their independence from the Russian empire. The enslaved states of Eastern Europe immediately declared their independence from Russian domination and proclaimed their freedom from decades of Soviet tyranny.

The long prophesied Jewish exodus from Russia occurred during the years of anarchy following this breakup of the seventy-year-old communist Soviet Empire. The Jews have endured centuries of persecution in Russia since the introduction of the czars. During the rule of the czars in the nineteenth century, Russian

Jews were forced to live under severe restrictions. In the years following the Communist Revolution in 1917, the Jews suffered decades of continual repression. Despite the Soviet agreement to the Helsinki Accord on Human Rights by President Gorbachev, most Jews were prevented from immigrating to the West or to Israel. Hundreds of thousands of Jews applied for exit visas without success in the years preceding the breakup of the Soviet Union.

The "glasnost" policy of Soviet leader Mikhail Gorbachev led to the disintegration of the Soviet Union. Many believe that God destroyed the "evil empire" of Russian communism to free His chosen people to return as exiles to the Promised Land. Despite the dissolution of the USSR, the vast majority of Jews in Russia still live with persecution and prejudice. In the last seven years over one-half million Russian Jews have left Russia to join their brothers in the Promised Land. However, over four million Russian Jews remain trapped in Russia and its associated states in the Commonwealth of Independent States. Despite continuing obstacles, over one million Jews have applied for visas to leave Russia recently.

As in the days of the Egyptian Pharaoh, God is saying, "Let my people go," and the Russian reply is identical to Pharaoh's, "Not Yet!" However, Scripture declares that God will miraculously deliver "all" of His people from Russia just as He did from Egypt some thirty-five centuries ago.

The prophet Ezekiel, who prophesied about the coming Russian-Arab invasion of Israel in Ezekiel 38 and 39, declared, "Therefore thus saith the Lord God; Now will I bring again the captivity of Jacob, and have mercy upon the whole house of Israel, and will be jealous for my holy name;...When I have brought them again from the peoples, and gathered them out of their enemies' lands, and am sanctified in them in the sight of many nations" (Ezekiel 39:25, 27).

The prophet Zechariah also spoke of the coming exodus of the Russian Jews when he wrote, "Ho, ho, come forth, and flee from the land of the north, saith the Lord: for I have spread you abroad as the four winds of the heaven, saith the Lord" (Zechariah 2:6).

## When Will This Final Exodus Occur?

The Jews have celebrated the Exodus from Egypt every year on the night of Passover for more than thirty-five hundred years. This final exodus from Russia will be so miraculous that God declares that Israel will celebrate this coming Russian exodus at their Passover Suppers, rather than the traditional celebration of the ancient Exodus from Egypt.

The prophet Jeremiah prophesied about the final release of the Jews of the North in these words: "Therefore, behold, the days come, saith the Lord, that it shall no more be said, The Lord liveth, that brought up the children of Israel out of the land of Egypt; but, The Lord liveth, that brought up the children of Israel from the land of the North, and from all the lands whither he had driven them: and I will bring them again into their land that I gave unto their fathers" (Jeremiah 16:14–15).

It is highly probable that this second exodus will occur on the actual anniversary of the first Exodus, namely, on the Feast of Passover, based on the previous anniversary pattern demonstrated in Israel's history. The Bible records in Exodus 12:41-42 that God instructed the Jews to celebrate Passover "forever" on the fourteenth of Nisan in remembrance of how God had saved them from the centuries of bondage in Egypt. However, in Jeremiah 16:14–15, after describing the exodus from Russia, God tells Israel that, in the future, they will celebrate this "Russian" exodus rather than the one from ancient Egypt. The probable reconciliation of these seemingly contradictory scriptural statements is that the Jews will be miraculously freed from Russia on the very same day, during Passover. Thus, the nation of Israel will continue to commemorate its ancient Passover Supper as commanded on the evening of the fourteenth of Nisan, but will, from that point on, commemorate its second and more recent exodus "from of the land of the North." If this prophesied second exodus occurs on Passover, it will continue the pattern of biblical anniversaries discussed in previous chapters.

The Jews of Russia will be joined in their return to the Holy Land by a multitude of Jews from many other countries as God miraculously returns them to the Promised Land: "Behold, I will bring them from the north country, and gather them from the coasts of the earth, and with them the blind and the lame, the woman with child and her that travaileth with child together: a great company shall return thither" (Jeremiah 31:8).

When millions of Jews from Russia and other countries return to the Promised Land, Israel will experience the fulfillment of many of the Bible's ancient prophecies. The presence of the Ark of the Covenant in Jerusalem will probably prompt the national religious leadership of Israel to rebuild the Temple. The political-military vacuum created by the destruction of the military power of Russia and the Arab nations in the War of Gog and Magog will set the stage for the closing events of this age. These key events are leading us inexorably toward the Battle of Armageddon and Christ's triumphant return to set up His Kingdom.

# 11

# *The Rapture*
# *The Hope of the Church*

For what is our hope, or joy, or crown of rejoicing? Are not even ye in the presence of our Lord Jesus Christ at His coming? (1 Thessalonians 2:19)

In many different Scriptures, Christ has promised His Church that He will come to take her home to be with Him before the time known as the Great Tribulation of the "last days."

> For the Lord Himself shall descend from heaven with a shout, with voice of the archangel, and with the trump of God: and the dead in Christ shall rise first: then we which are alive and remain shall be caught up together with them in the clouds, to meet the Lord in the air: and so shall we ever be with the Lord. Wherefore comfort one another with these words (1 Thessalonians 4:16–17)

During the last two hundred years, this belief in the imminent return of Christ for His Church has motivated and encouraged Christian missions to "Go ye therefore, and teach all nations, baptizing them in the name of the Father, and of the Son, and of the Holy Ghost" (Matthew 28:19).

This hope and belief in the near return of Christ has prompted the creation of numerous missionary societies in Europe and North America that have brought the gospel to every nation on earth in this generation. As Christians read the Scriptures concerning God's promises to the Church, they rejoice in the knowledge that our Lord has a unique future in store for them. However, along with the promises about His return to rapture all believers, Jesus warned that the Rapture would be followed by the most terrible time of persecution known in the history of man — the Great Tribulation.

The Great Tribulation is the special period of God's judgment spoken of by Christ and the prophets. It will commence three and one-half years after the future leader of the revived Roman Empire in Europe — the Antichrist — makes a seven-year covenant or defense treaty with Israel. Three and one-half years later, the Antichrist will break this treaty by entering the rebuilt Temple in Jerusalem, where he will seat Himself in the Holy of Holies and declare that he is god (see 2 Thessalonians 2:4). Israel will rebel against this blasphemy, causing the Antichrist to launch a reign of terror against all those who oppose his demand for worship. The Bible tells us clearly that this unparalleled time of tribulation, which will begin when the Antichrist enters the Temple, will last exactly 1260 days (see Daniel 12:7) — forty-two months of thirty days each (Revelation 13:5).

The event that will end this hell on earth will be the destruction of the Antichrist and the armies of the world at the Battle of Armageddon: "He gathered them together into a place called in the Hebrew tongue Armageddon" (Revelation 16:16). Jesus Christ will descend from heaven with His army of saints, the Church (Jude 14), and will destroy the Antichrist and his False Prophet with "the brightness of his coming" (2 Thessalonians 2:8).

In the book of Revelation, this period of three and one-half years is called "the Great Tribulation" (7:14) because an enormous destruction is prophesied in which over half of the planet's population will die in "the great wine press of the wrath of God" (Revelation 14:19). However, praise God! The Lord has promised us that He has not appointed His Church to wrath but rather to salvation.

The apostle Paul said, "For yourselves know perfectly that the day of the Lord so cometh as a thief in the night. . . . Ye are all the children of light, and the children of the day: we are not of the

*The Temple Mount.*
*Notice that the Dome of the Rock is 150 feet south of the true site of the original temple site (directly opposite the enclosed Eastern Gate).*

*The "sealed" Eastern Gate of the Temple Mount.*
*Grant and Kaye Jeffrey exploring the Eastern Gate.*

*Some Jewish believer has written "Welcome Messiah" on the "sealed" Eastern Gate where Christ will enter — Ezekiel 43:4–5.*

*Orthodox Jews worshipping at the Western Wall of the Temple Mount. (Notice Wilson's arch to the left of the Western Wall).*

*A model of the Third Temple, exhibited in Jerusalem.*
*(Note that the location of the Temple is in the northern portion of the*
*Temple Mount — opposite to the Eastern Gate).*

*A model of the Ark of the Covenant.*

*An Ethiopian mural showing the Ark of the Covenant. It illustrates Prince Menelik I, the son of King Solomon, taking the Ark to Aksum in Ethiopia.*

### EXPLANATION OF THE 44 PANEL SHEBA PAINTING, ADDIS ABABA, ETHIOPIA

THE ANCIENT ETHIOPIANS, 3000 YEARS AGO, WORSHIPED THE COBRA. IT WAS THE CUSTOMARY THING FOR PEOPLE TO OFFER THEIR FIRST BORN SON TO THE COBRA. A MAN CALLED AGABOS SAID TO THE PEOPLE, "LET US KILL THE COBRA FOR NOBODY WANTS TO LOSE HIS BELOVED SON." HE THEN ADDED THAT UPON THE DEATH OF THE COBRA HE WOULD THEN BECOME THEIR EMPEROR. AGABOS WAS THE FATHER OF SHEBA.

HOW PEOPLE WORSHIPED THE COBRA.
A DISCUSSION TO KILL THE COBRA.
THE POISON IS PREPARED FROM A CACTUS
THE MEN OFFERED THE POISONED FOOD TO A GOAT.
THE MEN TOOK THE GOAT TO THE COBRA.
THE COBRA WAS POISONED WHEN IT ATE.
HE SHOWED THE DEAD COBRA TO THE PEOPLE.
AGABOS BECAME EMPEROR AFTER KILLING THE COBRA.
HE AGREED WITH HIS PEOPLE THAT HIS DAUGHTER, SHEBA, SHOULD REIGN UPON HIS DEATH.
SHEBA'S FATHER DIED.
SHE TOOK HER FATHERS THRONE.
JERUSALEM MERCHANT BY THE NAME OF TAMRS COMES TO ETHIOPIA.
SHEBA ASKS ABOUT THE WISDOM OF SOLOMON. SHE SENDS A LETTER, ACCOMPANIED BY THE BEST PERFUME IN ETHIOPIA TO SOLOMON.
TAMRS RETURNED TO JERUSALEM CARRYING THE LETTER AND THE PERFUME.
HE PRESENTS SHEBA'S GIFTS TO KING SOLOMON.
QUEEN SHEBA TRAVELS TO JERUSALEM TO VISIT SOLOMON.
SHE TAKES A BOAT.
SHE ARRIVES AT KING SOLOMON'S PALACE.
KING SOLOMON IS INTRODUCED TO THE QUEEN.
KING SOLOMON HAS A RECEPTION FOR SHEBA'S ATTENDANTS. SHE LOOKS DOWN FROM THE BALCONY.
KING SOLOMON INVITES THE QUEEN FOR SUPPER. THE FOOD IS VERY SALTY.
SOLOMON ASKS SHEBA TO SPEND THE NIGHT WITH HIM. SHE REFUSES. SHE BEGS HIM TO TAKE AN OATH THAT HE WILL DO HER NO HARM. SOLOMON SAID " I WILL NOT TOUCH YOU UNLESS YOU TAKE ANYTHING THAT BELONGS TO ME HERE IN THIS HOUSE."
SOLOMON GRABBED THE SERVANT.
HE SLEPT WITH SHEBA'S MAID. SHEBA IS THIRSTY . WHEN THE SERVANT BRINGS WATER TO SHEBA, SOLOMON EMBRACES SHEBA. HE SAID, " YOU PROMISED ME NOT TO TAKE ANYTHING THAT BELONGS TO ME." HE SLEEPS WITH SHEBA.
HE GIVES HER A RING THE NEXT MORNING.
SHEBA ON HER WAY BACK TO HER LAND
MENELIK AND THE MAID'S CHILD BORN AT ABOUT THE SAME TIME.
MENELIK AND HIS BROTHER PLAY.
MENELIK ASKED THE NAME OF HIS FATHER.
SHEBA SHOWS HIM A PICTURE OF HIS FATHER, SOLOMON.
MENELIK AND THE RETINUE ON WAY TO VISIT KING SOLOMON.
MENELIK AND ATTENDANTS IN A BOAT ON WAY TO JERUSALEM.
MENELIK AND BROTHER INTRODUCED TO SOLOMON.
MELELIK ATTENDS CLASSES.
SOLOMON GIVES ARK OF THE COVENANT TO HIS MENELIK. ( TABLES OF THE LAW OF MOSES )
MENELIK RETURNS TO ETHIOPIA WITH ARK OF THE COVENANT
MENELIK GIVES ARK OF THE COVENANT TO HIS MOTHER.
SHEBA CROWNS MENELIK AND MAID'S SON OFFICIALLY.
SHEBA GIVES MENELIK THE OFFICIAL SEAL.
SHEBA MAKES A WILL BEFORE SHE DIES.
MONUMENTS OF AKSUM BUILT ACCORDING TO HER WISHES.

THE EMPERORS OF ETHIOPIA CLAIM DIRECT DESCENDENCY FROM MENELIK 1, THAT IS FROM KING SOLOMON OF JUDEA, AND THIS IS WHY – IN THE IMPERIAL COAT OF ARMS, ON THE MOUNUMENT OF ETHIOPIA, IN THE JEWELRY OF THE COUNTRY – THERE CAN BE FOUND, TO THIS DAY, HARMONIOUS COMBINATION OF THE JEWISH SEAL OF DAVID AND OF THE CHRIST ON A CROSS.

*The description of each panel of the Ethiopian mural depicting the story of Solomon, Queen Sheba, Prince Menelik, and the removal of the Ark of the Covenant.*

*Crown Prince Stephen Mengesha.*
*He is standing beside his great-grandfather, Emperor, Haile Selassie*
*"The Conquering Lion of Judah."*

*Prince Stephen Mengesha in discussion with the author, Grant Jeffrey.*

*The Repository of the Ark of the Covenant.*
*This building (bottom right of photograph) — the Church of Zion of Mary — was built over the ancient Repository of the Ark in Aksum, northern Ethiopia.*

*The Second Temple at the time of Christ.*
*This model of the Second Temple reflects the latest archeological discoveries. Notice that the open area to the south (left) of the Temple is the present location of the beautiful Dome of the Rock.*

*The Dome of the Tablets.*
*The flat stone at the base is the "Even Shetiyah," the foundation stone.*
*Notice that the Dome of the Rock is over 150 feet to the south.*

*Orthodox Jews from the Tribe of Levi studying Temple Worship in a*
*Yeshiva (Bible College) in the Old City of Jerusalem.*

*The author, Grant Jeffrey, and his wife Kaye in the Old*
*City of Jerusalem*

*Grant Jeffrey standing on the Mount of Olives opposite the*
*Temple Mount.*

night, nor of darkness. Therefore let us not sleep, as do others; but let us watch and be sober. . . . But let us, who are of the day, be sober, putting on the breastplate of faith and love; and for an helmet, the hope of salvation," (1 Thessalonians 5:2, 5–6, 8).

Before looking at the many additional Scriptures that prove conclusively that the Church will be in heaven with Christ during the Great Tribulation, it may be instructive to examine the mistaken teaching, which has recently resurfaced, that attempts to prove that the Church will live through the Great Tribulation and thus experience "the wrath of God" described in Revelation 4–19.

## Why Do Some Teach That the Church Will Endure the Tribulation?

Even those who believe that the Church must experience the Great Tribulation generally admit that there are many clear Scriptures that appear to indicate that the Church will be in heaven during this period. However, three premises generally cause them to reject the pretribulation Rapture and accept the position called the "postribulation Rapture." The first premise is an emotional one. It is the contention that it would be unfair for the modern Church to escape to heaven scot-free. They point to the undeniable fact that the Church has known tribulation for thousands of years and that today many believers, such as those living in Muslim and totalitarian countries, are suffering severe persecution. These critics ask why our generation should expect to escape the martyrdom that other believers have experienced. While it is easy to understand such an emotion, it would be wrong to deny the doctrine of the pretribulation Rapture on this basis alone. The reality is that while many Christians have endured tremendous persecutions and tribulations, untold millions of believers have lived out their lives in times of peace. Furthermore, a point can be made that all Christians throughout history who have died either in peace or in persecution escaped the Great Tribulation.

An underlying misconception of many critics of the pretribulation Rapture is their incorrect and unscriptural belief that the Church will somehow be purified by enduring the Great Tribulation. They mistakenly feel that the modern Church, as the Bride of Christ, must endure the wrath of the Antichrist to purge her sins. The apostle Paul declared "That he might present it to himself a glorious church, not having spot, or wrinkle, or any such thing; but that it should be holy and without blemish" (Ephesians 5:27).

Nevertheless, while the longing for purification of the Church is correct, the Scriptures declare repeatedly that we are purified solely by the completed work of Christ on the Cross. There is no justification of our sins that can make us righteous and holy but the justification that comes from the atoning blood of our Lord applied to our hearts when we repent of our sins. The belief that we can somehow be purified by enduring the Tribulation reveals a misunderstanding of the doctrine of God's unmerited grace. If the Lord delays His return much longer, the rising tide of sin, rampant immorality, and anti-Christian laws, plus the drift toward "Big Brother" totalitarian government, will inexorably lead to tremendous persecution for the Church. However, such persecution and tribulation of Christians will not constitute the Great Tribulation.

Some critics have claimed that those who teach the hope of the pretribulation Rapture are guilty of leaving Christians unprepared for the possibility that they might have to endure the persecution of the Tribulation period. However, in thirty years of teaching Bible prophecy, I have not witnessed anyone who believes in the pretribulation Rapture who has taught that Christians are immune from all end-time persecution. The prophecy teachers, myself included, who believe God promises an escape from the Tribulation "wrath of God" also warn believers that persecution is coming, even in North America, if the Lord tarries much longer. The doctrine of the pretribulation Rapture is no guarantee that Christians can avoid paying the supreme price of martyrdom. Recent studies in *The National and International Religious Report* reveal that as many as 300,000 believers die as martyrs around the world every year. The postribulation Rapture position can rob the Church of her blessed hope. Jesus promised, "I also will keep thee from the hour of temptation, which shall come upon all the world, to try them that dwell upon the earth" (Revelation 3:10).

The second and more important reason why some are teaching that the Church will be present during this terrible time is the failure to distinguish between God's plan for Israel and His plan for the Church, especially concerning the prophecy revealed by Christ in Matthew 24. They often acknowledge that there is strong biblical evidence for a pretribulation Rapture; however, they inevitably come back to their interpretation of Matthew 24, which seems to indicate that the Rapture follows the events of the Great Tribulation.

In the passage in Matthew 24, Christ is on the Temple Mount explaining to His Jewish disciples the events that will occur in Israel and in other nations that will lead to the return of Christ as their Jewish Messiah. The disciples' question that Jesus was answering concerned the coming of Israel's long-promised Kingdom, not the coming of Christ for His Church (which they did not even know about). It is easy to forget that, at this point, before the crucifixion of our Lord and the coming of the Holy Spirit at Pentecost, there was no such thing as a Christian Church. If you had told one of the disciples during the week before Christ's crucifixion that someday there would be an organization based on Christ's teachings, called the Church, and that 99 percent of its members would be uncircumcised Gentiles who would follow neither Jewish law nor offer Temple sacrifices, he would probably have fallen off his chair in shock and disbelief. One of the classic mistakes in interpretation is to take this conversation between Christ and His Jewish disciples concerning the messianic kingdom and read back into it the reality of the Christian Church, which did not come into existence until the Jews rejected Christ and God breathed life into His Body of believers on the day of Pentecost.

Since Christ does not mention the Church to His disciples in this conversation, the plain interpretation is that Israel is the primary focus of the prophecy of Matthew 24. Matthew 24 speaks of the Great Tribulation, and beginning at verse 15, Christ states that the Antichrist will set up the "abomination of desolation" (a supernatural statue of the Antichrist) to be worshiped in the Temple. In verses 40 and 41, Jesus says, "Then shall two be in the field; the one shall be taken, and the other left. Two women shall be grinding at the mill; the one shall be taken, and the other left." A vital question for students of the Bible is the identity of these people who "shall be taken." Does this prophecy refer to the Church or does it reveal God's plans for the Tribulation saints who become believers after the Rapture?

This chapter tells us that at the end of the Great Tribulation, God will send His angels and "they shall gather together his elect from the four winds, from one end of heaven to the other" (verse 31). These "elect" are the people who become believers during the

Great Tribulation of three and one-half years. This gathering together is not the Rapture. This gathering of Tribulation believers takes place at the end of the Tribulation, whereas the Rapture of the Church occurs sometime prior to the beginning of the Great Tribulation when Antichrist sets himself up as "god" in the Temple. Notice that the *angels* "gather the elect" (verse 31), whereas, at the time of the Rapture, "The Lord himself shall descend from heaven with a shout, with the voice of the arch-angel, and with the trump of God: and the dead in Christ shall rise first" (1 Thessalonians 4:16–17). This gathering of the "elect" Tribulation saints will occur at the conclusion of three and one-half years — a period of time for which there are the most detailed prophecies found in the Bible.

The Bible describes many Tribulation events that must occur prior to the "gathering" of the Tribulation saints and thus, it cannot be correctly described as "imminent." These facts have caused many scholars to believe that this "gathering" is, therefore, a different event than the "Rapture" of the Church. However, when we turn our attention to the coming of Christ for His Church, we find that there are no warnings or signals given to indicate the time of the Rapture. The Rapture can literally occur at any time.

The third reason postribulationist writers attack the pretribulation Rapture doctrine results from their claims that it cannot be true because no Church writer or Reformer ever taught this doctrine until approximately 170 years ago, when it was introduced by John Darby, a Plymouth Brethern. Their argument that no one ever saw this "truth" throughout eighteen hundred years of Church history has been very effective, causing many Christians to abandon their belief in the pretribulation Rapture. The only problem with their assertion that no one in the early Church taught the pretribulation Rapture is that it has been found to be incorrect.

Obviously the truth about the time of the Rapture can be found only in Scripture. The Protestant Reformation was based essentially on this return to the authority of the Bible. The Latin phrase *sola Scriptura*, meaning "Scripture alone," became the rallying cry of the Reformers who ignored centuries of tradition and church councils in their insistence that truth could only be discovered in the Word of God.

While the resolution of this issue must be based on our interpretation of Scripture, it is important to answer the errors of our opponents, who disparage "the blessed hope" of the Rapture with misinformation, unmindful of the modern rediscovery of the truth about the pretribulation Rapture.

## A Discovery That the Pretribulation Rapture Was Taught in the Early Church

During the summer of 1994, after more than a decade of searching, I discovered several fascinating manuscripts that contain clear evidence of the teaching of the pretribulation Rapture in the early church.

### Ephraem's Teaching on the Pretribulation Rapture

For all the saints and Elect of God are gathered, prior to the tribulation that is to come, and are taken to the Lord lest they see the confusion that is to overwhelm the world because of our sins.

*On the Last Times, the Antichrist, and the End of the World,*
by Ephraem the Syrian, A.D. 373

The early Christian writer and poet Ephraem the Syrian (who lived from A. D. 306 to 373) was a major theologian of the early Byzantine Eastern church. He was born near Nisbis, in the Roman province of Syria, near present-day Edessa, Turkey. Ephraem displayed a profound love of the Scriptures in his writings, as illustrated by several of his written comments quoted in the *Works of Nathaniel Lardner* (1788, vol. 4): "I esteem no man more happy than him, who diligently reads the Scriptures delivered to us by the Spirit of God, and thinks how he may order his conversation by the precepts of them." To this day, his hymns and homilies are used in the liturgy of the Greek Orthodox and Middle Eastern Nestorian Church. While the sixteen-volume Post-Nicene Library includes a number of homilies and psalms by Ephraem the Syrian, the editors noted that he also wrote a large number of commentaries that have never been translated into English.

Ephraem's fascinating teaching on the Antichrist has never been published in English until now. This critically important prophecy manuscript from the fourth century of the Church era reveals a literal method of interpretation in its teaching of the premillennial return of Christ. More importantly, Ephraem's text reveals a very clear statement about the pretribulational return of Christ to take His elect saints home to heaven to escape the coming Tribulation. In addition, Ephraem declares his beliefs in a literal Jewish Antichrist, who will rule the Roman Empire during the last days; in a rebuilt Temple; in the two witnesses; and in a literal Great Tribulation, lasting 1,260 days. It is also fascinating to note that he taught that the War of Gog and Magog would precede the tribulation period. I discovered another text by Ephraem, called *The Book of the Cave of Treasures*, which reveals that he taught that Daniel's Seventieth Week will be fulfilled in the final seven years at the end of this age and will conclude with Christ's return at the Battle of Armageddon to establish His Kingdom.

The following section includes key passages from Ephraem's important text, written about A.D. 373, translated by Professor Cameron Rhoades, professor of Latin at Tyndale Theological Seminary.

> 1. Most dearly beloved brothers, believe the Holy Spirit who speaks in us. Now we have spoken before, because the end of the world is very near, and the consummation remains. Has not the first faith withered away in men?

> 2. *We ought to understand thoroughly therefore, my brothers what is imminent or overhanging.* Already there have been hunger and plagues, violent movements of nations and signs, which have been predicted by the Lord; they have already been fulfilled, and there is not other which remains, except the advent of the wicked one in the completion of the Roman kingdom. Why therefore are we occupied with worldly business, and why is our mind held fixed on the lusts of the world or the anxieties of the ages? Why therefore do we not reject every care of earthly actions and prepare ourselves for the meeting of the Lord Christ, *so that He may draw us from the confusion, which overwhelms the world?* Believe you me, dearest brothers, because the coming of the Lord is nigh, believe you me, because the end of the world is at hand, believe me, because it is the very last time.

> *Because all saints and the Elect of the Lord are gathered together before the tribulation which is to about to come and are taken to*

*the Lord, in order hat they may not see at any time the confusion which overwhelms the world because of our sins* (italics added). And so, brothers, most dear to me, it is the eleventh hour, and the end of this world comes to the harvest, and angels, armed and prepared, hold sickles in their hands, awaiting the empire of the Lord.

3. When therefore the end of the world comes, there arise diverse wars, commotions on all sides, horrible earthquakes, perturbations of nations, tempests throughout the lands, plagues, famine, drought throughout the thoroughfares, great danger throughout the sea and dry land, constant persecutions, slaughters and massacres everywhere.

6. When therefore the end of the world comes, that abominable, lying and murderous one is born from the tribe of Dan. He is conceived from the seed of a man and from a most vile virgin, mixed with an evil or worthless spirit.

7. But when the time of the abomination of his desolation begins to approach, having been made legal, he takes the empire. . . . Therefore, when he receives the kingdom, he orders the temple of God to be rebuilt for himself, which is in Jerusalem; who, after coming into it, he shall sit as God and order that he be adored by all nations . . . then all people from everywhere shall flock together to him at the city of Jerusalem, and the holy city shall be trampled on by the nations for forty-two months just as the holy apostle says in the Apocalypse, which become three and a half years, 1260 days.

8. In these three years and a half the heaven shall suspend its dew; because there will be no rain upon the earth . . . and there will be a great tribulation, as there has not been, since people began to be upon the earth . . . and no one is able to sell or to buy of the grain of the fall harvest, unless he is one who has the serpentine sign on the forehead or the hand. . . .

10. And when the three and a half years have been completed, the time of the Antichrist, through which he will have seduced the world, after the resurrection of the two prophets, in the hour which the world does not know, and

on the day which the enemy or son of perdition does not know, will come the sign of the Son of Man, and coming forward the Lord shall appear with great power and much majesty, with the sign of the word of salvation going before him, and also even with all the powers of the heavens with the whole chorus of the saints. . . . Then Christ shall come and the enemy shall be thrown into confusion, and the Lord shall destroy him by the Spirit of his mouth. And he shall be bound and shall be plunged into the abyss of everlasting fire alive with his father Satan; and all people, who do his wishes, shall perish with him forever; but the righteous ones shall inherit everlasting life with the Lord for ever and ever.

To summarize the key points in Ephraem's text on the last days:

1. Ephraem's manuscript lays out the events of the last days in chronological sequence. Significantly, he began with the Rapture using the word "imminent"; then, he described the Great Tribulation of three and one-half year's duration under the Antichrist's tyranny, followed by the Second Coming of Christ to earth with his saints to defeat the Antichrist.

2. Significantly, at the beginning of his treatise in section 2, Ephraem used the word "imminent" to describe the Rapture occurring before the tribulation and the coming of the Antichrist. "We ought to understand thoroughly therefore, my brothers what is imminent or overhanging."

3. He clearly described the pretribulation Rapture: "Because all saints and the Elect of the Lord are gathered together before the tribulation which is to about to come and are taken to the Lord, in order that they may not see at any time the confusion which overwhelms the world because of our sins."

4. He then gives the purpose of God for rapturing the Church "before the tribulation": so that "they may not see at any time the confusion which overwhelms the world because of our sins." Ephraem used the word "confusion" as a synonym for the tribulation period.

5. Ephraem described the duration of the "great tribulation" (the last half of the seven-year tribulation period) in sections 7, 8,

and 10 as follows: "forty-two months," "three and a half years," and "1260 days."

6. He summarized, "There will be a great tribulation, as there has not been since people began to be upon the earth" and then described the Mark of the Beast system.

7. He declared that Christ will come to the earth after the "three and a half years" Tribulation period in section 10: "And when the three and a half years have been completed, the time of the Antichrist, through which he will have seduced the world, after the resurrection of the two prophets . . . will come the sign of the Son of Man, and coming forward the Lord shall appear with great power and much majesty."

Dr. Paul Alexander, perhaps the most authoritative scholar on the writings of the early Byzantine church, concluded that in *The Last Times, the Antichrist, and the End of the World*, Ephraem taught that the Lord would supernaturally remove the saints of the Church from the earth "prior to the tribulations that is to come." Ephraem wrote that the saints will be "taken to the Lord lest they see the confusion that is to overwhelm the world because of our sins." Dr. Alexander believed that this text was written by some unknown writer in the sixth century, but he concluded that it was derived from an original Ephraem manuscript (A.D. 373). Other scholars, including the German editor Professor Caspari, who wrote a German commentary on this Latin manuscript in 1890, believed that Ephraem's manuscript was written by Ephraem himself in A.D. 373. Professor Cameron Rhoades, professor of Latin at Tyndale Theological Seminary, translated Ephraem's Latin text into English at the request of my friend Dr. Tommy Ice and myself.

## Ephraem and Daniel's Seventieth Week — The Tribulation Period

A question naturally arises in the mind of Bible students about how long Ephraem believed the Tribulation would last. While Ephraem correctly describes the Great Tribulation as three and one-half years, his other writings reveal that he believed that the whole tribulation period, "that sore affliction," would last "one week" of seven years. Ephraem's book, *The Book of the Cave of Treasures*, written about A.D. 370, taught about the genealogy of

Christ. He wrote that the sixty-ninth week of Daniel 9:24–27 ended with the rejection and crucifixion of Jesus the Messiah.

> The Jews have no longer among them a king, or a priest, or a prophet, or a Passover, even as Daniel prophesied concerning them, saying, *After two and sixty weeks Christ shall be slain,* and the city of holiness shall be laid waste until the completion of things decreed'. (Daniel 9:26). That is to say, for ever and ever [italics added].
>
> *(Book of the Cave of Treasures,* p. 235).

In Daniel's prophecy he foretold that Jerusalem would be rebuilt "even in troublesome times" during the initial period of "seven weeks" of years (forty-nine years). Daniel foretold that this initial period of seven "weeks" of years would be immediately followed by a further period of sixty-two "weeks" of years, ending with the cutting off of the Messiah (483 years). The combined total of sixty-nine weeks of years (seven weeks plus sixty-two weeks) concludes with the rejection of Christ. As quoted above, Ephraem taught that Jesus Christ was slain at the end of the combined sixty-nine weeks of years.

However, in the section of his book dealing with the future War of Gog and Magog, Ephraem wrote about the final (seventieth) week of Daniel as follows.

> *At the end of the world and at the final consummation* . . . suddenly the gates of the north shall be opened . . . They will destroy the earth, and there will be none able to stand before them. *After one week of that sore affliction* [Tribulation], *they will all be destroyed in the plain of Joppa* . . . . Then will the son of perdition appear, of the seed and of the tribe of Dan . . . He will go into Jerusalem and will sit upon a throne in the Temple saying, 'I am the Christ,' and he will be borne aloft by legions of devils like a king and a lawgiver, naming himself God . . . *The time of the error of the Anti-Christ will last* two years and a half, but others say *three years and six months"* (italics added).

Although there are some curious elements in his description of prophetic events, it is clear that Ephraem believed that the Seventieth Week of Daniel's prophecy of the Seventy Weeks will be fulfilled during the final seven years of this age when the

Antichrist will appear. This evidence of a belief in a "gap" or "parenthesis" between the sixty-ninth and seventieth week of Daniel 9:24–27 from a fourth-century Christian writer is significant. It is worthwhile to note that this teaching that there would be a "gap" or parenthesis between Daniel's sixty-ninth week and the seventieth week of years was taught also by others in the early church, including the Epistle of Barnabas (A.D. 110) and the writings of Hippolytus (A.D. 220).

## Scriptural Indications of a Pretribulation Rapture

Scripture presents five definite indications that support the pretribulation Rapture:

First, in the first three chapters of Revelation, the Church is mentioned nineteen times as being on earth. However, in Revelation 4–19, which describes the Great Tribulation in great detail, there is not one mention of the Church on the earth.

During this period, the Church is described as participating in the Marriage Supper of the Lamb and at the "bema" judgement seat before Christ in heaven. An interesting point is that Revelation 6:17 and 7:1–8 prophesy that before the great day of God's wrath comes, the angels will hold back their judgement "till we have sealed the servants of our God on their foreheads" (verse 3). The prophet then describes that the angels "sealed an hundred and forty and four thousand of all the tribes of the children of Israel" (verse 4). The passage then describes that 12,000 from each of the named tribes of Israel are sealed for divine protection. This description of the sealing of the servants of God exclusively from the twelve tribes of Israel, before the wrath of God is unleashed in the Great Tribulation, would strongly indicate that the reason the Church is not mentioned is because it is already safely in heaven at this time.

Second, Revelation 4 tells us that when John was "in the Spirit" and was "raptured" up to heaven to stand before the throne of heaven, he saw twenty-four elders with crowns on their heads. But Paul says, in 2 Timothy 4:8, that "henceforth there is laid up for me a crown of righteousness, which the Lord, the righteous judge, shall give me at that day: and not to me only, but unto all them also that love his appearing." Second Corinthians 5:10 speaks of that day when "we must all appear before the judgment seat of Christ; that every one may receive the things done in his body, according to that he hath done, whether it be good or bad."

Therefore, the fact that the twenty-four elders, representing the Church, already have their crowns in his prophetic vision indicates that John was taken to a time just after the Rapture and saw the rewarding of crowns to the raptured Christians at the judgment seat. After he witnesses the Rapture to heaven, he then sees the sequential series of judgments of the Great Tribulation occurring upon the earth.

Third, as mentioned earlier, Matthew 24 describes the events of the Tribulation and focuses on Israel, not the Church. Jesus says that those in Judea (not North America) should flee to the hills (verse 16). Matthew records that the Jews should pray that it does not occur on the Sabbath (verse 20). The reason for this is that, after the Temple is rebuilt, the rabbinical restriction of a "Sabbath day's journey" will again be in effect.

This rabbinical requirement (an interpretation of God's instruction in Exodus 16:29 forbidding "work" on the Sabbath) prohibits a Jew from walking (or fleeing) more than two thousand cubits (3,000 ft.)from where he finds himself at the beginning of the Sabbath day. Obviously, these Jewish restrictions have no meaning for a Christian, who is not under the Law. Jesus was referring to the Jews during the Tribulation, not the Church.

Fourth, Paul tells the Thessalonians that "God hath not appointed us to wrath, but to obtain salvation by our Lord Jesus Christ" (1 Thessalonians 5:9). Verse 11 advises us to "comfort yourselves together, and edify one another, even as also ye do" because of this fact. In what manner would we comfort each other if our only hope is to endure through three and one-half years of the wrath of God? Notice that Paul contrasts two separate and opposite destinies. He reminds the Church that its destiny is the Lord's salvation and that the Church has not been appointed by God to the wrath of the Great Tribulation.

Fifth, one of the strongest proofs that the Rapture will precede the revealing of the Man of Lawlessness, the Antichrist, is found in 2 Thessalonians 2:1–9. The church at Thessalonica was confused, and they felt apprehensive that the great Day of the Lord could occur at any moment. Paul appeals to their memory of his teaching about "the coming of our Lord Jesus Christ, and by our gathering together unto him" (verse 1), and tells them not to be troubled by the incorrect teaching that Armageddon awaits the Church. He very specifically points out, "That day shall not come, except there come a falling away first, and that man of sin be revealed, the son of perdition" (verse 3).

This "revealing" of the Antichrist does not occur when he is born, nor even probably when he makes a seven-year treaty with Israel (see Daniel 9:27). He will be "revealed" in his satanic nature when he seats himself in the rebuilt Temple in Jerusalem, claiming to be god and demanding worship as god. It is this act that reveals his satanic character as Antichrist and confirms that he has been totally possessed by Satan.

Paul also says that the Man of Sin (or lawlessness) will only be revealed "in his [appointed] time" (verse 6). He clearly indicates that there is an individual who, by his supernatural power, hinders or restrains the Antichrist "until he be taken out of the way" (verse 7). "And then shall that Wicked be revealed, . . . even him, whose coming is after the working of Satan with all power and signs and lying wonders" (verse 8).

Several suggestions have been offered by scholars as to the identity of the supernatural power of whom Paul says, "The one who now holds it back will continue to do so till he is taken out of the way" (2 Thessalonians 2:7 NIV). Some have thought the restrainer of Antichrist is human government, but that suggestion is disproved by the fact that governments or kingdoms will continue after Antichrist is revealed (see Revelation 13:7) and by the fact that the singular personal pronoun "he" is used. Others have suggested that the Church is the "he"; however, nowhere else in Scripture is the Church addressed as "he," nor does the Church have any power except that which God manifests through it. The "He" whom Paul says is holding back "the man of sin" is none other than the Holy Spirit.

Prior to Christ's ascension to heaven, He promised His disciples that the Holy Spirit would come to empower the Church and that He would never leave it. In John 14:16–17, Jesus promised that the Holy Spirit would abide in His Church forever in His role as the Counselor. He even said that the Counselor could not come until He had ascended (John 16:7). However, unless the Holy Spirit is taken out of the way in His office as Counselor, the Antichrist will not be able to be revealed. John 16:8-11 makes it clear that the Holy Spirit is He that restrains the Antichrist: "And when he is come, he will reprove the world of sin, and of righteousness, and of judgment: of sin, because they believe not on me; of righteousness, because I go to my Father, and ye see me no more; of judgment, because the prince of this world is judged."

Since we have been assured by Jesus that the Father "shall give you another Comforter, that he may abide with you for ever" (John 14:16), it is probable that when the Holy Spirit removes Himself as the restrainer of the Antichrist, it is because the Church (the Bride of Christ) has already been raptured and is in heaven at the Marriage Supper of the Lamb.

It is worthwhile to remember that the Holy Spirit, as part of the Trinity, will continue to act throughout earth and heaven as He acted in Old Testament times, prior to His coming at Pentecost in A.D. 32. It is only in His role or office as the Comforter of the Church and the restrainer of the Antichrist that He will remove Himself. The third person of the Trinity was, is now, and always will be omnipresent.

The day is coming, though it is known only to God Himself, when he will call every Christian, living and dead, to meet Him in the air and return home to heaven to the great Marriage Supper of the Lamb. Since it is imminent, it could happen without warning at any moment. All we know about its timing is that it has not occurred yet and that it will occur before the Great Tribulation begins.

The Father tells the Church "to wait for his Son from heaven, whom he raised from the dead, even Jesus, which delivered us from the wrath to come" (1 Thessalonians :10).

# 12

# *The Antichrist and the Revival of the Roman Empire*

Thou, O king, sawest, and behold a great image. This great image, whose brightness was excellent, stood before thee; and the form thereof was terrible. This image's head was of fine gold, his breast and his arms of silver, his belly and his thighs of brass, his legs of iron, his feet part of iron and part of clay. Thou sawest till that a stone was cut out without hands, which smote the image upon his feet that were of iron and clay, and brake them to pieces.

(Daniel 2: 31-34)

### Daniel's Vision of a Revived Roman Empire

Daniel rose from being a slave in exile to become the prime minister of the greatest empire of the ancient world due, in part, to his God-given ability to interpret the dreams and visions of King Nebuchadnezzar of Babylon. One of the king's dreams that Daniel interpreted was of a great statue composed of different metals. Daniel revealed that this image symbolized the future course of world empires until the end of this age. He said that there would be only four world empires from Babylon, in 606 B.C., to the time of the Second Coming of Christ, who would then introduce His heavenly and eternal "Stone" Kingdom with Himself as Messiah-King.

This vision of the great image revealed that each stage of these four empires would decrease in value (head of gold, chest of silver, thighs of bronze, legs of iron, and feet of both iron and clay), but also would increase in strength. As Daniel 2 indicates, the first empire was Babylon (Daniel 2:37–38). Historians and Bible scholars agree that the second empire was Media-Persia; the third, Greece; and the fourth, the Roman Empire. The iron legs represent Rome in its divided empire stage. The empire that is still to come, represented by the feet with ten toes, is the revived Roman Empire, appearing in its final form during the period leading up to the Battle of Armageddon.

One of the most amazing aspects of this prophecy is that it predicted that no matter what ambitious men would dream of attempting, no world empire would ever successfully replace the Roman Empire. Mohammed, Charlemagne, Genghis Khan, Frederich Barbarossa, Napoleon, the British Empire, Adolf Hitler, and the Russians have all attempted to build a fifth world empire, but each in turn has failed. The future is in the hands of God (2:45), and He has decreed that this last world power will be a revival of the ancient Roman Empire within a confederacy of ten nations, based upon the territory of the old Roman Empire.

## The Antichrist-Leader of the Revived Roman Empire

Several years later, Daniel had a parallel vision of this final stage of the revived Roman Empire: "After this I saw in the night visions, and behold a fourth beast, dreadful and terrible, and strong exceedingly; and it had great iron teeth: it devoured and brake in pieces, and stamped the residue with the feet of it: and it was diverse from all the beasts that were before it; and it had ten horns. I considered the horns, and, behold, there came up among them another little horn, before whom there were three of the first horns plucked up by the roots" (Daniel 7:7–8).

The interpretation of this vision indicates that after these ten nations have formed a ten-nation "Roman confederacy," the "little horn" — the new leader of Western Europe (the Antichrist) — will seize three of the nations by force. Then the other seven nations apparently will submit and join him. Although he will rule for seven years (9:27), his absolute power over all of the nations of the earth and over the new believers, the "tribulation saints," will only last 1260 days, from his sacrilegious entrance into the new Temple in Jerusalem (Daniel 7:25) to the final Battle of Armageddon, when he will be destroyed by Christ.

Probably, this revived Roman Empire of ten nations will follow closely the geographical outlines of the ancient one. The map (figure 1) illustrates the extent of ancient Rome. Rome never conquered Ireland, and it is significant that Great Britain has lost the southern Republic of Ireland and may eventually withdraw from Northern Ireland. Also, Scotland was never conquered by Rome. Emperor Hadrian's legions built Hadrian's Wall to separate Roman England from free Scotland in A.D. 121; it kept out the invaders for almost two hundred years. In this light, it is fascinating to follow the negotiations of the Scottish nationalists who are seeking independence for Scotland since the development of the incredibly valuable North Sea oil off the northern shores of Scotland.

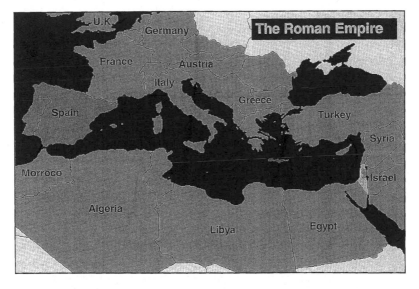

*THE FOURTH KINGDOM OF DANIEL — THE ROMAN EMPIRE*
*THE REVIVAL OF THE ROMAN EMPIRE*
*Figure 1*

A tremendous upheaval has led to the breakup of the Russian Empire, the Commonwealth of Independent States. The future defeat of Russia, when she attacks Israel, may create an opportunity for a dynamic European leader to seize control of the three eastern European nations which will break free in the chaos of Russia's military defeat. These three nations were apparently once part of the ancient Roman Empire and have been caught, like three rib bones, in the jaws of the Russian bear since 1945. If these three nations escape Russian domination when God defeats Russia and its allies (see Daniel 7:5–8), they may become the first successful conquest of the Antichrist on his road to world power.

In June 1979 Europe held its first election for the European Parliament (the first directly elected, multinational assembly in history), which was set up to deal with European community problems. This is a natural development of a process which began in 1958 with the founding of the European Common Market (officially known as the European Economic Community or E.E.C.) and the North Atlantic Treaty Organization (NATO). At that time, Europe, unknowingly, took its first tentative steps toward the long-prophesied ten-nation confederacy based on the ancient Roman Empire. Interestingly, the E.E.C. is based on the Treaty of Rome, which was signed in Rome on March 25, 1957. Jean Monnet, was one of the inspirers of this union, revealed the ultimate objective of the union when he said, "Once a common market interest has been created, then political union will come naturally." Henri Spaak, Belgium's foreign minister who signed the Treaty of Rome, admitted that these leaders were consciously recreating the Roman Empire.

Results from a poll in a report from Brussels in January 1985 showed that 52 percent of Europeans supported the idea of transforming the present union of European states into a true confederacy to be known as the United States of Europe. This proposed confederation would go well beyond the current economic union, to involve a defense and political union, similar to the union of Canada's provinces or the union of the states of America. All of these actions are the embryonic stages of the final revival of the Roman Empire foreseen by the prophet Daniel. The European Union is now rushing toward a common European currency.

### The Last Seven Years: Daniel's Seventieth Week

In an earlier chapter we saw the absolute precision of the fulfillment of Daniel's vision of the Seventy Weeks of years. Jesus

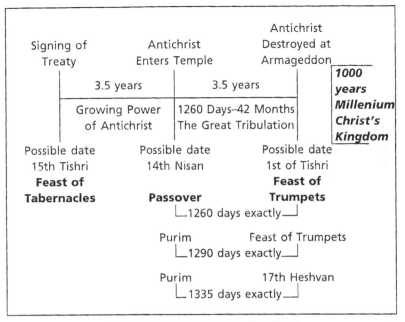

DANIEL'S SEVENTIETH WEEK
SEVEN-YEAR TREATY BETWEEN ANTICHRIST AND ISRAEL
*Figure 2*

Christ was "cut-off" (9:26) on Palm Sunday, A.D. 32, exactly to the day that the sixty-nine "weeks" of years terminated. That left one remaining "week" of years (seven years) to be fulfilled at the end of this age, just before Christ returns at the Battle of Armageddon to set up the Kingdom that has been postponed almost two thousand years because Israel rejected her Messiah.

Figure 2 illustrates this Seventieth Week of seven years that will commence with a seven-year treaty made with Israel by the Antichrist, the leader of the ten-nation revived Roman Empire. This treaty will guarantee Israel's security. After almost fifty years in a state of war with her Arab neighbors, Israeli citizens bear the highest taxes for defense of any nation in the world. It is easy to see why Israel will be tempted to make a defense treaty and covenant with the Antichrist and his European empire in the hope of finally being able to rest from their eternal vigilance. As indicated in chapter 6, it is possible that this treaty will be signed in the fall of some future year, on the anniversary of Israel's Feast of

Tabernacles, the fifteenth day of the month Tishri. "And he shall confirm the covenant with many for one week: and in the midst of the week he shall cause the sacrifice and the oblation to cease, and for the overspreading of abominations he shall make it desolate, even until the consummation, and that determined shall be poured upon the desolate" (Daniel 9:27). This prophecy focuses on Israel, not the Church. The vision was given to a Hebrew prophet in answer to his question as to what will happen to his people, Israel, in the future.

In other words the Antichrist, the world dictator, will force the Jews "in the midst of the week" (after three and one-half years) to stop the sacrifices in the rebuilt Temple. Then he will set up an idol of himself (the abomination) in the Temple to be worshiped as "god" until he is destroyed at the end of the seven years when Christ returns. This period, from his defiling the Temple until his destruction, will last exactly 1260 days (Daniel 7:25; 12:6–7; Revelation 13:5), or forty-two months of thirty days each. Revelation 13:3,14–18 tells us that the Antichrist will be killed and miraculously rise from the dead through Satan's power at the exact midpoint of the last seven years, apparently after he stops the daily sacrifice.

It is possible that this will occur on Passover, with his resurrection occurring a few days later on the Feast of Firstfruits (the seventeenth of Nisan, in the spring). This would allow him to imitate Christ as "Messiah" and to pretend to fulfill the biblical prophecies about Christ's first coming.

Interestingly, this scenario would fit the pattern of biblically significant events occurring on Jewish feast days. As predicted in the Bible, his time of total power over the tribulation saints lasts only 1260 days, or forty-two months of thirty days each (Revelation 13:5). This period of 1260 days, the second half of Daniel's Seventieth Week, would bring us to the first day of Tishri, the Feast of Trumpets, a day on which we can expect the Antichrist's destruction at the prophesied Battle of Armageddon (Joel 2:1–2, 15). It is fascinating to consider the curious details that the prophet Daniel supplies to supplement this future history. In Daniel 7:25 he describes the Antichrist's power over the holy people for three and one-half years ("a time and times and the dividing of time" — 360 days + 2 × 360 days + 1/2 of 360 days = 1260 days). However, Daniel is told in his last vision that the Antichrist's defeat would occur 1290 days "from the time that the daily sacrifice is taken away." The prophet also wrote: "Blessed is he that waiteth, and cometh to the thousand three hundred and five and thirty [1335] days. (Daniel 12:11–12)

In all the commentaries I have searched, I have never found an adequate explanation of how these three different numbers of days could be reconciled in the career and death of the Antichrist at the Battle of Armageddon.

Let me offer a possible scenario that might fit these prophetic scriptural indications of the exact duration of the Great Tribulation (see figure 2). In keeping with the pattern of biblical anniversaries, it is possible that the Antichrist will stop the daily sacrifice in the Temple on the Feast of Purim, which occurs thirty days before the Feast of Passover (the beginning of the 1290 days). Some thirty days later (the beginning of the 1260 days) on Passover, someone, possibly a Jewish believer, will kill this tyrant. However, he will rise from the dead due to the supernatural power of Satan, which, apparently, God will allow in this unique case to accomplish His purpose (Revelation 13:3–8, 15–18). He may be possessed by Satan on Passover in exactly the same manner as was Judas Iscariot (Luke 22:1–3). This will be the true revealing of the Man of Sin in his satanic-possessed nature as the Antichrist. (see figure 2)

Thus, these two periods, the 1260 days and the 1290 days, would end on the same day, the Feast of Trumpets, at the Battle of Armageddon. However, the first event, the stopping of the daily sacrifice would occur thirty days before the Passover on the Feast of Purim, the anniversary of that day recorded in the book of Esther 3:13, when Haman, the ancient enemy of the Jews, sought to destroy the entire Jewish race. If this interpretation is correct, then 1335 days from the Feast of Purim would bring us up to a day known in the biblical calendar as the 17th day of Heshvan, three and one-half years later (45 days after the Battle of Armageddon and the death of Antichrist at the Second Coming of Christ). It is fascinating that this day of blessing, according to the prophet Daniel in chapter 12:12, is the exact anniversary of the day that God destroyed all life on earth in the Flood in the days of Noah. The 17th day of Heshvan is the day the forty days of rain began and the fountains of the deep opened to destroy man's sinful rebellion. Another key anniversary connected with the 17th day of

Heshvan is the great day of blessing brought about when Lord Balfour made the famous Balfour Declaration in November 2, 1917 — the declaration that Palestine would become a Jewish national homeland for the first time in almost two thousand years. It would certainly be consistent for God to commemorate this anniversary by ushering in the final blessings of the promised millennial kingdom on that significant day.

Only time will tell whether or not this is the correct interpretation.

### The Final Battle of Armageddon

The great Battle of Armageddon will occur in northern Israel and extend down the great Valley of Jezreel, below the mountain of Megiddo. The name Armageddon comes from *har* for "mountain" and "Megiddo," the ancient city that overlooks this enormous plain. It is also known as the Valley of Jehoshaphat (the valley of God's judgement). According to Revelation 16:16, this ancient battleground will be the scene of the most devastating military confrontation in human history.

The battles will rage over a two-hundred-mile-long zone southward, toward the city of Jerusalem. The battle carnage will be so terrible that horses will sink into the resulting mire of blood, bodies, and mud until the blood reaches "to the horses' bridles" (Revelation 14:19–20). If you have ever seen some of the awful war photos of the quagmire of blood and mud produced by artillery and modern conventional weapons, you can imagine how this whole fertile valley could turn into a bloodbath under the assault of the massive 200-million-man army of the "Kings of the East" against the combined armies of the Western nations led by the Antichrist.

With Russia already destroyed in the earlier battle of Magog, and America probably somewhat isolationist, the political-military vacuum will have been filled by a resurgent Europe under the leadership of the Antichrist. The other major political-military super-power will be a combination of the vast populations of China, Southeast Asia, and India, together with the technological and economic leadership of a remilitarized Japan. Already, China and Japan have signed a thirty-year treaty of cooperation. In this new situation, the Antichrist and the revived Roman Empire will have guaranteed Israel's security and her probable control of the oil supplies of the Middle East. From a geopolitical standpoint, Israel's strategic position at the meeting point of Europe, Africa, and Asia has always made the control of this land essential for a world empire. The power, whether East or West, that controls Israel and the Middle East oil will control the world.

The prophet Daniel describes that while the Antichrist is at his headquarters in Jerusalem, he will be attacked by African and Arab nations led by a "King of the South" (Egypt) and another group of nations led by a "King of the North" (probably Syria). When his forces quickly defeat these attacks, he will conquer Egypt, Libya, and Ethiopia (Daniel 11:40–43). However, the oriental nations of the world that resent his totalitarian dictatorship will finally decide that this is the time to attack the Antichrist in Israel and win world power. As these nations to the East (China, India, Japan, etc.) and the North (the remaining parts of Russia), begin to mobilize their vast armies for this final decisive battle, the Antichrist will gather all the remaining nations of the West still under his control and will bring them to Israel to face the approaching armies of the "Kings of the East" (Daniel 11:44–45). The prophet John tells us that God will miraculously dry up the great river Euphrates to allow this enormous 200-million-man army to cross over the river to approach northern Israel (Revelation 16:12–16).

The angel's prophecy that the army of the Eastern nations would contain 200 million men naturally shocked the prophet John (Revelation 9:13–16). The entire population of the Roman Empire in the first century was only about 200 million men, woman, and children. Naturally, it was hard for John and, indeed, for many Bible commentators over the years to believe that the angel "literally" meant that one side alone in this Battle of Armageddon would contain such an enormous number of soldiers. Until World War II, only twelve battles in human history have been fought with more than 50,000 soldiers on both sides. It is only in this century that we have seen the complete mobilization of a nation's resources for war. According to *The War Atlas*, the worldwide arms buildup has now created armies that can field 570 million soldiers when all reserves are called up.

My wife, Kaye, and I visited China in 1986. As we stood on Tian'An Men Square in Bejing, the largest square in the world, we were shocked to see that the reports about the results of the one-child policy in China were true. Before us on the square, out of the hundreds of thousands of families out for a Sunday stroll, there were almost no young Chinese girls in evidence. There were at least nine young boys for every girl. In my research I had discovered that the result of the rigorously enforced one-child policy in China since 1978 is that out of all live births, nine boys are born for every female child. When we questioned Chinese officials about these reports and our own eyewitness impressions, they confirmed that the 9:1 ratio of boys to girls is a fact. The Chinese have developed several reliable methods to determine the sex of the fetus early in a pregnancy. Since they are only allowed one child, most Chinese couples choose to abort the female fetus and keep trying until they conceive a male fetus. If a woman has a second pregnancy, she is forced to abort it. If she becomes pregnant a third time, she is forced to undergo sterilization.

Whenever a Chinese couple successfully avoids the authorities and has a second child, a fine is levied equal to one year's income. Naturally, the Chinese would like to have their family name continue and to have a male child return from school at age eighteen to help contribute to the family income. A girl will not continue the family name, and she will go to live in her husband's home and help support his parents, not her own. For all these reasons, most Chinese couples abort female fetuses and try to bear one male child. For thousands of years the male-female balance of human populations has remained close to fifty-fifty. For the first time in history, human political decisions, biological-testing techniques, and self-interest have combined to produce a massive sexual imbalance in the population of the largest nation on earth (one-quarter of the world's population). The social, political, and military ramifications of an excess 125 million young men without hope of ever being married and finding stability in a home are already giving nightmares to the political planners in China.

The officials I spoke with went on to say that although the one-child policy was essential to stop famine in China, this unexpected disproportion of boys to girls was already being discussed in party meetings as potentially the greatest social problem that China would face in the next decade. With a base population of 1.2 billion people today, this imbalance of boys to girls will produce an unprecedented situation in human history. By the year 2005, China will have an excess of 125 million Chinese boys of military age, with no girls for them to marry and no prospects of their ever having a family of their own. This same phenomenon is now being reported in India, Korea, and other Asian countries. When this group of 125 million military-age young men is added to the armies that these huge countries already possess, it is possible to see that the biblical prophecy of a 200-million-man army from the "Kings of the East" is not only literally possible, it is a terrible reality facing our world as we approach the year 2000. Two thousand years ago God described the consequences of such events in telling John that the "Kings of the East" would have an army of 200 million.

During this incredible Battle of Armageddon, Christ will return from heaven with His heavenly army (the millions of saints described in Jude 14–15) and destroy the nations of the world that have joined in battle to destroy Israel and each other. Christ will destroy the Antichrist and the False Prophet and their armies. He will defend Jerusalem and all who call upon His Name for protection (Zechariah 12:1–9). Jesus Christ will visibly return in glory as the "King of Kings and Lord of Lords" to set up His Kingdom forever (Revelation 19:11–16).

All of Israel's major events have occurred on the anniversaries of the feast days and fast days of their Jewish liturgical calendar. It would be consistent if this same pattern held and these final climatic events which usher in the Millennium were to occur on the last three significant feast days of the year — the Feast of Trumpets, the Day of Atonement, and the final Feast of Tabernacles.

Only the events themselves, of course, will prove whether or not these patterns of biblical anniversaries will continue to be prophetically fulfilled during Israel's final crisis, the Battle of Armageddon.

# 13

# God's Prophetic Time Cycles

Remember the former things of old: for I am God, and there is none else; I am God, and there is none like me, declaring the end from the beginning, and from ancient times the things that are not yet done, saying, My counsel shall stand, and I will do all my pleasure. (Isaiah 46:9–10)

One cannot study the Bible for long without being struck forcibly by the wondrous phenomenon that a great number of historical and prophetic events concerning the Jews have occurred according to precise time cycles. If you were to discover, while studying the history of any other nation, that many significant events occurred according to precise time cycles, you would be justified in concluding that some supernatural power was intervening in the affairs of that nation. Whenever we examine the historical dates and significant events of any other nation, we discover that events occur at random, with no discernible pattern of anniversaries. It is only when we turn to the history of Israel that a different phenomenon appears. God has revealed His sovereignty and prophetic foreknowledge through His appointment of historic events for Israel according to precise cycles of time.

Scripture records several significant biblical time cycles concerning the history of Israel. The most important periods consist of 40 days, 40 years, 70 years, 430 years, 490 years, and 2,520 years.

Some of these cycles are well known to us. Some, unless you are a student of prophecy, may not be as familiar.

## The Forty-Day Cycle

In addition, there are thirteen periods of forty days recorded in the Old and New Testament that are significant times of probation and testing.

| | |
|---|---|
| The duration of rainfall in the Flood | Genesis 7:4,12 |
| Israel mourns for Jacob | Genesis 50:3 |
| Moses on Mount Sinai | Exodus 24:18 |
| Moses intercedes for Israel | Deuteronomy 9:25 |
| Moses' second time on Mount Sinai | Exodus 34:28 |
| Moses' second fasting period | Deuteronomy 9:18 |
| The 12 spies search Canaan | Numbers 13:25 |
| Goliath challenges Israel | 1 Samuel 17:16 |
| Jonah's forty days and Nineveh | Jonah 3:4 |
| Elijah's fasting journey | 1 Kings 19:8 |
| Ezekiel lies forty days on his right side | Ezekiel 4:5 |
| Jesus fasts and is tempted by Satan | Matthew 4:2 |
| From Jesus' Resurrection to His Ascension | Acts 1:2 |

Recognizing the symbolism of the forty-day period, some Christians celebrate the forty days of Lent as a time of self-denial and spiritual preparation.

## The Forty-Year Cycle

Probably the best known cycle is the forty-year cycle. This period appears repeatedly throughout Israel's history in connection with a time of testing and probation. The Scriptures record twelve of these forty-year cycles:

| | |
|---|---|
| Moses in Egypt | Acts 7:23 |
| Moses in Midian | Acts 7:30 |
| Israel in the wilderness | Deuteronomy 8:2 |
| Israel under the judge Othniel | Judges 3:11 |
| Israel under the judge Barak | Judges 5:31 |
| Israel under Gideon | Judges 8:28 |
| Israel enslaved by the Philistines | Judges 13:1 |
| Israel under the judge Eli | 1 Samuel 4:18 |
| Israel under King Saul | Acts 13:21 |
| Israel under King David | 2 Samuel 5:4 |

Israel under King Solomon            1 Kings 11:42
Israel under King Joash            2 Chronicles 24:1

### The Seventy-Year Cycle

The Bible speaks of three historically significant events in Israel's history that each spanned seventy years.

*1.   The Babylonian Captivity*           *606 B.C. to 536 B.C.*

This seventy-year captivity began with Nebuchadnezzar invading Judea (Daniel 1:1–2) and ended with the decree issued by King Cyrus in 536 B.C., which authorized the Jews to return to Jerusalem.

God has always been precise in His dealing with Israel in terms of its stewardship of the land. When Israel crossed the Jordan River to enter the Promised Land, they entered a special covenant relationship with God that was expressed by the law of the Sabbath of the land. According to this law, every seven years Israel was to let the land lie fallow and not harvest the crops. God promised that He would provide a bumper crop in the sixth year to carry them over the "Sabbath year" of rest for the land and provide enough seed to plant again in the eighth year of the cycle.

This act of obedience would demonstrate Israel's total trust and obedience to God. At the end of the seventh cycle of the forty-ninth year, God promised to supply enough food to feed them during both the forty-ninth and the fiftieth years. Then the cycle would resume (Leviticus 25:1–13,18–22.). This fiftieth year was known as the Year of Jubilee — the year in which the land would lie at rest, all debts would to be cancelled, and all slaves would be set free. This Jubilee Year became a symbol and a promise of the Great Jubilee, that day when true liberty would be realized as the Messiah came to set up His Kingdom and proclaim liberty to all humans.

There is no scriptural evidence that Israel ever faithfully kept the law of the Sabbath of the land by letting the land lie fallow for a whole year. Once Israel adopted a monarchy under King Saul in 1096 B.C., for the first time, the law of the Sabbath of the land could have been enforced by royal decree. However, Israel did not obey God in this matter, and 490 years later, in 606 B.C., she had missed keeping this Sabbath a total of seventy times. Moses prophesied more than 850 years earlier that Israel would disobey this Sabbath law and would go into captivity for her disobedience.

"Then shall the land enjoy her sabbaths, as long as it lieth desolate, and ye be in your enemies land; even then shall the land rest; . . . because it did not rest in your sabbaths, when ye dwelt upon it" (Leviticus 26:34–35).

The year 606 B.C. was a Year of Jubilee, and therefore it was also a Sabbath-rest year for the land. The prophet Jeremiah records that in one last weak attempt at partial obedience, "King Zedekiah had made a covenant with all the people which were at Jerusalem, to proclaim liberty unto them." (Jeremiah 34:8). However after freeing their Hebrew slaves, the princes and the aristocracy broke their solemn covenant of liberty that they had made before God and enslaved their servants again. In anger God declared, "Ye have not hearkened unto me, in proclaiming liberty, every one to his brother, and every man to his neighbor: behold, I proclaim a liberty for you, saith the Lord, to the sword, to the pestilence, and to the famine; and I will make you to be removed into all the kingdoms of the earth" (Jeremiah 34:8,17). If Israel would not voluntarily keep the Sabbath of the land seventy times in 490 years, God would keep it for them.

The record of 2 Chronicles 36:17–21 declares that God specifically took Israel into captivity in Babylon from 606 B.C. to 536 B.C. "to fulfill the word of the Lord by the mouth of Jeremiah, until the land had enjoyed her sabbaths; for as long as she lay desolate she kept sabbath, to fulfill threescore and ten years" (verse 21).

In other words, God decided to force Israel to keep the Sabbath of the land to make up for the missed seventy years of letting the land rest (Jeremiah 25:11). After the completion of this seventy-year period God fulfilled His word: "That after seventy years be accomplished at Babylon I will visit you, and perform my good word toward you, in causing you to return to this place" (Jeremiah 29:10).

2. *The Babylonian Desolations*                    *589 B.C. to 520B.C.*

This overlapping seventy-year period of "desolations" began with the conquering of Israel's land and the besieging of Jerusalem by Nebuchadnezzar on the tenth day of the tenth month, Tebeth, 589 B.C., and ended seventy biblical years later (biblical years of 360 days each) to the exact day in 520 B.C., the twenty-fourth day of Chisleu, when the foundation of the Second Temple was laid (see Haggai 2:18). The interval between these dates is exactly seventy biblical-prophetic years, which equals 25,200 days (70 × 360 days = 25,200 days). This precision of fulfillment using this 360-day year is one of the strong proofs that God still observes the ancient 360-day biblical year in calculating the interval or duration for prophetic periods.

3. *The Restoration Period*             *515 B.C. to 445 B.C.*

This period began with the dedication of the Second Temple on Passover, 515 B.C. (Ezra 6:15–22), and ended exactly seventy years later with the decree by the Persian King Artaxerxes authorizing Nehemiah to rebuild the walls of Jerusalem in the month of Nisan, 445 B.C. (Nehemiah 2:1, 7).

## The Four-Hundred-Thirty-Year Cycle

There are two significant periods of 430 years recorded in Scripture.

1. *The Abrahamic Covenant To the Exodus*       *430 years*

God made a covenant with Abraham that his descendants would inherit the Promised land on Passover, the fourteenth of Nisan (Genesis 15:18). The Exodus occurred 430 years later on Passover. "It came to pass at the end of the four hundred and thirty years, even the selfsame day it came to pass, that all the hosts of the Lord went out from the land of Egypt" (Exodus 12:41; cf., Galatians 3:17). On the same day, the fourteenth of Nisan, God later commanded the Israelites to observe the annual Passover forever.

2. *The Closing of the Old Testament To Christ's Public Ministry*
                                     *430 Years*

Malachi wrote the last book of the Old Testament in 396 B.C., and the canon of the Old Testament was closed by the Great Synagogue. In Malachi 3:1 he prophesied: "Behold, I will send my messenger, and he shall prepare the way before me: and the Lord, whom ye seek, shall suddenly come to his temple." Jesus commenced His public teaching, which forms the beginning of the New Testament period, 430 biblical years later. The period from 396 B.C. to the fall of A.D. 28 equals 430 biblical years (note: only one year between 1 B.C. and A.D. 1). This period is equal to 423.8 calendar years.

## The Four-Hundred-Ninety-Year Cycle

The entire chronology of God's dealing with Israel (from the birth of Abraham to the final setting up of Christ's kingdom on earth) is marked with five startlingly precise periods of 490 years. In several of these periods, an unusual principle is revealed: During the time Israel is in total disobedience, God's hand is removed from them and prophetic time is suspended. The time is, in a sense, not counted.

When God set forth the regulations for a Nazirite — a person who made a vow of separation to the Lord — He said that if the person broke any of the regulations for Nazirites, "The previous days do not count, because he became defiled during his separation" (Numbers 6:12 NIV). Israel is, by analogy, a "Nazirite" nation set apart as holy to God. When they were "defiled," God omitted these periods of disobedience from His divine chronology as though time had stopped.

1. *The Birth of Abraham To the Exodus*                     *490 Years*

Abraham was seventy-five years old when he left for Canaan. From the giving of the covenant to the Exodus was 430 years (Exodus 12:40). However, we need to subtract the fifteen years of rebellion when Abraham disobeyed God and chose to have a son by Hagar. Abraham lost faith in God's promise of a son by Sarah and disobeyed God by trying to create an heir his own way with Hagar. Ishmael lived in Abraham's house fifteen years until Abraham trusted God to miraculously produce Isaac, the promised seed. The total period from the birth of Abraham till the Exodus is 490 years, as God counts the time: 75 + 430 = 505 years; this sum minus the 15 years of Abraham's disobedience equals 490 years.

2. *The Coronation of King Saul in 1096 B.C. To the*
   *Babylonian Captivity in 606 B.C.*                      *490 Years*

This period is discussed in detail in the section on the seventy-year cycle.

3. *The Dedication of the First Temple in 1005 B.C. To the*
   *Decree of Artaxerxes to Rebuild Jerusalem in 445 B.C.*    *490 Years*

This is a period of 560 years. When we subtract the seventy years of Babylonian captivity, as a time of disobedience not counted, the remaining total is 490 years.

4. *The Dedication of the First Temple in 1005 B.C.*
   *To the Dedication of the Second Temple in 515 B.C.*    *490 Years*

It is a remarkable fact that the First Temple under Solomon was dedicated on the Feast of Tabernacles, the fifteenth day of Tishri, and the Second Temple was dedicated to God by Ezra, the scribe, on the same day of the Feast of Tabernacles 490 years later (see 1 Kings 8:2, 65); Nehemiah 8:14–18).

5. *Daniel's Vision of the Seventy Weeks*    *490 Years*

Daniel's Seventy Seeks was discussed fully in chapter 2. The period from 445 B.C. (March 14) to A.D. 32 (April 6) is 483 biblical years to the day. The "final week" of seven years will be fulfilled in our generation to seal up the vision (see Daniel 9:24–27). This will complete the 490 years.

As we review these remarkable periods of 490 years in God's dealings with Israel, we are reminded of God's sovereignty in precisely controlling Israel's history. Thousands of years ago God declared: "My counsel shall stand, and I will do all my pleasure" (Isaiah 46:10). Truly, it is God that is unfolding His will in human history.

## Two-Thousand-Five Hundred-Twenty-Year Cycle

The 2,520 cycle is the largest and most unique of all prophetic periods. There are three time cycles of 2,520 years indicated in the Scriptures.

1. *The Babylonian Captivity To Israel's Rebirth in 1948*    *2520 Years*

This cycle of 2520 years has already been fulfilled in the period from the end of the worldwide captivity to the rebirth of Israel, exactly as prophesied by the prophet Ezekiel (chapter 4:4–6)

The end of the Babylonian captivity in 536 B.C. to the rebirth of Israel on May 15, 1948, is a period of exactly 2,520 biblical years. (See chapter 3 for a full discussion.)

2.  *The Times of the Gentiles*                    *2520 Years*

This period began with the Babylonian Captivity and continues through 2520 biblical years into our generation. Over the
centuries many students of prophecy have interpreted the "times
of the Gentiles," referred to by Christ in Luke 21:22–24 and by Paul
in Romans 11:25–27, as being a period of 2,520 years.

> For these be the days of vengeance, that all things which
> are written may be fulfilled. . . . And they shall fall by the
> edge of the sword, and shall be led away captive into all
> nations: and Jerusalem shall be trodden down of the Gen-
> tiles, until the times of the Gentiles be fulfilled.
>
> (Luke 21:22, 24)

> For I would not, brethren, that ye should be ignorant of
> this mystery, lest ye should be wise in your own conceits;
> that blindness in part is happened to Israel, until the full-
> ness of the Gentiles be come in.          (Romans 11:25)

3.  *The Times of Israel in the Land*              *2520 Years*

This cycle of 2520 years began with the entry of Israel into the
Promised Land in 1451 B.C. and continued until A.D. 70, when it
was interrupted by the destruction of Israel's national existence.
After almost two thousand years, Christ will return to set up their
millennial kingdom of 1000 years. The 1520 years from 1451 B.C. to
A.D.70 plus the 1000 years of the promised kingdom give us a total
of 2520 years.

Can any reasonable person believe that all of this has occurred
simply by chance? It seems far more logical to this writer that we
are observing an incredible display of God's sovereignty and that
this phenomenon suggests that God is controlling the destiny of
His chosen people.

# 14

# *Does Prophecy Reveal the Time of Israel's Final Crisis?*

> Behold, I will make thee know what shall be in the last end of the indignation [the Great Tribulation]; for at the time appointed the end shall be.　　　　(Daniel 8:19)

The angel was sent to Daniel to answer his question as to how long it would be until God would finally set up His eternal Kingdom on earth. The answer the angel gave was that the appointed time was set and that it would occur a long time after the life of Daniel. However, Daniel was not left in darkness concerning his question; he was given many interesting time indications of when Israel's final appointment with destiny would come. In this chapter we will examine some of these prophecies as they relate to Israel and her final crisis, the Battle of Armageddon, and the coming of her Messiah-King.

## Man's Appointment in the Valley of Decision

Over twenty-five centuries ago God set an appointment for Israel and the nations that will not be postponed, no matter what man wishes. God described through His prophets "The Great Day of the Lord" in which mankind will finally see Jesus Christ, not as "a suffering servant," but rather as the conquering "King of Kings and Lord of Hosts."

> And I heard, but I understood not: then said I, O my Lord, what shall be the end of these things? And he said, Go thy way, Daniel: for the words are closed up and sealed till the time of the end. Many shall be purified, and made white, and tried; but the wicked shall do wickedly: and none of the wicked shall understand; but the wise shall understand. . . . But go thou thy way till the end be: for thou shalt rest, and stand in thy lot at the end of the days.
>
> (Daniel 12:8–10, 13)

One of the most misunderstood subjects in the study of prophecy is the determination of the time of Israel's final crisis. The reason for this misunderstanding is that we often confuse God's prophecies concerning Israel with those prophecies concerning the Rapture of the Church. No one, including this author, will ever know the day of the promised Rapture, when the saints are resurrected, until that day arrives. There are no events that must occur prior to Christ calling His Church home to heaven. In fact, if Christ had raptured the Church in the first century, the end-time events would still have occurred on schedule in this generation without contradicting a single prophecy about the final crisis for Israel in our lifetime. For this reason, this chapter is not about the Rapture of the Church but about "the last days" of the nation of Israel before her Messiah returns in glory.

In the book of Joel, the prophet declares that, first, God will end the long captivity of Judah and Jerusalem; then He "will also gather all nations, and will bring them down into the valley of Jehoshaphat, and will plead with them there for my people and for my heritage Israel, whom they have scattered among the nations"(Joel 3:2)

"Let the heathen be wakened, and come up to the valley of Jehoshaphat: for there will I sit to judge all the heathen round about" (verse 12); "Multitudes, multitudes in the valley of decision: for the Day of the Lord is near in the valley of decision" (verse 14).

## Can We Know Anything About the Time of Israel's Final Crisis?

For many years, sincere and prudent Christians have been warned against looking into the prophecies of the Bible for indications of God's timing and specific signs leading up to the "last days."

Usually these well-intentioned warnings have hinged on two factors: one is based on an interpretation of certain Scriptures, which we will examine; the other is based on the history of prophetic interpretation.

### The Scriptural Interpretations

The scriptural passage, which is usually quoted out of context, is the following: "But of the times and seasons, brethren, ye have no need that I write unto you. For you yourselves know perfectly that the Day of the Lord so cometh as a thief in the night." (1 Thessalonians 5:1–2)

At first glance, this verse would seem to state that we, as Christians, should be content to be as ignorant of the time of the Day of the Lord as a householder who is unaware of the hour a thief will choose to break into his house at night. If this were the correct interpretation, we would willingly join those who dismiss prophecy about the last days as useless speculation. However, when we wish to clearly understand a scriptural passage, we must look at the whole context of the passage, not just the passage itself. When we examine fully 1 Thessalonians 5:1–10, we will see that precisely the opposite message is conveyed to the Church by Paul, namely, that we are not to be ignorant of the time of the Day of the Lord as it relates to Israel and the nations.

Earlier in his letter to the Church, Paul exhorted them to remain faithful and sanctified until "the coming of our Lord Jesus Christ with all His saints" (1 Thessalonians 3:13). He comforted them with the knowledge that "we which are alive and remain shall be caught up together with them [those who have already died in the faith] in the clouds to meet the Lord in the air" (1 Thessalonians 4:17).

The phrase "caught up" is translated from the Latin word *rapere*, which means "to snatch away." This is the source of the word *Rapture*, the word many Christians use to describe the resurrection of the believers in the Church and their transformation into immortal spiritual bodies that will be gathered together to be with Christ forever.

Paul then continues his instructions in 1 Thessalonians 5:1–11, by informing the Church that the children "of the night" and "of darkness" (the unbelievers) will be overtaken by surprise. For them, "the Day of the Lord" will come as "a thief in the night." "They shall not escape." He then states that it should be totally different for the Christians, "the children of the light, and the children of the day."

Paul says, "But ye, brethren, are not in darkness that that day should overtake you as a thief. Ye are all the children of light, and the children of the day: we are not of the night, nor of darkness. Therefore let us not sleep, as do others [the children of the night, unbelievers]; but let us watch and be sober" (1 Thessalonians 5:4–5).

"For God hath not appointed us to wrath, but to obtain salvation by our Lord Jesus Christ. . . . Wherefore [because of these facts] comfort yourselves together, and edify one another, even as also ye do" (1 Thessalonians 5:9,11). Far from telling us to ignore prophecy and the signs of the last days, Paul specifically warns us to be watchful, hopeful, and joyful as we see the beginning signs of "the last days" because it means the Rapture is close at hand.

Moses, in Deuteronomy 29:29, told us that, "the secret things belong unto the Lord our God: but those things which are revealed belong unto us and to our children for ever, that we may do all the works of this Law." God has revealed many of the details of our immediate future through His many precise prophecies.

If we choose to ignore the warning signs that the last days are fast approaching, then we will be like the church at Sardis, which Christ warned by saying, "Be watchful, and strengthen the things which remain . . . If therefore thou shalt not watch, I will come on thee as a thief, and thou shalt not know what hour I will come upon thee" (Revelation 3:2–3).

For many Christians, the one real objection to inquiring into the time of the "last days" is their misunderstanding of a statement of Jesus to His disciples. Jesus said, "But of that day and that hour knoweth no man, no, not the angels which are in heaven, neither the Son, but the Father" (Mark 13:32).

Many Christians have understood this verse to be an absolute, universal statement regarding prophetic interpretation that applies not only to Christ's disciples in A.D. 32, but also to the Christians of every generation including ours, the generation that is witnessing the signs leading to His Second Coming. It is important to study this verse in its context. Jesus had just finished prophesying that the generation that is alive when Israel becomes a nation will live to see the fulfillment of all of the prophecies of the "last days. The whole passage reads,

> But of that day and that hour knoweth no man, no, not the angels which are in heaven, neither the Son, but the Father. Take ye heed, watch and pray; for ye know not when the time is. For the Son of man is as a man taking a far journey, who left his house, and gave authority to his servants, and to every man his work, and commanded the porter to watch. Watch ye therefore: for ye know not when the master of the house cometh, at even, or at midnight, or at the cock crowing, or in the morning: lest coming suddenly he find you sleeping. And what I say unto you, I say unto all, Watch. (Mark 13:32–37)

Please note that even in this passage where Christ states that, at that time, no one knew the "day nor the hour," He commands that the believers' response to the uncertainty of the exact time of His coming must be eternal watchfulness, not sleep or lack of interest in His return.

## Two Key Questions

The two key questions to be answered in any fair inquiry into the appropriateness of this study are simply these: (1) Is the statement of Christ in Mark 13:32 a universal statement for all time, thereby prohibiting careful, prudent consideration and study as we see the signs of the approach of the last days? or (2) Is Christ's statement a description of the lack of knowledge His disciples had about this subject during the generation almost two thousand years ago, before the Church or the New Testament existed?

It is important to remember that Christ made this statement to His Jewish disciples prior to His crucifixion, before the existence of the Church had been revealed and before most revelations of the New Testament prophecies had been given, especially the book of Revelation. Obviously like all other statements, the

Scripture passages must be studied in context. Before His death and resurrection, much of the truth about His Second Coming was veiled from His followers. The very fact that there would be a future Church was unknown to all but God at the time of Jesus' remark to His disciples.

Consider the fact that during the Great Tribulation, anyone who has access to a Bible will be able to calculate the 1260 days (see Revelation 11:2; 11:3; 12:6; 13:5; and Daniel 7:25) from the time Antichrist enters the rebuilt Temple to the exact day when the Battle of Armageddon will occur. God revealed such a specific time prophecy to encourage those who become believers during the Great Tribulation to resist the Antichrist. The persecution resulting from the Mark of the Beast system during those final three and one-half years, will be so horrible that God felt it was essential to assure believers that it would not go on forever, but would end 1260 days after it began with the defeat of the Antichrist.

These facts suggest that Christ's statement, "But of that day and hour knoweth no man," was not an universal, unlimited pronouncement for all time, but rather, it was a description of the limited knowledge of the time of the "last days" that would prevail from the first century until the final generation, of which Christ prophesied, "This generation shall not pass away, till all be fulfilled" (Luke 21:32).

The closing chapter of the book of Daniel reveals that just before the end, believers will finally understand the things he prophesied.

> Daniel, close up and seal the words of the scroll until the time of the end. Many will go here and there to increase knowledge [of these prophecies]. . . . Go your way, Daniel, because the words are closed up and sealed until the time of the end. . . . None of the wicked will understand, but those who are wise will understand.
>
> (Daniel 12:4, 9–10, NIV)

Daniel was told to seal the vision "until the time of the end." The clear implication is that, as "the time of the end" approached, the visions and their meaning would be unsealed. While unbelievers will never understand, believers will begin to "understand" as the crisis approaches.

After Christ ascended to glory, He gave an additional revelation to His Church through the prophet John. The book of Revelation removes some of the veil from future events and reveals new information, including some precise prophecies about time periods that cast a new light on some Old Testament prophecies about "the time appointed" when "the end shall be" (Daniel 8:19).

### The Historical Problem

The second reason many Christians have been warned against looking into prophecy is the historical fact that in the past many commentators have incorrectly interpreted the time of the end. Subsequent events have often proven their interpretations were incorrect. The truth is that in any area of study, scholars will often make errors that will seem obvious to those who come after them. This is so even in the exacting field of science.

Unfortunately, the area of Bible prophecy seems to be the only area where such early mistakes have led to the suggestion that the whole area of study be abandoned. In any other area of study, we learn from the mistakes of the pioneers and, using the knowledge we have gained, we move on to develop more sound conclusions. Almost all previous commentators on prophecy have miscalculated the true length of the biblical year (360 days) which the prophets used and, consequently, they have miscalculated the time periods involved in many of the prophecies. In addition, the "historical" school of interpretation has unfortunately insisted that the prophecies of Daniel and Revelation, which refer clearly to the 1260 literal days of the reign of Antichrist, must be interpreted as a period of 1260 years (on the day-year theory — the idea that whenever a prophecy says a day, it automatically must mean a year). This day-year interpretation was used by some great scholars, including Rev. John Cummings, Dr. Grattan Guinness in his *Approaching End of the Age,* and Bishop Newton in his *Dissertations on the Prophecies.* They tried in vain to force the period of the Roman Catholic papacy into this time cycle, setting dozens of commencement and termination points for such a 1260 day-year period, all without success.

However, we would be mistaken if we failed to heed the direct command of Christ to "watch and pray" simply out of a disappointment with the mistakes of past commentators.

## The Time of the Rapture is Unknowable

One paramount point to remember is that the time of the Rapture of the Church is not indicated in the Scriptures. No one will know when this event is to take place until the moment it occurs. Then the Christians will be raptured to meet Christ in the air and return with Him to the Marriage Supper of the Lamb in heaven. The reason we cannot know the time is, while there are many specific time indications for Israel's "last days," there are no time predictions for the Church.

I am not a prophet, nor have I received a revelation from God about the time of the end. I am simply a student of Scripture who would like to share with others the results of my research for their own consideration. These time cycles are simply logical deductions and calculations based on the same principles developed from the earlier time cycles proven by the history of Israel to have been fulfilled precisely. There are many Scriptures that indicate that the Lord has set His appointment with destiny for Israel from the beginning of time. However, we must always recognize that God is sovereign and may choose to delay His appointed judgment of the world.

The apostle Peter told us that "the Lord is not slack concerning His promise, as some men count slackness; but is long-suffering toward us, not willing that any should perish, but that all should come to repentance. But the day of the Lord will come as a thief in the night" (2 Peter 3:9).

In the days of Jonah, God responded to the national repentance of Nineveh by cancelling the prophesied judgment that was to have begun in forty days. He alone is sovereign and will choose the time. Since the Lord delayed His prophesied judgment of Nineveh because of their repentance, we cannot know if God might delay His coming once again.

Nevertheless, if these prophetic time cycles continue to run their course, mankind is approaching the most awesome and significant crisis in history. Only time and the passage of events will reveal whether the Lord will continue these appointed cycles and bring them to their conclusion in our generation.

Part of the reason for our increased understanding of these Scriptures is that we enjoy the privilege of viewing biblical prophecies from the vantage point of this final generation, especially since so many prophecies have already been fulfilled partially.

The analysis of fulfilled prophecies allows us to confirm the correct principles of interpretation, such as the biblical-prophetic 360-day year, and come to a more accurate understanding of how these end-time prophecies may be fulfilled.

In my library I have more than three thousand volumes on prophecy, some of them published as early as 1650. It is interesting to note that during the first two centuries of the Christian era, early writers such as Julias Africanus, Cyprian, and Hippotylus show a far greater understanding of prophecy than most medieval Christian commentators until the time of the Reformation. Unfortunately, with all of the other theological concerns of that time, the Reformers seldom wrote on prophecy. In fact, John Calvin's commentary on the Bible includes every single book except the prophetic book of Revelation. Most of the Reformers had personally suffered under the persecution of the medieval Church and its Inquisition. When they did address prophetic subjects, quite understandably, they focussed primarily on the Antichrist and his Babylonian mystery-religion system as described in the book of the Revelation.

It is only during the last two hundred years that the focus has finally returned to the one-quarter of Scripture that is composed of prophetic themes. That is one reason why a clearer understanding of the Rapture and the first Resurrection is found in the writings of commentators of the last two centuries. If current students of prophecy can see further, it is simply because, as Sir Isaac Newton said, quoting Bernard of Clairvaux in his fascinating treatise called *Observations on Daniel and the Revelation*, we "stand on the shoulders of those giants who went before us."

In the next chapter we will consider some possible answers to Daniel's question, "How long shall it be to the end of these wonders?" (Daniel 12:6). This is no longer a question of idle prophetic speculation but, rather, it is a question whose answer will vitally affect every person alive. For the Christian believer, the approach of the "last days" promises the imminent return of Jesus Christ when "we which are alive and remain shall be caught up together with them in the clouds to meet the Lord in the air; and so shall we ever be with the Lord" (1 Thessalonians 4:17), before the Great Tribulation commences.

For the Jew, the coming tragic "time of Jacob's trouble" threatens to be the greatest of all persecutions. However, this seven-year period will mercifully climax in the triumphant victory of their long-awaited Messiah, who will lead them into their promised Kingdom. For unbelievers, the impending cataclysmic events will push them into making their eternal choice as to whether they will follow Christ or Satan during the judgments of the Tribulation period.

As we have seen in previous chapters, the Lord has fulfilled many of Israel's prophecies with incredible precision. Since God says, "I am the Lord, I change not" (see Malachi 3:6), we can expect that those same amazing time cycles and biblical anniversaries that are evident in Israel's past will repeat themselves now that Israel is once again an independent nation on the world stage. The same God who guided Israel's actions in the early scenes of world history has already set the stage for the final act. The countdown to Armageddon commenced on May 15,1948, when Israel rose from the valley of "dry bones" to become a mighty nation.

A healthy degree of caution is certainly in order as we examine these interpretations of future time cycles. Many sincere students of prophecy have previously calculated dates for the fulfilling of these events, only to see the dates come and go, disproving their calculations. The result, of course, is that the world and most Christians tend to ridicule or ignore all prophecy completely. However, this attitude is unjustified. What other area of study, biblical or otherwise, is abandoned because earlier efforts failed to arrive at a complete understanding of the subject? If scholars had abandoned the study of such sciences as geology or physics simply because earlier theories proved to be inaccurate, there would be few scientists and little scientific knowledge today.

We learn from the failures as well as the successes of early biblical scholars. We must avoid being dogmatic in setting dates so that we can have an open mind to interpret the data carefuly and purposefully. Time alone will reveal whether or not we have correctly understood a specific prophecy.

Several factors influence our ability to accurately interpret the specific times of unfulfilled prophecy. First, some prophecies are written in such a way that they can only be fully understood after they have been fulfilled. Then, we can look back and see the incredible precision of their fulfillment. Second, there is, at present, some uncertainty regarding the precise dating of some of the very early historical events (before 606 B.C.) in the life of Israel.

This factor hinders us from determining with absolute assurance the exact commencement dates of a few of the prophetic time cycles. In addition, research reveals that there were numerous changes to the calendar during the last two thousand years.

However, these problems notwithstanding, Jesus rebuked the spiritual leaders of Israel for not recognizing the signs of the Messiah's coming, which had been extensively prophesied in the Old Testament. In light of the tremendous number of prophecies regarding "this generation" and Christ's command to "Watch," we should prudently inquire into what Scripture reveals about the timing of these important future events.

In the next chapter, we will consider these prophetic time cycles and examine the scriptural indications of the signs that we are approaching the final days for Israel's last crisis and the coming of the Messiah.

# 15

# *Prophetic Time Indications*

But now [God] commandeth all men every where to repent: because he hath appointed a day, in which He will
judge the world in righteousness by that man [Jesus]
whom He hath ordained.                    (Acts 17:30–31)

Behold, I will make thee know what shall be in the last end
on the indignation; for at the appointed time the end shall
be.                                        (Daniel 8:19)

### Prophetic Time Cycles

When one considers the astonishing precision with which the
Lord has prophesied the past events in the history of Israel, it is
more than likely that within the Scriptures, there are some indications of the time He has set for the appointed future events of
Israel's final crisis.

As the pattern of God's precise historical timetables for Israel
unfolded in my studies, I began to wonder if these exact time
cycles and biblical anniversaries would continue to apply now
that Israel was back in the Promised Land. Several years ago, in
my study of the prophecy of Ezekiel 4:4–6, I discovered that his
unusual vision of the end of the worldwide captivity of Israel had
been fulfilled precisely on May 15, 1948. It seemed possible that
God's system of prophetic time cycles for Israel and the nations

might still be in effect. In the light of this understanding, I would like to prayerfully share with you the results of many years of careful Bible study. There are several major prophetic time cycles that terminate in our generation. The fact that they independently conclude at the same "appointed time" in the next decade is intriguing.

### "One Day Is with the Lord as a Thousand Years"

The apostle Peter was taught by Jesus for three years before His crucifixion and for another forty days following His resurrection. During this time, Christ opened the Scriptures to His disciples concerning the prophecies about Himself (see Luke 24:25–27, 45). As a result of this time of intensive training, Peter discussed the Lord's Second Coming in his epistles, knowing that this event was far into the future. He wrote, "Knowing this first, that there shall come in the last days scoffers, walking after their own lusts, And saying, Where is the promise of his coming? for since the fathers fell asleep, all things continue as they were from the beginning of the creation" (2 Peter 3:3–4).

Peter then explained to the Church that there was one particular fact regarding this apparent delay of the "last days" of which they should be aware: "But, beloved, be not ignorant of this one thing, that one day is with the Lord as a thousand years, and a thousand years as one day. The Lord is not slack concerning his promise, as some men count slackness; but is long-suffering toward us, not willing that any should perish, but that all should come to repentance" (2 Peter:8–9). The "day" he spoke about referred to the days of the creation week (see Genesis 1–2), as a microcosm of the seven days of the great Sabbath Week of God's historical dealing with His creation — mankind (see figure 1). Just as the creation and the replenishing of the earth took six days and then God rested on the seventh day, so there would be six thousand years and then the great Sabbath rest of one thousand years (the Millennium), as described in Hebrews 4:4, 7–9 and Revelation 20.

A number of evangelical scholars believe that scientific evidence suggests a much longer duration for man's existence than the six thousand years indicated by a normal reading of the chronological account in the book of Genesis. However, for purposes of this discussion, I will take the same position taken by virtually all the earlier commentators, Jewish and Christian, from the first century until the mid-nineteenth century. I will interpret the scriptural account by its common-sense meaning. When Jesus Christ and His apostles referred to Adam, Enoch, and Noah, they referred to these men as historical characters. Furthermore, none of the inspired writers of the New Testament indicate that either the historical accounts of Genesis or its chronological details are to be understood in a symbolic, mythical, or nonliteral manner. Since the Bible was given as a God-inspired revelation of truth to all generations — past, present, and future, it seems odd and unlikely in the extreme to think that God would allow the writers to include detailed chronological data that clearly indicates a six thousand-year duration from Adam, if in fact, man was created millions of years ago.

Early Christian writers, including Lactantius, dealt with this controversy seventeen centuries ago because, even then, there were prevalent theories from Plato, Cicero, and the Chaldeans that man has existed on this planet for "many thousands of ages." In his *Divine Institutes* (chap. 14), Lactantius states, "But we, whom the Holy Scriptures instruct to the knowledge of the truth, know the beginning and the end of the world (age), respecting which we will now speak in the end of our work, . . . Therefore let the philosophers, who enumerate thousands of ages from the beginning of the world, know that the six thousandth year is not yet completed, and that when this number is completed the consummation must take place."

| 5th Day<br>1000 Years | 6th Day<br>1000 Years | 7th Day<br>1000 Years<br>Millenium |
|---|---|---|
| 1 B.C.<br>Christ's Birth<br>Feast of<br>Tabernacles | A.D. 1000 | Feast of<br>Tabernacles |

*"A DAY IS WITH THE LORD AS A THOUSAND YEARS"*
*THE GREAT SABBATH WEEK*
*Figure 1*

The Scriptures do not give any date for determining when the universe was originally created. However, the chronology of the Old Testament suggests that the time of the creation of man, Adam and Eve, occurred approximately 4000 B.C. The Bible lists precisely the age of each patriarch (i.e., Lamech, 182 years) when the next patriarch (i.e., Noah) was born. Even if the next patriarch in the recorded genealogy was a great-grandson, rather than a son, this method of listing the age when the next patriarch was born provides an exact, continuous chronology of the generations.

Thus, the time interval between Adam and Abraham is precise, and the possibility of missing gaps in the recorded genealogy would not seriously alter the duration of this period. The long, overlapping life spans of Adam, Lamech, Shem, and Abraham indicate how easily the accurate history of this time period could have been passed down intact from generation to generation. Quite aside from this, the inspiration of the Holy Scriptures by God assures us that the facts recorded are accurate and reliable.

There is much discussion among Christians about how to reconcile the prevailing theories of the age of the earth and of man with the Scripture records. However, there are many dating techniques that suggest that the earth and moon may be far younger than the 4.6 billion years given in most textbooks today. As just one small example of the mounting scientific evidence for a younger solar system, consider the recent landings of man on the moon's surface. Because the moon has no atmosphere, scientists had calculated that billions of years of falling meteoritic dust would have accumulated as a thick layer on the moon's surface of up to two thousand feet in depth. There was concern that our lunar spacecraft would sink deeply into this light dust. If you remember, the lunar landing module had very long legs and huge landing pads to prevent it from sinking out of sight. Much to the surprise of the scientists, it turned out that there was less than two inches of moon dust on the surface. Recent measurements of the influx of meteoritic dust confirm the scientists' earlier calculations that the layer should be two thousand feet thick if the moon is, in fact, 4.6 billion years old. The existence of only two inches of dust is just one more piece of evidence that the solar system may be less that ten thousand years old.[1]

Despite this ongoing controversy, the Genesis account also indicates that there were two distinct processes and stages of creation. The original creation of the universe is described in

Genesis 1:1, "In the beginning God created the Heaven and the Earth." No date is indicated for this event, and it is possible that it took place in the dateless past. Recent scientific discoveries concerning the background radiation of the universe suggest both the immediate creation of the universe out of nothing and the fact that this initial creation of matter took place billions of years ago.

The creation story continues with a much-debated phrase that, along with other supporting Scripture, indicates that there was a dramatic change in the condition of God's creation. Genesis 1:2 states that, at some time after the original creation, the world *became* "without form and void" (*tohu va bohu* — Hebrew for waste, destruction, and emptiness). The books of Isaiah, Jeremiah, and Ezekiel seem also to refer to the destruction of the original creation, apparently in connection with the rebellion of Satan and his demonic angels in the dateless past. Genesis 1:3 takes up the second part of the creation story by describing the re-creation of life on this planet and concludes, in verse 28, with God's command to "be fruitful and multiply and replenish the earth."

Early Jewish and Christian writers believed that this re-creation of the earth and the beginning of man's history from Adam occurred approximately four thousand years prior to the time the New Testament was written. In 1650, Archbishop Ussher calculated back from the birth of Christ, based on the dates and chronological data given in the Scriptures, and arrived at the date of 4004 B.C. as the year of Adam's creation.

There is a document known as the *Epistle of Barnabas* that was written to the early churches. Many early church leaders, including Origen and Jerome, believed this document to be genuine. Even though it has never been part of the Bible and may not have been written by the Barnabas of the New Testament, it is valuable as extra-biblical information concerning the history and the early teachings of the Church, just as the works of early historians such as Josephus add to our knowledge of the Scriptures. As you know, Barnabas was the first partner of the apostle Paul on his missionary journeys. In this epistle, Barnabas speaks of the creation account in Genesis:

> And God made in six days the works of His hands; and He finished them on the seventh day, and He rested on the seventh day and sanctified it. Consider, my children, what

that signifies, He finished them in six days. The meaning of it is this: that in six thousand years the Lord God will bring all things to an end. For with him, one day is a thousand years; as Himself test)fieth, saying, behold this day shall be as a thousand years. Therefore children, in six days, that is, in six thousand years, shall all things be accomplished. And what is it that He saith, and He rested the seventh day; He meaneth this; that when His Son shall come, and abolish the season of the wicked one [the Antichrist], and judge the ungodly; and shall change the sun and the moon, and the stars, then He shall gloriously rest in that seventh day.[2]

King David, in Psalm 90:4 referred to the same symbolic time scale when he said, "For a thousand years in thy sight are but as yesterday when it is past, and as a watch in the night."

Early church commentators, including Methodius, Bishop of Tyre, point out that the reason Adam died at the age of 930 years (Genesis 5:5) and did not live past one thousand years was because God had prophesied that, "In the day that thou eatest thereof (the forbidden fruit) thou shalt surely die" (Genesis 2:17). Since a day was equal to a thousand years in God's sight, Adam had to die before the day (1000 years) was completed.

Another church father, Irenaeus, commenting on the book of Genesis in his book *Against Heresies* (A.D. 150), stated a belief held by the early church: "This is an account of the things formerly created, as also it is a prophecy of what is to come. For the day of the Lord is as a thousand years; and in six days created things were completed; it is evident, therefore, that they will come to an end at the sixth thousand years."[3]

Using the interpretations of Barnabas and Irenaeus, we can calculate a time line of the last two thousand years since the birth of Christ (see figure 1). The two-thousand-year period preceding the beginning of the "seventh day" is calculated from the fifteenth of Tishri, the Feast of the Tabernacles, in the year 1 B.C., when Jesus was born. In the Gospel of John, the apostle says, "The word became flesh, and tabernacled [dwelt] among us" (John 1:14 RSV margin). It is possible that John is referring to the fact that Jesus was born on the anniversary of the Feast of Tabernacles, the fifteenth of Tishri, 1 B.C. (the anniversary of the dedication of both

Temples and the coming of the Shekinah Glory). The chronological data provided by Luke 3:1–3, confirms that Christ was born in 1 B.C. and the Church taught this during the first centuries of the Christian era. (See "The Date of the Nativity of Christ" in the appendix.)

If these calculations are correct, and Christ was born at the beginning of the fifth day (1 B.C.), then the fifth and sixth days (lasting two thousand years) have nearly elapsed. We can look for the beginning of the seventh day (the Millennium, the thousand years of peace in Revelation 20:2–6) to commence on the fifteenth of Tishri, the first day of the Feast of Tabernacles, at some point in our generation — two thousand years from Christ's birth. The difficulty in being more precise is that there were many serious revisions in the calendar during the last two thousand years. Therefore, we can only be certain of the date of the end of the two-thousand-year-period within a range of perhaps a dozen years.

In the writings of the Christian writer Methodius, in A.D. 300, we find the following reference to the Feast of Tabernacles:

> For since in six days God made the heaven and earth, and finished the whole world . . . and blessed the seventh day and sanctified it, so by a figure in the seventh month, when the fruits of the earth have been gathered in, we are commanded to keep the feast [of Tabernacles] to the Lord, which signifies that, when this world shall be terminated at the seventh thousand year, when God shall have completed the world, He shall rejoice in us. . . . Then, when the appointed times shall have been accomplished, and God shall have ceased to form this creation, in the seventh month, the great resurrection-day, it is commanded that the Feast of our Tabernacles shall be celebrated to the Lord.[4]

### "After Two Days He will Revive Us: In the Third Day He will Raise Us Up"

The Jews taught that God's dealing with His people would be encompassed within a "Great Sabbath Week" lasting seven thousand years. The prophet Hosea, in his messianic prophecy of the final restoration of Israel, apparently referred to this prophetic time cycle.

Come, and let us return unto the Lord: for he hath torn, and he will heal us; he hath smitten, and he will bind us up. And after two days will he revive us: in the third day he will raise us up, and we shall live in his sight. Then shall we know, if we follow on to know the Lord: his going forth is prepared as the morning; and he shall come unto us as the rain, as the latter and former rain unto the earth. (Hosea 6:1–3)

In interpreting the meaning of these "two days," we must remember that the biblical year in history and prophecy has only 360 days. Therefore, one thousand prophetic years would contain only 360,000 days (1,000 × 360). This is equal to 985.626 years according to our present calendar. Many Jewish and Christian authorities interpret the Great Sabbath as the final seventh day of one thousand years, following the six thousand years ( 6 × 1000 years) since the day of Adam.

In the Gemara, a commentary on the Talmud, Rabbi Ketina states the following:

The world endures six thousand years and one thousand it shall be laid waste [that is, the enemies of God shall be destroyed!, whereof it is said, 'The Lord alone shall be exalted in that day.' As out of seven years every seventh [is a] year of remission, so out of the seven thousand years of the world, the seventh millennium shall be the millennial [1000 years] years of remission, that God alone may be exalted in that day.[5]

Bishop Latimer, writing in 1552, had a similar understanding of this one-thousand-year period, which will start around the year 2000:

The world was ordained to endure, as all learned men affirm, 6000 years. Now of that number, there be passed 5,552 years [as of A.D. 1552], so that there is no more left but 448 years.[6]

Even during the Reformation, there were Christian scholars who understood that the sabbatical week of seven thousand years indicated that the time of the "last days" would occur in our generation.

One of the oldest books in my library is *The Chronology on the Old and New Testament*, written by Archbishop Ussher in 1650. In this Latin volume, Ussher, who had access to many ancient church manuscripts which were subsequently and tragically lost in the burning of early Irish churches during the savage Irish wars, calculated that the Millennium would begin near the year 2000.

Rabbi Elias, who lived two hundred years before Christ, said,

> The world endures six thousand years: two thousand before the law, two thousand under the law, and two thousand under Messiah.[7]

The Christian scholar Lactantius (A.D. 300) held a similar view. In the seventh volume of his *Book of Divine Institutions*, he wrote the following:

> Because all the works of God were finished in six days, it is necessary that the world should remain in this state six ages, that is six thousand years. Because having finished the works He rested on the seventh day and blessed it; it is necessary that at the end of the sixth thousandth year all wickedness should be abolished out of the earth and justice should reign for a thousand years.[8]

Writings could be produced in great numbers from other early church fathers, including Victorinus, Bishop of Petau, Hippotylus, Justin Martyr, and Methodius, to illustrate the early Church's belief that the Millennium would commence upon the completion of six thousand years from Adam. This widespread evidence, together with 2 Peter 3:8, is a strong argument that this belief was the genuine teaching of the apostles and the early Church. It is unfortunate, but perhaps providential, that changes in the calendar make it impossible to calculate with precision when the two-thousand-year period will end, except to note that it must occur in our generation.

### Three Important Cautions

In regard to the foregoing interpretations, it is vital to remember three important factors:

First, these are only interpretations and not prophetic revelations. Although I believe these interpretations are valid, only time itself will prove whether or not they are accurate.

Second, even if these interpretations of the correct time of the completion of these appointed prophetic time cycles are valid conclusions, God is sovereign and may accelerate or postpone "the time appointed."

Third, even if these interpretations regarding the time of the Great Tribulation and the beginning of the Millennium are correct, the time of the Rapture of the Church still cannot be determined. The time of the Rapture is known only by God. It is possible that the Rapture is not even set to occur on a certain day. It may well be that, in His sovereignty, God has ordained a certain number of souls that He will gather into that "peculiar people," the Church, before His return. When the Church is completed, God may call us home to heaven.

Second Peter 3:12 suggests that Christians should be "looking for and hasting unto the coming of the day of God" by evangelizing a lost world to find faith in Jesus Christ. Many students of prophecy believe that the Rapture will be immediately followed by Daniel's Seventieth Week (which begins when the Antichrist signs a seven-year treaty with Israel) or by the "revealing" of the Antichrist, when he sets himself up as "god" in the rebuilt Temple in Jerusalem. However, there is no biblical indication that the Rapture will occur on either of these occasions.

The time of the Rapture is known only to God, and it could occur at any time, from today until the day when the Holy Spirit is removed as the restrainer so that the Antichrist can "reveal" himself in the Temple. Once the Antichrist reveals his nature, the focus of God's program for man will be centered upon Israel, the "two witnesses," and the 144,000 Jewish witnesses. The revelation of the Antichrist is the last possible moment that the Rapture could occur, if our interpretation of the many Scriptures regarding the Rapture is correct. During the Tribulation period, from the Rapture until the return of Christ with His saints at the Battle of Armageddon, the Church will participate in the Marriage Supper of the Lamb and enjoy Heaven (Revelation 4–19).

*Notes to Chapter 15*

1. Stuart Ross Taylor, *Lunor Science: A Post-Appolo View* (New York: Pergamon Press, Inc., 1975), 84, 92.

2. Barnabas, "The Epistle of Barnabas," *Ante-Nicene Fathers* (Grand Rapids: Eerdmans Publishing Co., 1987), 1:146–147.

3. Irenaeus, "Against Heresies," *Ante-Nicene Fathers* (Grand Rapids: Eerdmans Publishing Co., 1987), 1:557.

4. Methodius, "The Banquet of The Ten Virgins," *Ante-Nicene Fathers* (Grand Rapids: Eerdmans Publishing Co., 1987), 6:344.

5. Bishop Thomas Newton, *Dissertations On The Prophecies* (London: 1817), 2:373.

6. Archbishop Jacob Usher, *Chronology of The Old and New Testaments* (Verona: 1750).

7. Bishop Burnett, *The Sacred Theory of The Earth* (London: 1816), 408.

8. Lactantitius, "The Divine Institutes," *Ante-Nicene Fathers* (Grand Rapids: Eerdmans Publishing Co., 1987), 7:211.

# 16

# *Prophetic Signs of the Second Coming*

For the Lord himself shall descend from heaven with a shout, with the voice of the archangel, andwith the trump of God: and the dead in Christ shall rise first: Then we which are alive and remainshall be caught up together with them in the clouds, to meet the Lord in the air: and so shall we ever be with the Lord. Wherefore comfort one another with these words.     (1 Thessalonians 4:16–18)

During the early centuries following the ascension of Jesus into heaven, Christians often greeted one another by saying, "Maranatha," which means "the Lord cometh." Despite constant persecution from both the pagans and the officials of the Roman government, the early Christians rejoiced in the certain knowledge that Jesus had prophesied that He would someday return to establish His Kingdom on earth. These believers knew that Jesus rose from the dead on the third day following His crucifixion — as He had foretold during His ministry. Jesus Christ was seen by many people during the forty days following His resurrection. Thirty years after Jesus ascended to heaven in the sight of His followers, the apostle Paul wrote, "After that, he was seen of above five hundred brethren at once; of whom the greater part remain unto this present, but some are fallen asleep" (1 Corinthians 15:6). The truth of His death and resurrection was widely known and taught by the early Church, encouraging a widespread expectation of His glorious return to destroy evil and establish His righteous government on earth forever.

The Second Coming of Jesus Christ is the greatest single theme in Scripture. While there are approximately three hundred prophecies in the Old Testament that foretold the first coming of Christ, there are more than eight times as many verses describing the Second Coming. In total, some 2400 verses throughout the Old and New Testaments reveal God's promises about the return of Jesus Christ. The enormous number of prophetic verses about the Second Coming underlines the vital importance of this event in God's plan for mankind. Consequently, we dare not ignore the prophetic signs pointing to the nearness of His return.

Significantly, the first prophecy in the Bible (Genesis 3:15), which God addressed to Satan after Adam and Eve's sin, predicted three major events in the redemptive plan of God, concluding with the Second Coming of Christ. The first event was the virgin birth of Jesus ("her seed"); the second event was Satan's apparent victory when Jesus was crucified ("thou shalt bruise his heel"); the third event will be fulfilled at the Battle of Armageddon when Jesus Christ will defeat Satan ("thy head") and his seed, the Antichrist ("it [her seed, Jesus] shall bruise thy head"). The New Testament book of Jude recalls that the righteous patriarch Enoch was raptured to heaven before the Flood. Jude revealed that Enoch prophesied about the Second Coming, when the Lord would return to earth with millions of His saints. "Enoch, also, the seventh from Adam, prophesied of these, saying: 'Behold, the Lord cometh with ten thousands of his saints, to execute judgment upon all'" (Jude 14–15).

The prophet John recorded our Lord's final prophecy in the final verses of the book of Revelation: "And, behold, I come quickly; and my reward is with me, to give every man according as his work shall be" (Revelation 22:12). Jesus Christ's final message to His Church concludes with these words: "He which testifieth these things saith, Surely, I come quickly. Amen. Even so, come, Lord Jesus" (Revelation 22:20).

## Prophetic Signs of the Return of Christ

For thousands of years students of the Bible's ancient prophecies have pondered the question of whether they would live to witness the return of Christ to redeem the earth. Many Christians living in our generation naturally long for the return of Jesus Christ. Skeptics remind us that past generations of believers also longed for the Second Coming but died with the promise still unfulfilled. These skeptics naturally ask, "Why should we believe that our generation is the one that will witness the return of Christ when other generations were disappointed in their hopes?" After thirty years of careful Bible study, I am convinced that the overwhelming evidence concerning the fulfillment of these predictions in our generation points to the return of Jesus Christ in our lifetime. Jesus and the other prophets described a number of specific prophecies that would occur in the lifetime of those who would see Him return with their own eyes. Is ours the generation that will see Christ coming for His Church? The answer to this question has profound implications for our lives as Christians, our witnessing, and our life priorities.

In this chapter and the chapter following, we will examine a number of significant prophecies made more than two thousand years ago that are being fulfilled in our generation. Each individual prophecy is a unique and significant event that has not been totally fulfilled in any past generation. The unique nature of many of these predictions suggests strongly that these prophecies are unlikely to be fulfilled a second time in another future generation. Our Lord Jesus Christ warned us to watch carefully for these prophetic signs: "And when these things begin to come to pass, then look up, and lift up your heads; for your redemption draweth nigh" (Luke 21:28). Let's examine the most significant predictions that point to Christ's imminent return.

### 1. A Warning about the Rise of False Christs

"And Jesus answered and said unto them, Take heed that no man deceive you. For many shall come in my name, saying, I am Christ; and shall deceive many" (Matthew 24:4–5). It is significant that Christ's first specific prophetic warning involved the rise of false messiahs and false prophets in the last days. The first false messiah arose about a hundred years after Christ. It is fascinating to note that there are no historical references to any false messiahs appearing until the years following the death and resurrection of Jesus of Nazareth. The Jewish scholar C. G. Montefiore wrote, "Of false Messiahs, we know of none among the Jews until Bar Cochba in 131 C.E." The genuine article always precedes the appearance of counterfeit ones.

Simon Bar Cochba, a Jewish rebel commander led his conquered people in a furious revolt against their brutal Roman conquerors in A.D. 132. Many of the Jews joined the rebellion in the vain hope that Bar Cochba was their genuine messiah. The great Jewish rabbinical scholar Akiba announced that Simon Bar Cochba was the true messiah. This encouraged many Jews to join his desperate revolt. Despite the tremendous initial Jewish victories over the Romans during the first few years, six Roman legions of Emperor Hadrian invaded Israel and decisively defeated the Jewish army on the ninth day of Av (August) in A.D. 135 (the very same day the Babylonians and Romans destroyed the Temple centuries before). Hadrian's legions killed over one-half million Jewish soldiers in a desperate battle several miles southwest of Jerusalem. Tragically, as a result of the war, more than three million Jews were slaughtered throughout the eastern provinces of the Roman Empire, and millions of Jews were sold into abject slavery. The Roman Senate passed a law prohibiting the Jews from approaching Jerusalem, their conquered capital. The defeat of the Jews, doomed rebellion by following a false Messiah led to their exile from the Promised Land for almost eighteen hundred years.

During the following centuries, false messiahs would arise from time to time, including Moses of Crete in the fifth century. He promised the Jews of Crete that he would miraculously part the waters, allowing his followers to march across the Mediterranean Sea to the Promised Land. In the seventeenth century a Jew living in Turkey named Shabbethai Zebi claimed he was the Messiah and attracted a vast following. Many influential rabbis throughout the Middle East and Europe acclaimed him as the true messiah. Finally the Turkish Sultan arrested him for sedition. The Sultan threatened to test Zebi's supernatural claims by having his archers shoot arrows at him to see if his claimed "miraculous" powers would ward off the deadly missiles. Realizing that he was doomed, Zebi converted to Islam to save his life and died in disgrace a few years later. In our generation, hundreds of thousands of Jewish followers of the deceased Rabbi Schneerson, who died in 1991, still believe that he was the promised messiah and that he will soon rise from the dead.

The truth is that no other person in history has ever fulfilled even a fraction of the forty-eight specific biblical prophecies about the coming Messiah except Jesus of Nazareth. As outlined in a previous chapter, the historical evidence is overwhelming that Jesus is the true Messiah. He is the only one who has fulfilled every one of the specific messianic prophecies. A respected Jewish rabbi named Abarbanel wrote extensively in the fifteenth century about the qualifications of the coming Messiah. Abarbanel noted that one of the qualifications of the true Messiah would be that the Gentiles will seek after him and acknowledge his claims (Micah 4:1–4). In fulfillment of this qualification of the Messiah, hundreds of millions of Gentiles throughout history in every nation on earth have devoted their lives to following Jesus Christ's teachings and worshiping Him as their Messiah and God.

Throughout history a false messiah has appeared approximately once every century since the days of Christ. Millions of people today are longing for a messiah who will lead them to a transcendent experience. Significantly, we are experiencing an explosion of false christs in our generation, exactly as Jesus prophesied two thousand years ago. A report from Los Angeles indicated that hundreds of individuals in California currently claim they are the messiah. In England someone who calls himself Lord Maitreya periodically publicizes claims that he is the Christ. Every few years Benjamin Creme issues full-page ads that appear in major newspapers around the world announcing the advent of the messiah in the person of the Lord Maitreya. These imposter messiahs in our generation include such figures as the deceased David Koresh, Rev. Sun Myung Moon, Charles Manson, Jim Jones, Ron L. Hubbard, and many others. Recently a New Age cult called Heaven's Gate encouraged thirty-nine of its members to commit suicide following the leadership of Marshall Applewhite and his partner Bonnie Nettles, who took the names Do and Ti. He claimed to be the messiah and stated that his partner Bonnie was "God the Father." Never before has the world seen so many false messianic claims. As we approach the year 2000 we will see a virtual flood of false messianic figures and false prophets declaring that they are the only hope for mankind. The rising number of false messiahs in our generation is preparing our society for the spirit of Antichrist worship in the last days. We are witnessing the beginning of attitudes that will manifest themselves some day in the worship of the Antichrist in the Temple in Jerusalem.

## 2.   Wars and Rumors of Wars

Jesus Christ said, "And ye shall hear of wars and rumours of wars: see that ye be not troubled: for all these things must come to pass, but the end is not yet. For nation shall rise against nation, and kingdom against kingdom . . ." (Matthew 24:6–7). Twenty-five centuries ago, the prophet Joel saw a divine vision concerning our generation and prophesied the following message: "Proclaim ye this among the Gentiles; Prepare war, wake up the mighty men, let all the men of war draw near; let them come up. Beat your plow shares into swords, and your pruning hooks into spears: let the weak say, I am strong" (Joel 3:9–10).

Throughout history mankind has endured thirteen years of war for every single year of peace. However, since 1945 the number of wars has increased tremendously. As dozens of new nations demanded independence and old empires disintegrated, more than three hundred wars were fought since World War II. A military study, *The War Atlas*, concluded that the world has not known a single day since World War II without some nation waging a war or conflict somewhere on earth. Despite thousands of peace treaties, the last one hundred years has truly become "the century of war." As a result of the obvious dangers, most nations have joined worldwide military alliances in which only the stars are neutral.

Far more sobering than the increasing frequency of war is the fact that modern scientific discoveries and massive military budgets have combined to produce devastating new weapons of mass destruction that have the potential, for the first time in history, to destroy humanity. Despite the constant affirmations about the nations' desire for peace, weapons labs and armories are producing nuclear, chemical, and biological weapons, together with astronomical numbers of conventional weapons, in virtually every nation on earth. Consider some of the following facts and ask yourself where we are heading.

The standing armies of the world today contain hundreds of millions of soldiers. The major powers could mobilize hundreds of millions of troops if needed for war. According to the Reshaping International Order Report issued by the Club of Rome, almost 50 percent (some 500,000) of all scientists on earth are working on weapons research. Research indicates that almost 40 percent of all scientific research funding worldwide is focused on arms research. The international arms trade exceeds $1 trillion annually. If only a small fraction of this enormous investment was redirected "from swords into plowshares," we could permanently solve the Third World's food, sanitation, and health problems. The armament factories of Russia, China, and the Western nations are producing sophisticated weaponry at a truly awesome rate. China is the now the world's fifth largest arms supplier — after Russia, the United States, Britain, and France — selling some $2 billion annually. Many of the Chinese weapons are direct copies of Western or Russian arms, but they are much cheaper. China's arms salesmen are fuelling a massive arms race in the Middle East, with huge sales of sophisticated missiles and low-cost copies of Russian rifles, tanks, and planes. China has recently sold more tanks to Africa than have all western countries combined. A poor African nation can buy four Chinese T-59 tanks for the price of one M-1 tank from the United States. China is also selling intermediate-range missile systems to many Arab regimes that are preparing for war with Israel. Iraq, Iran, and Libya now possess long-range missiles with biological and chemical warheads capable of destroying Paris or London. For the first time since the Middle Ages, Europe faces a formidable military threat from the Muslim Arab nations who are absolutely committed to the destruction of both the Jews and Christians.

Despite years of peace negotiations between the PLO, the Arab states, and Israel, the continuing tensions in the Middle East are developing into a time bomb that could soon explode into a devastating war. This war may involve the use of nuclear, chemical, and biological weapons. Although these nations have been discussing peace for decades, the twenty-one Arab nations surrounding Israel have accumulated more than three times the artillery and tanks possessed by the combined European armies of NATO. Despite America's support of Israel, the United States has sold staggering amounts of sophisticated Abram's M-1 tanks, advanced anti-tank missiles, communications gear, and the most effective F-16 fighter planes in the American arsenal to the Arab states dedicated to the destruction of the Jewish state. The Arab nations have no significant enemies other than Israel. Consider the implications. Over the last fifty years, NATO has built up a huge sophisticated military force to confront the massive armies of Russia, the fourteen nations of the C.I.S., and the nations of eastern Europe. However, the Arab nations confronting the tiny nation of Israel have amassed huge armies that exceed NATO's military forces by more than one-half million soldiers. There is no conceivable reason for the Arab states to devote such huge financial, technical, and manpower resources to their military forces unless they are absolutely committed to the annihilation of the Jews of Israel.

The Jewish state is confronted with a combined Arab military force far larger than the combined armies of North America and Europe, the countries that make up the forces of the NATO alliance. In light of the repeated Arab threats to destroy Israel, Israel cannot safely agree to surrender the military control of the West Bank. If the 80,000-man Palestinian army of the PLO controlled the high mountainous region of the West Bank of Israel in a future war, the combined Arab armies could easily attack across the remaining narrow band of land along the Mediterranean Sea connecting northern and southern Israel. At certain points this vital and strategic strip of coastal land connecting northern and southern Israel is only nine miles wide between the West Bank and the Mediterranean Sea. Israel's military control of the strategic depth of the West Bank is essential, according to all military studies, to absorb and withstand the assault of combined Arab tank and infantry forces. Numerous military studies by the U.S. Joint Chiefs of Staff have concluded that if Israel ever surrenders military control of the West Bank, the Arab armies would be able to cut Israel in two within a few hours using their overwhelming Arab armored tank forces. If Israel negotiates the surrender of the military control of the West Bank to Arafat and the PLO and allows the creation of a Palestinian state, Israel will not likely survive the coming war with the combined Arab armies. UN Security Resolution 242, the resolution that governs the continuing peace negotiations, guaranteed that Israel would retain "recognized and secure borders." Without the military control of the West Bank, Israel cannot win the next war. In addition, without the control of the West Bank and the Golan Heights in the north, Israel would be forced to use its nuclear weapons almost immediately following a powerful Arab attack.

Five of the ten major arms-importing nations in the world are in the Middle East. Even the poorest of the Third World countries borrow hundreds of millions of dollars annually to buy huge supplies of modern, sophisticated weapons. As soon as the western nations design a new version of a weapon, their arms salesmen sell the obsolete version of that weapon system to a Third World country. As a result of this cycle of arms build-up, there is now one military weapon and the equivalent of four thousand pounds of explosives for every man, woman, and child worldwide.

Consider the destructive power possessed by the thirty Trident submarines that represent only one-third of the present American nuclear arsenal. At a cost of $3 billion dollars apiece, each submarine can fire twenty-four missiles with up to fourteen individually targeted D5 warheads per missile. These advanced super-accurate missiles can deliver their lethal thermonuclear warheads from a submerged ocean location over ten thousand miles away to detonate within one hundred yards of their target. Each Trident D5 nuclear warhead is five times more powerful than the atomic bomb that devastated Hiroshima. Every one of these thirty submarines has the capability to destroy 408 separate enemy cities or military bases. As a result of modern weapons technology, we have progressed to the point that one single Trident submarine can deliver more devastation than all of the combined weapons used by both sides in five years of warfare during World War II. According to the Center for Defense Information, we know that the U.S. military has experienced ninety-six serious nuclear accidents, each one bringing us one step closer to nuclear Armageddon. The tragic history of thousands of years of warfare suggests that these nuclear weapons will ultimately be used someday in a future conflict.

For thousands of years mankind has engaged in deadly warfare. However, throughout the last fifty centuries, most battles involved only a few thousand participants. Nations previously lacked the means of totally destroying the enemy country. However, our century has perfected the art of mass warfare by which all nations unite to annihilate the opponent and obtain unconditional surrender. Global military spending now exceeds $1 trillion every year according to the U.S. Arms Control and Disarmament Agency. A trillion dollars is so large a number that it is hard to comprehend the true magnitude of the dollars mankind now invests in preparation for war. To put it in perspective, the cost of a single Exocet air-to-ship missile exceeds the combined annual income of more than ten thousand people in many Third World countries. Massive military spending has distorted our priorities. For example, western countries are spending less than one-half of 1 percent of their annual military budgets on foreign aid.

Over 200 million people have died as a result of warfare since 1900. Since 1945, ten nations, including Israel, have accumulated more than sixty thousand nuclear warheads in their growing arsenals. According to the book *The Fate of the Earth*, by Jonathan Schell, the Russians possess enough nuclear warheads to destroy every single American military target several times over. After that, they would still have eight thousand nuclear missiles left over. If the Russians then targeted every U.S. city and town, in order of decreasing population size, they would still have enough one-megaton nuclear warheads (eighty times the power of the Hiroshima bomb) to destroy every single town in America with a population of fifteen hundred people or more. It should be obvious from these calculations that in a future world war the Russians, the Chinese, and the American military would run out of meaningful military and civilian targets long before they ran out of nuclear warheads. Jesus Christ prophesied that the Antichrist's armies, represented by the red horseman of the Apocalypse, will ride forth to destroy many nations during the Great Tribulation (Revelation 6:3–4). Surely, even now, we can hear the approaching hoof beats.

Jesus also warned, "For then shall be great tribulation, such as was not since the beginning of the world to this time, no, nor ever shall be. And except those days should be shortened, there should no flesh be saved: but for the elect's sake those days shall be shortened" (Matthew 24: 21–22). When you consider the enormous problems facing mankind — disease, famine, ecological disasters, and tens of millions of homeless people — you recognize the terrible moral vacuum at the core of our modern civilization, which chooses to spend trillions of dollars on the tools of annihilation rather than begin to solve the massive problems facing humanity.

The words of President Eisenhower, as reported in the *New York Times* on April 17, 1953, still challenge us today:

A life of perpetual fear and tension; a burden of arms draining the wealth and the labor of all peoples; a wasting of strength that defies the American system or the Soviet system or any system to achieve the true abundance and happiness for the people of this earth. Every gun that is made, every warship launched, every rocket fired signifies, in the final sense, a theft from those who hunger and are not fed, those who are cold and are not clothed. This world in arms is not spending money alone. It is spending the sweat of its laborers, the genius of its scientists, the hopes of its children. We pay for a single fighter plane with a half million bushels of wheat. We pay for a single destroyer with new homes that could have housed more than 8000 people . . . This is not a way of life at all, in any true sense. Under the cloud of threatening war, it is humanity, hanging from a cross of iron.

The people of the world cry out for peace, but no rational nation can dare to unilaterally disarm before it's enemy does the same.

Jesus Christ described the final conflict facing mankind in these words: "Upon the earth distress of nations, with perplexity; . . . men's hearts failing them for fear, and for looking after those things which are coming on the earth: for the powers of heaven shall be shaken" (Luke 21: 25–26). Since the breakup of the Soviet Union in 1991, Russia and America have engaged in a complex series of disarmament treaties, producing a wave of euphoria among millions of people worldwide who hope that true peace is at hand. According to the historical research of author Sidney Lens, since 1945 more than six thousand disarmament negotiating sessions have taken place. Despite these disarmament treaties, very few nuclear bombs were actually destroyed. Unfortunately, most treaties allowed the older nuclear warheads to be simply recycled into new, more accurate missiles.

The biblical prophecies predict clearly that the world will experience a devastating world war involving all nations in the last days. The second red horseman of the Apocalypse represents the terrible world war during the final years of the seven-year

Tribulation period. "And when he had opened the second seal, I heard the second beast say, Come and see. And there went our another horse that was red; and power was given to him that sat thereon to take peace from the earth, and that they should kill one another; and there was given unto him a great sword" (Revelation 6: 3–4). The prophets Daniel and John predicted that the nations of the world would ultimately surrender their sovereignty to the Antichrist in the hope that he would provide security and true peace. Many politicians today believe that the only way to prevent such a devastating world war is for every nation to surrender its sovereignty to a future world government. However, the Scriptures warn that the earth will never know true peace until the Prince of Peace comes. Although men are desperately seeking peace, the Antichrist will only be able to produce a short period of false peace. The prophet John revealed that the first Horseman of the Apocalypse would be a rider on a white horse with a bow but no arrows. This symbol represents the Antichrist impersonating the true Prince of Peace, Jesus Christ, who will appear riding on a white horse during His triumphant return to earth (Revelation 19). John prophesied: "I looked, and behold, a white horse. And he who sat on it had a bow; and a crown was given to him, and he went out conquering and to conquer." The Antichrist will use men's deep longing for peace "to conquer" the world's nations and force them to join his world government.

U.S. Defense Secretary William Cohen warned, in his speech to a University of Georgia forum on terrorism, that the Internet is now providing a medium for terrorists to widely distribute instructions for building bombs as well as racist propaganda. He called for increased vigilance against terrorist use of unconventional chemical and biological weapons (including the deadly Ebola River Virus) that are now available to these terrorist groups. In addition, he warned ominously about the dangers presented by new electromagnetic weapons that might be used by terrorists or rogue Islamic nations to "punch holes in the ozone layer or trigger earthquakes or volcanoes" (*Toronto Star*, April 29, 1997).

Despite the fact that the 1972 Biological Weapons Convention unconditionally prohibited the developing, producing, and stockpiling of biological and chemical weapons, many Third World nations are now acquiring deadly chemical and biological weapons (CBW). Most of the world's nations, including Russia and the

United States, have ratified this arms agreement. However, many nations are secretly developing deadly biological and chemical weapons that will devastate unprotected populations in a future conflict. Some future dictator may be tempted to use these deadly CBW weapons because of their low cost and their ability to be used secretly against an enemy. These chemical and biological weapons are a tempting alternative for a Third World nation, compared to the enormous cost of developing a huge conventional army or producing a sophisticated nuclear capability. Some researchers have described biological and chemical weapons as the "poor man's nuclear bomb."

Syria, Iraq, Egypt, and Iran are rapidly developing advanced chemical weapons programs. Libya recently built two huge chemical and biological weapons plants located deep within the mountains at the edge of the southern Libyan desert. Over sixty German and Swiss companies have provided extensive chemical engineering services and the sophisticated laboratory equipment required to modify Libya's Russian-built SCUD missiles to carry chemical warheads. Many of these same European companies built Iraq's chemical-weapons facilities before and after the Gulf War and are still willing to sell their technological soul to the highest bidder. During the closing days of the Gulf War, the Prime Minister of Israel took the visiting German foreign minister to the ruins of an Israeli apartment building in Tel Aviv that had been destroyed by one of the thirty-nine Iraqi SCUD missiles that were targeted at the Jewish state. The prime minister showed him the German company's serial numbers on the modified SCUDs that Saddam Hussein launched against Israel. President Hussein of Iraq threatened to "burn half of Israel" with his advanced chemical weapons supplied by European countries. Despite his defeat in the war in the Gulf, and the continued UN sanctions, Saddam Hussein has now totally rebuilt his army. Over ten thousand Russian nuclear scientists and technicians continue to develop Iraq's secret nuclear arsenal, despite the presence of U.N. arms inspectors.

Chemical weapons were rarely employed in past wars, partly because of the universal repugnance against their use. Unfortunately, chemical weapons have proven to be both effective and deadly. In World War I chemical weapons killed almost one hundred thousand soldiers in Europe. In the Vietnam War, America unleashed hundreds of tons of chemical weapons, including herbicides such as Agent Orange, on Viet Cong areas in an attempt to defoliate the jungle cover. President Saddam Hussein repeatedly used massive amounts of chemical weapons against Iranian soldiers in the eight-year Iran-Iraq War. In the late 1980s, Saddam launched chemical attacks against his Kurdish minority, killing at least 13,000 villagers in Iraq's northern provinces. When American soldiers occupied southern Iraq at the end of the Gulf War, they discovered over one hundred thousand Iraqi chemical artillery shells ready for use. Tragically, thousands of American troops were exposed to these chemical weapons when U.S. soldiers blew up Iraqi chemical weapons following the allied victory. Many reports from Afghanistan and Cambodia confirm that chemical and biological weapons were used under Russian control. Despite the 1925 Geneva Protocol against chemical and biological warfare, many countries have stockpiled huge quantities of these doomsday weapons in case they are needed in a future conflict. Every western country has developed a stockpile of these deadly munitions.

A recent report from *Jane's Land Based Air Defence 1997–1998* revealed that Russia's military laboratories have developed a dangerous new variant of the deadly anthrax toxin that is impervious to antibiotics. Historically, anthrax has been a fatal disease affecting primarily sheep. However, if anthrax infects humans, they will die an agonizing death characterized by festering boils and severe pain. In addition, the report claims that Russian defectors admitted that three new nerve gases were recently developed that can be made easily from commonly available chemicals. The authoritative Jane's report declared: "It only needs this, or the new chemical nerve agents, to be independently discovered by an ostracized nation's scientists and then developed for missile delivery for an Armageddon situation to occur whereby the only reliable retribution may well be overwhelming nuclear response" (*Toronto Star*, April 4, 1997). All of these nations justify their chemical-weapons research based on the clause in the 1925 Geneva Protocol agreement that allows a country to conduct limited research for "defensive" purposes. However, it is obviously impossible to verify whether research on a new chemical or biological weapon in a secret research laboratory is truly defensive or offensive.

Israel has reportedly developed over three hundred nuclear weapons, including sophisticated neutron bombs that can destroy biological life with powerful nuclear radiation without creating a large explosion. Today an embattled Israel is surrounded by twenty-one powerfully armed Arab states with virtually unlimited military budgets. Naturally, Israel prefers to rely on her sole control of her nuclear arms rather than trust that the United States would risk its survival for the Jewish state in a future military confrontation in the Middle East.

Another fifteen Third World countries (including Cuba, Libya, and Iran) will join the nuclear club by the year 2000. Each of these nations will possess their own nuclear-armed ballistic missiles within a few years, in addition to the 20,000 remaining nuclear warheads in Russia that are still aimed at the cities of the West. Many of the militant Islamic leaders openly declare their goal to achieve the destruction of both Israel and America, the "great Satan." For the last fifteen years these Muslim states, including Libya, Iran, Syria, and Iraq, have spent untold billions of dollars in a desperate attempt to acquire the nuclear warheads that would allow them to destroy both Israel and her strongest ally, America. Despite these well-known threats, the president and Congress have refused to fund a realistic strategic defense against incoming missiles.

Intelligence sources in Europe confirm that the Russians have sold advanced nuclear missile technology to North Korea, enabling them to produce their own nuclear weapons. North Korea has already sold this nuclear technology to Iraq, Iran, Syria, and Libya. Western military-intelligence analysts admit that several of the Arab nations facing Israel are desperately trying to develop or buy nuclear weapons. The tragedy is that every arms race in history has ultimately resulted in the use of these weapons, regardless of the devastating consequences. The continued arms buildup in Russia, China, the West, the Middle East, and the Third World is setting the stage for the final Battle of Armageddon that will drench the world in blood.

3. *Famines*

"And I beheld, and lo a black horse; and he that sat on him had a pair of balances in his hand. And I heard a voice in the midst of the four beasts say, A measure of wheat for a penny, and three measures of barley for a penny; and see thou hurt not the oil and the wine" (Revelation 6:5–6). In his vision, the prophet John saw a worldwide famine so destructive that an entire day's wages ("a penny" was a laborer's daily wage in Rome) would only buy enough wheat to supply the needs of a single man. However, an unusual feature of this worldwide famine of the last days is that, side by side with absolute poverty will be found the "oil and wine" of enormous wealth.

Another prophetic warning sign that Christ gave us is that "there shall be famines" that would be widespread and devastating, and shall lead up to the final conflict (Matthew 24:7). That distant sound you hear while you stand comfortably on the platform waiting for your train is not an oncoming train; it is the sound of almost two billion banging, empty, rice bowls from the one-third of mankind who are facing hunger every day. Only thirty years ago the "Green Revolution" offered the promise of the end of hunger in our generation. Unfortunately we are faced with drought and famine conditions throughout potions of Africa, India, and Southeast Asia. Millions are at risk of famine in this decade in central Africa, India, North Korea, and China. Even today North Korea, Sudan, and China are unable to properly feed their populations. According to the Annual Study of the UN Population Fund, the amount of agricultural land is decreasing rapidly worldwide. Deserts are growing worldwide at the rate of 14.8 million acres every year. Over 26 billion tons of precious topsoil are lost each year, and the valuable tropical rain forests, which contribute significant amounts of our planet's oxygen, are shrinking inexorably by more than 27 million acres every year.

The deadly effect of population growth and diminished food resources is not a future problem; the disaster has already begun in Asia and Africa. The ghostly black horseman of the Apocalypse has waited through the centuries for that dreaded final trumpet call of worldwide famine. The appalling specter of widespread famine is here; the black horse of the book of Revelation, representing the coming famine, is about to begin his deadly ride. The world population is growing at the rate of more than 225,000 people every single day. This is equivalent to adding an additional medium-sized city to the earth's population every twenty-four hours. However, 90 percent of the 150 new babies born every minute will be born in the Third World, where food supplies are the lowest.

Rapid global population growth is one of the most dangerous problems facing the world as we approach the year 2000. The average rate of population-increase worldwide is approximately 2 percent, although it is much higher in those Third World countries that can least afford it. A rich country like Austria, with a very low rate of population growth, will take almost three thousand years to double its population. Meanwhile, a poor nation like Nigeria has such a high population growth-rate that it will double its already huge population in less than a dozen years. It is virtually impossible to increase food production quickly enough to prevent widespread famine and the coming disaster in Third World nations whose populations are exploding.

In order to place this worldwide average of 2 percent growth-rate of population in perspective, consider the following:

| Timescale | Years | World Population |
|---|---|---|
| From the beginning of man until Christ | ? | 300 million |
| From Christ to Columbus, 1492 | 1462 | 500 million |
| From Columbus to World War I, 1918 | 418 | 2 billion |
| From World War I to 1962 | 44 | 3 billion |
| From 1962 to 1980 | 18 | 5 billion |
| From 1980 to 2000 | 20 | 6 billion plus |

At the present rate of population growth, we are adding a billion new mouths to be fed every twenty years. While it took the time from the creation of man until World War I to produce a population of two billion people, that same number of new people will be added to our current population in the next forty years. At this rate of population growth, in only six hundred years there would be one person standing on every square meter of land on the globe. Obviously, catastrophe will overtake mankind long before that.

Scientists now estimate that the world's population exceeds six billion people. The people of Africa, South America, and Asia constitute 85 percent of the world's population. The population explosion and its resulting famine was created because scientists solved the 'death-rate' problem with DDT, antibiotics, and improved sanitation before introducing effective fertility-control measures to solve the "birth-rate" problem. The resulting imbalance between rising births rates and falling death rates has produced a nightmare of starvation and famine in those countries we thought we were helping. Meteorologists now predict worldwide climatic changes leading to drastic reductions in the food-growing capacity of Canada, the United States, Russia, and France. Yet it is Canada, the United States, France, and Argentina that produce the vital food-surplus reserves that supply food to the nations that cannot feed themselves. Recently, massive flooding in the totalitarian state of North Korea has produced unprecedented famine conditions, with millions reduced to eating rats and the bark from trees in a desperate attempt to stave off starvation. Scientists believe that millions of North Koreans will soon face starvation.

### The Loss of Precious Topsoil

Since World War II, man has destroyed more than 4.5 billion acres of the earth's vital topsoil. This is equal to an area of agriculturally devastated land much larger than China and India combined. So far, 11 percent of the globe's topsoil has been eroded. The tragic loss of topsoil has already doomed the hopes for self-sufficiency for many Third World countries. The Sahara Desert is expanding relentlessly southward, destroying both the topsoil and the agricultural life style of the Africans who have lived there for thousands of years. The daily burning of huge tracts of the Amazon Rain Forest, which produces a great quantity of the oxygen we breathe, is destroying one of the earth's last great resources. Despite widespread calls for a halt, the government and business leaders of Brazil are reluctant to stop the farming and mining interests that are relentlessly burning the precious rain forests. This mistake is tragically compounded by the fact that these rain forests also provide many of the new pharmaceuticals that are vital to medical research. Scientists estimate that a large percentage of the rare plants in the rain forest have not yet been identified. We could easily lose plants that could hold the cure for cancer or many other diseases.

In the beginning God gave man dominion over this planet. Man's role was to faithfully tend the earth for the benefit of mankind and all God's creatures. One of the tragic results of man's sinful rebellion is that we have squandered the precious treasures of the earth and oceans. We have now reached the point where we are contributing to the destruction of many different species of life. Greedy and wasteful farming practices, such as over-grazing and deforestation, and poor farming methods have devastated our most precious agricultural treasure, our rich top-soil. Recently the World Resources Institute in Washington, D.C. released a sobering, comprehensive study of the world's soil conditions. One of the areas hardest hit is located in the center of the vast prairie covering western Canada and the mid-western American states. This relatively small area, only 5.3 percent of the world's agricultural land, has literally been the "world's bread-basket" for many decades. However, the study documents the continued erosion of our best topsoil on this continent. Over 235 million acres are now considered "degraded."

Modern fertilizers and land-management techniques could restore a small portion of the North American topsoil loss but at an enormous cost. However, the vast majority (over 2 billion acres) of the global soil erosion has occurred in the poorest countries of Asia and Africa. They are too poor to even begin the costly soil-reclamation projects that are desperately needed to provide for their hungry people. Over 20 percent of the agricultural soils of Europe, Asia, Africa, and Central America have been "degraded." The latest figures reveal that our food reserves (grain and corn) are the lowest in decades. Wheat reserves are at their lowest historical levels. Our government has sent our reserve food to Russia, China, and Zaire.

M. S. Swaminathan, from the editorial board of *World Resources* 1992-93, states, "If we don't develop programs for soil health care, then global food security will be in great trouble." The problems of topsoil reclamation are twofold. First, the cost is extremely high, beyond the capacity of the Asian and African nations most in need of such projects. Second, while it takes at least six centuries to produce a single inch of topsoil, we have casually destroyed our precious soil heritage in only four decades. Even if massive funds were available, the most optimistic estimate is that it will take twenty years of hard work on a given area to restore the damaged soil.

One of the principle causes of Third World famine is that over one-third of the food produced worldwide is destroyed by rats and other vermin. In the cities of many developing countries, the population of rats now outnumbers humans.

Our American and Canadian forefathers who pioneered this continent discovered a land with up to four feet of topsoil that had accumulated over thousands of years. While it took a millennia to develop these rich topsoils, in less than two hundred years we have squandered all but three inches of the precious topsoil throughout most of our North American farmlands. Our soils are so depleted that farmers are forced to invest in enormous amounts of fertilizer to produce an economical yield. The moral tragedy is that an investment of only $10 billion (1% of the annual global armaments expenditure of $1 trillion ) spent in building fertilizer plants throughout the world would solve mankind's hunger problem within a few years. There is less food storage capacity and less food reserves today than at any other time in this century. While the ultimate solution to this problem will only come with the return of Christ, each of us as Christians must respond as our brother's keeper with the resources He has given into our hands.

## 4. Pestilences

Jesus Christ warned "there shall be famines and pestilences" (Matthew 24:7). It is the tragic experience of this century that pestilence follows famine and war, compounding their terrors. Jesus warned that worldwide "pestilence" would be a sign that we were living in the generation when He would return. The prophet John was given a terrifying vision of the coming holocaust during the last seven years of this age (known as the Tribulation period) when God would unleash the devastating plagues of the last days that would decimate one-quarter of the population of the world.

The World Health Organization (WHO) issued a report dated April, 1997, from Geneva stating that "at least 30 new infections diseases with no known treatment, cure, or vaccine have emerged in the past 20 years" as a result of the increase in air travel, growing urbanization, and poor sanitation. Despite the billions spent in the last decades battling these infections, many diseases of the past, including bubonic plague, are reemerging as deadly threats to mankind. The WHO reported that malaria, smallpox, diphtheria, and yellow fever are also making a comeback. Their report mentions that "the health food craze was also partially to blame for the increase in food-borne diseases because unprocessed food contained less preservatives (which protect food from disease)."

The new scourge of fifty-three sexually-transmitted diseases (STDs) is a modern form of pestilence that is a direct result of the sexual immorality and perversions of this generation. Some doctors estimate that as many as 40 percent of all single, sexually-active adults in North America are infected with sexually transmitted diseases. As our generation has chosen to sow the wind of immorality and lust, we have begun to reap the whirlwind of sexually transmitted disease, sterility, and death. The worst of all these STDs is the deadly virus known as AIDS, the most dangerous plague in the history of mankind. According to a 1993 report prepared for the U.S. president by the CIA, the AIDS virus will probably infect and destroy the lives of up to 75 percent of the population of Africa south of the Sahara Desert. If correct, this study predicts that over the next decade, 350 million lives in Africa alone will be lost to AIDS. Researchers estimate that up to 50 percent of the population of Uganda may already be infected with AIDS. More than 1.5 million children are now orphans, almost 10 percent of Uganda's population of 17 million. This is unprecedented for a nation that is not involved in a current war. The *Washington Post* reported on October 23, 1994 that up to 50 percent of those admitted to hospitals in central Africa are suffering from the AIDS virus. Its report indicated that "Africa was particularly susceptible to AIDS because of widespread venereal disease — which facilitates the spread of HIV infection." The World Health Organization estimated that over 30 million people are infected with full-blown AIDS, with more than half of those people living in Africa.

A recent medical study concluded that more than 25 percent of the population of Sub-Sahara Africa is now infected with AIDS. However, a fascinating research report by John and Pat Caldwell found that those African tribes that practiced male circumcision experienced a far lower percentage of AIDS infection than surrounding tribes that failed to circumsize their male children (*Scientific American*, March 1996). In areas where African tribes circumsize their sons, the AIDS infection rate is as low as 1 percent, quite close to Western European rates. However, those nations that do not circumsize their sons suffered from AIDS infection as high as 25 percent of the population. A recent report from Africa revealed that "nearly one million people in ZwaZulu-Natal (with 8.7 million people), the most populous province of

South Africa, may be infected with HIV by 1996" (*Reuters* , Oct. 26, 1995). A report by the *Washington Post* on October 23, 1994, by Susan Okie revealed that an American doctor, Anne Moore, examined a graveyard outside one Zambian town in 1993. Moore reported that she "was unable to find a single grave that was more than two years old" (*Washington Post*, October 23, 1994). However, the report acknowledged that "because of the stigma attached to the disease in Africa, AIDS deaths are rarely acknowledged."

Twenty African nations now refuse to publish accurate AIDS infection rates because the devastating information is treated as a national security secret. However, AIDS is also exploding in Asia, with estimates of up to one in three people in Thailand in danger of dying (*Toronto Star*, Oct. 13, 1991). Experts from the Thai Red Cross estimate that more than 500 people are infected with the deadly disease in Thailand every night. Health workers estimate that up to 96 percent of the prostitutes in Thailand are infected with the deadly AIDS virus. Studies in India suggest that the AIDS infection rate for prostitutes now approaches 60 percent. It is estimated that the average male in these cultures visits a prostitute several times a week, exposes himself to the possibility of AIDS, and then brings that possibility home to his wife.

Thus far, AIDS has produced a 100 percent death rate. Very few victims have survived longer than twelve years. The medical researchers believe that AIDS is primarily transmitted through homosexual practices in Europe and North America. For fifteen years the medical establishment has warned homosexuals of the deadly danger of contracting AIDS as a result of their dangerous sexual practices. However, a recent report by *Harper's Magazine* revealed that "years of AIDS education has probably produced almost no change whatsoever in the behavior that all gay men and their grandmothers know to be the most dangerous for transmitting HIV" (*Harper's Magazine*, May 1995).

Medical studies reveal that AIDS can also be transmitted from an AIDS-infected drug user through shared needles to another drug user. In addition, it can be transmitted from an AIDS-infected mother to her baby during birth, and through AIDS-contaminated blood transfusions. However, as a result of new testing procedures introduced in 1985, the Canadian Red Cross reported that the risk of contracting AIDS from a blood transfusion in North America or Europe is now less than one chance in

225,000. In fact, out of 12 million blood transfusions completed since 1985 in Canada, only nine patients receiving blood have contracted the AIDS virus. You now have a much higher chance of dying from anesthetics or being hit by lightening than from receiving a tainted blood transfusion in North America or Europe today.

However, if the AIDS virus ever mutates to an airborne virus like tuberculosis (TB), the world will experience a plague beyond anything experienced in human history. A study released in the spring of 1994 by the *AIDS & Public Policy Journal* revealed that the rate of AIDS infection for homosexual men now approaches a staggering 50 percent, with a 40 percent infection rate among young gay men and up to a 70 percent infection rate among older homosexuals. Studies indicate that over 1.5 million male homosexuals in North America alone will ultimately die from AIDS. AIDS is now the leading cause of death for men aged 18–45. The *Danish Medical Journal* revealed that AIDS is now the number one killer of young and middle-aged men in the large cities of Denmark, exceeding both heart disease and cancer (*International Express*, June 19, 1996).

Over eleven million people now die annually from tuberculosis worldwide due to a new deadly new drug-resistant strain. The Laboratory Centre for Disease Control in Ottawa, Canada reported that tens of thousands of North Americans have become infected with a new drug-resistant form of TB that kills over 70 percent of its victims (*Toronto Star*, Nov. 22, 1995). Our society has abused and over-prescribed antibiotics for colds and other ailments to the point that many people can no longer derive benefit from the antibiotics prescribed by doctors to defeat deadly diseases. An article by science reporter Joseph Hall revealed that researchers recently warned the American Association for the Advancement of Science that "overuse of antibiotics is leading to a world in which the drugs are no longer effective" (*Toronto Star*, Feb. 18, 1997). University of Washington biologist Marilyn Roberts warned the international science conference that "tons of antibiotics are being used as farm additives on plants and animals, doctors are over-prescribing them and they are being misused in developing countries."

One of the big problems is that the shortage and the expense of antibiotics in poor countries encourages patients to stop taking the drug after a few days, but before it can kill the strongest strains of the bacteria remaining in their bodies. This facilitates the development of stronger drug-resistant bacteria that no longer respond to traditional antibiotics. Roberts ominously predicted that "if we don't change the way we use these medications, they will lose their effectiveness to fight diseases." Increasing numbers of diseases are becoming drug-resistant. There is now a new type of malaria that causes paralysis and death. This new type of malaria has infected over 300 million victims worldwide, and it no longer responds to the traditional drug "quinine."

Today we face growing pollution and ecological problems that appear to be virtually insolvable. Scientists are discovering hazardous waste dumps hidden in every community, leeching out their toxic elements into our water supply. The problem of disposal of radioactive waste from nuclear reactors remains unresolved, yet we continue to produce radioactive materials in the vain hope that someday we will find a solution. Over 70,000 new chemicals, which never existed before in nature, were introduced into the earth's biosphere during the last four decades. Only ten thousand of these chemicals were ever tested as to their effect on humans. Even if a new chemical is harmless by itself, it may be deadly when combined with other chemicals. When we add to this deadly concoction thousands of new, environmentally untested chemicals created in laboratories every year, we may be creating problems and diseases for which there is no cure.

The California Public Interest Group has calculated that over 250 billion pounds of synthetic chemicals are produced every year in the United States. One report revealed that "45,000 [chemicals] are in commercial distribution, and it takes a team of scientists, 300 mice, two to three years, and about $300,000 to determine whether one single suspect chemical causes cancer" (Debra L. Dadd, *Non-Toxic, Natural and Earthwise*, published by Jeremy P. Tarcher, 1990). Almost two decades ago, the Toxic Substances Strategy Committee, in their 1980 report to the U.S. president concluded that up to 90 percent of cancers were caused by exposure to hazardous substances in our environment. Our lifelong exposure to thousands of harmful chemicals is causing 15 percent of U.S. citizens to develop a super-sensitivity to harmful chemicals in their environment. These super-sensitive patients develop symptoms including allergies, depression, headaches, and irritability as a result of their exposure to environmental poisons.

A recent article in the Toronto Star newspaper (May 28, 1997) reported from Dallas that a new drug-beating germ may be unstoppable. This report claimed that "A common bacterium that is the leading cause of hospital-related infections appears to be on the brink of becoming an unstoppable germ. A staph infection known as Staphylococcus aureus has for the first time defended itself against the last remaining drug capable of killing all its strains, U.S. scientists say."

The continued heavy usage of pesticides has resulted in the development of new strains of germs, known as "super bugs." These "super bugs" have developed resistance to pesticides and other chemicals. Recently, environmental studies revealed that children living in homes that use garden pesticides have a 600 percent greater risk of developing leukemia.

5. *Earthquakes in Various Places*

Throughout history earthquakes have traditionally signaled political changes to ancient nations. Jesus Christ and the Old Testament prophets prophesied that the last days leading up to the Battle of Armageddon would be characterized by increasingly severe earthquakes throughout the globe where they had previously been unknown. Jesus prophesied earthquakes would occur in "diverse" or strange places. (Matthew 24:7). Our century has experienced an unparalleled increase in the frequency and intensity of earth disturbances. Many previously stable areas that have never known earthquakes before are experiencing numerous quakes for the first time. Each decade of this century has experienced a massive increase in the number of earthquakes occurring worldwide. More than one million minor quakes occur every year that are registered by seismologists. Approximately one hundred thousand earthquakes are strong enough to be felt, with approximately one thousand causing some degree of physical damage. To illustrate this phenomenon of increasing major earthquakes, consider the records showing the major "killer" earthquakes recorded since 1900. These "killer" earthquakes are major disturbances that register more than 6.5 on the earthquake Richter scale. An earthquake that registers 6.6 on the Richter scale is double the size of one that registers 6.5.

## The Rise in Major "Killer" Earthquakes

| Decade | Number of Major Quakes |
|---|---|
| 1890 to 1899 | 1 |
| 1900 to 1909 | 1 |
| 1910 to 1919 | 3 |
| 1920 to 1929 | 2 |
| 1930 to 1939 | 5 |
| 1940 to 1949 | 4 |
| 1950 to 1959 | 9 |
| 1960 to 1969 | 13 |
| 1970 to 1979 | 56 |
| 1980 to 1989 | 74 |
| 1990 to 1995 | 125 |

*Source*: U.S. Geological Survey Earthquake Report (Boulder, Colorado)

It should be noted that this increase in earthquakes is not simply the result of better reporting. An earthquake of 6.5 is so destructive that historical records have always recorded these major killer quakes. Anyone who examines the record of massive increases in earthquakes in our century must acknowledge that this is extremely unusual. The increase is unprecedented in recorded human history and, in light of the Bible's prophecies, these statistics provide incontrovertible evidence that we are living in the last days. This rising earthquake activity will culminate in a series of enormous earthquakes during the time of the Great Tribulation. The Bible warns that the judgment of God will finally unleash the greatest earthquake in history, unprecedented in its destructive power. John prophesied that, "There were noises and thunderings and lightnings; and there was a great earthquake, such a mighty and great earthquake as had not occurred since men were on the earth"(Revelation 16:18 ). Many areas of North America are now rated extremely hazardous for future earthquakes — Washington, California, Tennessee, New York, and the Great Lakes region — with a rating of 4 out of a maximum danger rating of 5.

The Scriptures also warn that the prophesied Russian-Arab attack on Israel (the "War of God and Magog") prior to the seven-year Tribulation period will be marked by the strongest earthquake up until that point in history. The prophet Ezekiel warned that it will be so catastrophic that all men worldwide will recognize that God has intervened in this supernatural manner to save His chosen people (Ezekiel 38: 19–20). Although this particular earthquake will be centered in the Middle East and Russia, the Bible declared that massive earthquakes would destroy cities worldwide during the last days. The prophet Haggai suggested that this great earthquake accompanying the Russian-Arab invasion would probably occur on the twenty-fourth day of the ninth month of the Hebrew calendar (December), the day before the festival of Hanukkah in some future year (Haggai 2: 6–7,18–21).

### 6. *All These are the Beginning of Sorrows*

Jesus told His disciples that the fulfillment of these initial prophecies would only signal the beginning of "the birth pains" of the coming Tribulation period, which is quickly approaching its appointed hour (Matthew 24:8). After revealing these initial predictions, Jesus gave His disciples a series of additional specific prophecies that would characterize the generation in which He would return to establish His messianic kingdom. The phrase the "beginnings of sorrows" indicates that the fulfillment of these prophetic signs will signal the approaching return of Christ in the same way that the increasing labor pains of a pregnant woman indicate the nearness of her impending delivery. As these prophecies are fulfilled one after another, we are to realize that His Second Coming is very near. The fulfillment of the prophetic signs that follow will indicate clearly to the generation that experiences them that they are living in the generation known to the rabbis as the "footsteps of the Messiah."

### 7. *Then Ye [Jews] Shall Be Hated of All Nations for My Name's Sake*

The name of the Jewish state is *Israel* which means, "Prince of God." God gave the name Israel to Jacob and his descendants forever. Jesus warned His Jewish disciples that one of the characteristics of the last days would be an increase of prejudice and hatred of the Jews in all nations worldwide (Matthew 24:9). Our generation has witnessed the appalling genocide of the Holocaust, during which Hitler's S.S. men killed over six million Jews in a methodical and diabolical plan of execution. Persecution continues in Russia, where over two million Jews still reside. Hatred of the Jews is expressed in vicious anti-Semitic cartoons and editorials in all Arab newspapers, including Egypt (which is supposed to be a peace partner of Israel). Vile propaganda against the Jews can be found in bookstores throughout the Arab world. It is significant that not one Arab country, nor Egypt, or Iran, contains a single official map that acknowledges the nation of Israel existing in the Middle East. In every map, the Arab states have replaced the Jewish state of Israel with the word "Palestine," providing full proof that they do not believe that Israel has any right to exist in any part of the Middle East. Tragically, during the last few years, there have been many terrorist attacks worldwide against Jewish synagogues and graveyards.

The United Nations is faced with hundreds of serious issues each year. However, during the last thirty years, the General Assembly has spent enormous amounts of time in debates and condemnation of one of its smallest member nations — Israel. An automatic majority of Russia's allies (including fourteen former republics), the twenty-one Arab states, and their Third World allies can be counted on to vote in favor of any resolution condemning Israel, no matter how one-sided or unfair it is. For example, after Israel's government recently opened an archeological tunnel leading from the Western Wall to the Via Delorosa in the Arab-Christian quarter of Jerusalem, the PLO falsely claimed that Israel was undermining the Muslim religious buildings on the Temple Mount. The tunnel has existed for over twenty-five centuries until it was explored in 1968 and opened at the southern end. There are no Muslim religious sites within five hundred yards of the new northern tunnel opening. Despite these well-known facts, the PLO launched a renewed Intifada that resulted in the deaths of numerous Israelis and Palestinians. After a few months of furious protests, the PLO stopped talking about the tunnel because its continued usage by thousands of tourists was causing no problems whatsoever. However, the PLO had created a huge publicity crisis and involved all of the nations of the world, including the United Nations, in debating a nonexistent problem purely for propaganda purposes against Israel. This is a typical Palestinian political approach to the so-called "peace process."

When a psychologically disturbed Jew, Baruch Goldstein, murdered thirty-nine Muslims, the whole world, including the United Nations, condemned Israel for months, as if the Jewish state was somehow responsible for this tragic massacre. However, when a disturbed Jordaninan soldier recently shot and killed seven innocent Jewish school girls, there was no condemnation of Jordan from Israel or the nations in the UN. Significantly, the leader of the opposing party in Jordan's parliament, and its religious authorities, have applauded this massacre of Jewish children. The reaction of the world's statesmen and the international media to Middle Eastern events, depending on whether the perpetrator is Jewish or Arab, is a strong indication of the world's continuing hatred against the Jews.

One final example of the different reaction of the world to actions of the Arabs as compared to the Jews is the following item in a recent newspaper. The *Associated Press* reported on May 6, 1997, that Yasser Arafat's PLO Justice Minister, Freih Abu Medein, announced, "The death penalty will be imposed on anyone who is convicted of selling one inch to Israel. Even middlemen involved in such deals will face the same penalty." Within three weeks, Palestinian groups murdered three Arab real-estate businessmen whom they claimed sold property to Jews. Incredibly, there has been no negative criticism or reaction from the UN or the world's media to this immoral and totalitarian anti-Semitic law that is similar in spirit to what we would have expected from the German Nazi Party in the 1930s. Why is there such a deafening silence when such an abomination occurs as the demand for the death of a human being who chose to sell his property to someone of another race? Can you imagine the world outcry in the media and at the UN if the Jewish state had proposed to execute anyone who sold his property to an Arab?

## 8. *The Love of Many Will Grow Cold*

Millions of people are experiencing alienation and family breakdown during these last few decades (Matthew 24:12). The economic and social forces attacking the family have reached the point that the historically normal "nuclear family" of two parents and their own biological children now represent a minority in North America. Transitory relationships are the norm for many, with divorces exceeding marriages in numerous communities. Many North American and European hospitals annually register more abortions than live births. The head of Russia's medical establishment stated that an average of seven million babies are aborted annually in that country. Many Russian women admit to having had eight or more abortions. In North America, the abortion figure exceeds one and one-quarter million every year. The combined worldwide death toll from abortion since 1945 exceeds the battlefield casualties in all of the wars during these decades. Christ warned that a denial of natural love will be a condition of the end times as mankind approaches the Great Tribulation period. "The love of many shall wax cold" (Matthew 24:12).

The transitory nature of modern society has destroyed the sense of community and mutual support that characterized the life of past generations. In only forty years, our society has been transformed from a community in which our grandparents knew every one of their neighbors to our present, alienated society, in which most of us do not even know who is living next door, let alone down the road. The rise of violent crime, child abuse, wife-battering, and even abuse of aging parents are sad fulfillments of Jesus Christ's two-thousand-year-old prophecy that warned that as we enter the final countdown, "the love of many will grow cold."

Reports from human-rights activists in Asia reveal that China executed 1,419 prisoners in 1993, according to Amnesty International. Harry We Hongda, a Chinese dissident and activist, and Sue Lloyd-Roberts of the BBC reported that the Chinese government is murdering healthy prisoners, allowing doctors to harvest body organs. There is a growing demand for healthy organs for transplanting to wealthy and powerful members of the Communist Party. The Chinese news agency, Xinhua, reported that almost ten thousand kidney transplants occurred in one hundred hospitals. The study estimates that approximately 90 percent of these organ transplants were taken from prisoners who were executed solely to provide their organs. Some foreigners travel to China to have an immediate transplant operation rather than wait in line for years in their home country. One Japanese man paid $30,000 for a kidney transplant. The January, 1995 report by Harry We Hongda in *Open Magazine*, a Chinese-language Hong Kong monthly, quoted a Chinese medical staff person as follows:

We make arrangements with the executioners to shoot in the head so that the prisoner dies very quickly, instantly, and the survival rate of organs is considerably higher [than from shooting through the heart] . . . We drive the surgical van directly to the execution site . . . As soon as the prisoner is executed, . . . [and] upon completion of necessary procedures by the police and the court, the body is ours . . . We buy the whole body. . . . From a legal point of view, once a prisoner has been shot, he no longer exists as a human being." One Chinese doctor offered to arrange a transplant for a reporter for a fee: "In two to three weeks, we can get a living kidney. . . . A team of surgeons will be dispatched for removal and delivery of the organ at a fee of $9,500. . . . We get customers from Hong Kong, Taiwan, the U.S., and from all over the world.

The human rights investigators visited the Organ Transplantation Research Center at the Tongji University of Medical Sciences located in Wuhan City, one of China's largest transplant hospitals. When they interviewed a patient about his operation, he declared, "All five of us in this hospital had our kidney transplants done on the same day. . . . All came from young prisoners, all under 25 and very healthy. . . . They were executed at 11 a.m., and we had our operations at 2 p.m." Although Chinese law forbids the harvesting of organs without a patient's permission, a police official told the investigators that during the last decade prisoners were never asked to give consent before their organs were harvested (The *Independent* , June 1995). Many of these "prisoners" are Chinese citizens jailed for their Christian faith.

Another horrifying example of the "love of many waxing cold" is revealed in similar reports from southern India indicating that numerous people are operated on without their consent or knowledge to harvest their kidneys for transplants to wealthy patients. Incredibly, corrupt doctors in Bangalore, India have illegally operated on up to one thousand poor villagers. These doctors have sold their harvested kidneys for as much as $18,000 to foreigners desperate for a transplant. A report by Tini McGirk in the *Independent on Sunday* from London, U.K. on April 2, 1995, revealed a widespread medical racket exists in India to harvest the organs of unsuspecting people. One policeman found four men stumbling along a road. When asked their problem, each man lifted his shirt to reveal identical long scars from their groin to their back. These men told the officer, "Our kidneys have been robbed." Each of these men were offered jobs by the medical clinic. Then they were told to take a blood test, which allowed a doctor to inject them unknowingly with a sedative. When they awoke hours later, each man had had a kidney surgically removed by the corrupt doctors, who then sold their stolen organs to a hospital as a transplant kidney. Unfortunately, this horrific situation is not rare. The newspaper report found that as many as fifty such illegal operations were performed in India every day. These stories remind one of late-night Frankenstein horror movies, but tragically the evil in the hearts of men in these last days is being revealed in all its horror, exactly as Jesus Christ warned two thousand years ago.

More than 2.7 million children are abused each year in the United States, according to the National Committee for the Prevention of Child Abuse (*U.S.A. Today*, April 23, 1992). Who can read the tragic statistics of rising child abuse and sexual assault without tears? Behind these figures are precious lives of children and women who will bear these terrible emotional scars for years. How can someone do this to a defenseless woman or child? Surely this rising tide of sexual violence is occurring because a spirit of lawlessness is rampant in our world. The natural protective love of men for children and women is being perverted by Satan as sin grows in men's hearts.

A study called "Rape in America" was recently completed by the National Victim Center and the Medical University of South Carolina. It interviewed over 4000 women and projected that over 683,000 women are raped each year in America. Their three-year study estimated that over twelve million women — one woman in eight — were raped at some point in their lives. These horrifying figures are three times higher than the crime statistics produced by the F.B.I. and the Justice Department. Only 16 percent of those women who were raped decided to report the assault to the police.

The ordeal of a sexual-assault trial and the lack of sympathy from police officers toward the female victim are significant factors in the low reporting of this terrible crime. The study found that only 22 percent of these sexual assaults were committed by a stranger. In many cases the attack came from someone the woman knew quite well. One of the most disturbing factors in this study is that 31 percent of the women stated that they were raped before the age of seventeen.

The hardness in some men's hearts is not confined solely to the actions of individual men. Governments are now displaying a brutality that staggers the mind. Red China is now selling kidneys, hearts, and other organs of executed prisoners as organ transplants at high prices. According to a judge in Brazil, young homeless street kids have been kidnapped off the streets by police death squads, and taken to medical clinics where they were killed. Their organs were then implanted in wealthy clients from around the world who would not wait their turn to receive a normal donor organ. The love of many people is becoming ice cold as natural affection and respect for God's laws disappears.

### The Rise of Violence

The average child in America watches television more than six hours a day. A study by the American Psychological Association, released in February 1992, reveals that elementary students will observe over 8000 violent television murders and over 100,000 other acts of violence by the time they graduate from elementary school. During their years in high school these students will witness another 100,000 acts of violence. Television is now the main source of information for 65 percent of Americans. For 35 percent of the population (including all young children) television is virtually the only source of information and news. The National Coalition on Television Violence reports that more than 50 percent of television cartoons teach violence and anti-social behavior as the norm. Every hour a viewer will witness an average of nineteen acts of violence. This wholesale exposure to non-stop video violence is desensitizing people to its horror. While broadcasters piously claim their programs do not influence behavior, they then sell one-minute segments of television advertising time to large corporations for hundreds of thousands of dollars. Why? These advertisers are not donating these millions to charity. Do you think corporations would pay millions for television advertising unless their daily marketing studies proved that television can definitely change viewer's behaviour? If a sixty-second commercial can change our buying behavior, it is dishonest for broadcasters to piously claim that the surrounding sixty-minutes of explicit sex and violence will have no effect on the viewer's subsequent behavior.

As an example of recent media trends, allegations were made

that the fantasy role-playing game "Dungeons and Dragons" was linked to over 125 murders and suicides. Yale University completed a recent study observing the effect of cartoon violence on children's behavior. They reported an 88 percent increase in child violence, including choking, the destruction of property, and infliction of pain to animals after watching television cartoons. Parents should watch one whole Saturday morning of television cartoons to determine if the content therein is acceptable for their children.

Over three thousand separate studies during the last thirty years explored the relationship between violence in our media and the subsequent behavior of viewers. According to the American Psychological Association Task Force on Television and Society, "There are 30 years of studies, and you'd be hard pressed to find one that didn't find a relationship between the violent programs children watch and the way they behave"(*Knight-Ridder* newspapers, May 15, 1992). Many prisoners, including serial killer Ted Bundy, have claimed that violent pornography is absolutely essential to their sexual fantasies and violent life style. Police who are involved on a daily basis with these criminals state that they usually find violent pornography or satanic material in the homes of criminals charged with violent sexual crime. However, the liberal media and their political supporters in Washington dishonestly deny that this violent material can cause people to imitate this criminal behavior.

In the wake of the tragic Los Angeles race riots several years ago, many citizens realized how close we are to the total breakdown of law and order. Studies after the "Rodney King" riot reveal that these riots were well planned. Black businessmen had been warned to identify their shops. The gangs prepared weapons and incendiary materials for starting fires in advance of the trial verdict. Today police estimate that there are 150,000 gang members in some 1000 gangs in Los Angeles County alone. Each year these gangs use greater violence as they acquire Uzi machine guns and chinese assault rifles. Recently police estimated that more than 36 percent of all murders in Los Angeles were committed by gang members. In 1996, Chinese agents were accused of smuggling 2,000 fully automatic machine guns for sale to L.A. gangs on cargo ships owned by the same company who is attempting to lease a naval base south of Los Angeles, a plan that President Clinton has endorsed and facilitated.

For decades the liberal educators and intellectuals demanded that we remove prayer, the Ten Commandments, and Christian values and principles from our schools. They succeeded to the point that it is now illegal to pray or hold a Bible study in most American schools. Meanwhile, teachers openly teach Hindu religious values under the guise of transcendental meditation and visualization exercises. They have sown the wind of value-free education, and we are now reaping the whirlwind of mindless destruction.

### 9. *The Gospel of the Kingdom Shall Be Preached in All the World*

"And this gospel of the kingdom will be preached in all the world as a witness to all the nations, and then the end will come" (Matthew 24:14). One of the most significant prophecies about the Second Coming included Christ's promise that "this gospel of the kingdom will be preached in all the world." The gospel is truly being preached throughout the world in the last days. The growth of the Church throughout the globe during our generation is astonishing! In the Muslim nation of Indonesia, more than 20 percent of the population has recently accepted Christ. Despite decades of dedicated missionary efforts, by 1900 only 3 percent of Africans had become followers of Jesus Christ. However, in this century over 45 percent of the five hundred million people living in Africa have become born-again Christians. In Russia, the end of the Cold War allowed the widespread introduction of the gospel. The availability of Russian Bibles and the tremendous dedication of Russian pastors has resulted in over one hundred million Russian Christians. In South Korea the gospel was rejected until WWII, despite the valiant efforts of western missionaries. However, as the winds of the Holy Spirit began to move throughout Asia, following World War II, researchers now estimate that up to 40 percent of the Korean population have declared their faith in Christ. In the two-thousand-year history of the Church, we have never seen such an astonishing move of God as we are witnessing today.

## The Spectacular Growth of the Christian Church

Despite the pessimistic statements of some writers that the population of the earth is growing faster than the growth of the Church, the truth is that the gospel is being preached in all the world with astonishing success during these last days. A 1991 study by the National Council of Churches concluded that church membership is growing at twice the rate of the overall population growth throughout the world. Their study noted that the greatest growth was in evangelical churches.

A fascinating study by the Lausanne Statistics Task Force examined the progress of evangelism during the last five centuries. Their researchers concluded that the growth of the church throughout the globe is far greater than previously reported. The number of born again Christians has grown three times faster than the world's population in the seventeen years since 1980. The historically verifiable records of the Lausanne Statistics Task Force reveal an incredible growth in the number of Christians world-wide.

## The Explosive Growth of Christian Faith

In 1430 one person in 99 of the world's population was a Christian
In 1790 one person in 49 of the world's population was a Christian
In 1940 one person in 32 of the world's population was a Christian
In 1970 one person in 19 of the world's population was a Christian
In 1980 one person in 16 of the world's population was a Christian
In 1983 one person in 13 of the world's population was a Christian
In 1986 one person in 11 of the world's population was a Christian
In 1997 one person in 10 of the world's population was a Christian
*Source*: Lausanne Statistics Task Force on Evangelism

Consider these figures carefully. The Church is actually winning a significant remnant of the world's population to faith in Jesus Christ during these last days! In only sixty years, the number of Christians throughout the world has grown by an astonishing 1300 percent. The evangelical Church has grown worldwide from only forty million in 1934 to 540 million born-again Christians today. Meanwhile the world's population has grown by only 400 percent. Christian radio broadcasts are now reaching almost half of the world's 360 "mega-languages," covering 78 percent of the earth's population, according to the broadcasting group World By

2000. Evangelical broadcasters are now preaching the Gospel daily to every language group throughout the globe. The combination of tremendous evangelism efforts by mission organizations, the dedication of more than one million national pastors, and the work of Christian broadcasters and publishers is rapidly fulfilling the Great Commission in our lifetime.

One of the little known miracles of the last days is the tremendous accomplishment of the Wycliffe Translators and other organizations in translating the Bible into the language of millions who have not yet heard the gospel. The Scriptures have now been translated into 3,850 languages representing virtually every nation, tribe, and dialect on the earth. These 3,850 languages include 98 percent of the world's present population. Television, radio, and the Internet now transmit the message of Jesus Christ instantaneously throughout the world. Researchers have calculated that more than 85,000 people accept Jesus as their personal Savior every day. Over one thousand new churches are formed every week in both Asia and Africa. Although these new converts to Christianity initially worship in homes or the outdoors, buildings are quickly constructed as these churches grow.

Our generation has witnessed the greatest explosion of the Christian Church since the Day of Pentecost in Jerusalem two thousand years ago until today. For example, there were less than one million Chinese Christians at the time of the communist takeover in mainland China in 1949, after a century of faithful missionary work by Hudson Taylor and others. However, the growth of the Church in China since 1949 has been staggering, despite tremendous persecution and the executions of untold millions of believers in concentration camps. Today, the lowest estimates calculate that there are more than 110 million true followers of Christ in the underground Church in communist China. As many as 25,000 people accept Christ in China every day. In 1985 my wife Kaye and I visited China. Our hearts were touched by these precious people. Despite the terrible persecution, millions of men and women have found spiritual reality in the person of Jesus Christ. There are now more than eighty thousand missionaries and millions of foreign national workers effectively spreading the Gospel throughout 181 nations worldwide.

Revelation 7:9–17 assures us that a great number from every nation will accept Jesus as Lord during the Great Tribulation after the Rapture has taken all living believers to heaven with Christ. The two witnesses and the 144,000 Jewish witnesses will preach the same message as John the Baptist, "Repent ye; for the kingdom of heaven is at hand." God will not leave mankind without a witness to Jesus Christ after the Rapture. Despite the terrible persecution, this gospel of the Kingdom will reach every tribe on earth. At the end of the seven-year Tribulation, the angels will gather these living tribulation saints together for protection from the wrath of God that will be unleashed at the Battle of Armageddon. The angels will gather these living tribulation saints from the four corners of the earth for protection from the wrath of God (Matthew 24: 31, 39–42). This passage tells us that this rescue of the tribulation saints will occur when Christ returns in glory to defeat Antichrist's armies at Armageddon. When Christ returns to earth, He will be accompanied by the millions of raptured saints; they are the Christians who were present at the Marriage Supper of the Lamb in heaven during the duration of the seven-year Tribulation period on earth. Jude 14 reveals that "the Lord cometh with ten thousands [millions] of His saints."

Another example of the fulfillment of the prophecy about "the gospel being preached in all the world" is unfolding today in the exploding distribution and expansion of the gospel message into every nation on earth (Matthew 24:14). Every year more than 300 million Bibles, New Testaments, and Scripture selections are distributed throughout the world. As one example, evangelist Reinhard Bonnke and his team travel throughout Africa with the largest tent meetings in the history of the world. Their tent can seat approximately thirty-four thousand people who listen to the gospel and receive healing from Christ. At the present growth-rate, over 50 percent of the population of Africa will be born-again believers by the year 2000.

The massive explosion of the gospel message in Asia is equally as astonishing as it is in Africa. One hundred years ago, Asia was a spiritual wasteland. Before WWII, it is estimated that Korea had fewer than two hundred Christians. However, today, as many as 50 percent of South Koreans now follow Jesus Christ. There are now eight churches in South Korea with memberships of more than 100,000 Christians. Almost two thousand years ago, Jesus Christ told His disciples that one of the most significant signs of His return would be the preaching of the gospel to all nations. Our

Lord Jesus Christ then added these significant words: "And then shall the end come."

## 10. The Apostle Paul's Warning Signs of The Last Days

This know also, that in the last days perilous times shall come. For men shall be lovers of their own selves, covetous, boasters, proud, blasphemers, disobedient to parents, unthankful, unholy, without natural affection, truce breakers, false accusers, incontinent, fierce, despisers of those that are good, traitors, heady, high minded, lovers of pleasure more than lovers of God; having a form of godliness, but denying the power thereof: from such turn away.

(2 Timothy 3: 1-5)

The apostle Paul wrote to Timothy and warned him of these prophetic signs that would characterize the last generation, who will see Jesus Christ return to establish His Kingdom on earth. This prophecy is so accurate in its characterization of today's world that it could have been written by any colomnist for this morning's newspaper. This prophetic catalog listing the symptoms of our disintegrating society reveals that the world is only one step away from disaster.

Millions in our society have become addicted to tranquilizers, sleeping pills, and drugs such as Prozac. Anxiety prevails throughout the world, and even our children have lost faith in the future. America has become a victim of its self-indulgence and rampant materialism. We are exposed to expressions of blasphemy to God in music, television, and daily conversation. Widespread child abuse, millions of abortions, runaway homeless children, childhood prostitution, and societal indulgence of homosexuality are spiritual plagues upon our lands.

We are suffering from an epidemic of ingratitude and dishonesty in both word and deed. Western society is deluged with an overload of sensuality through the media and in advertisements. Sadly, many churches have lost the first love of their relationship with Christ. Many liberal churches have become empty, dried-out spiritual husks preaching a "social gospel" stripped of its inspiration, authority, and its supernatural proclamation of Jesus Christ, the Son of God.

Nevertheless, our Lord admonished endtime believers that

"when you see these things begin to happen, then look up and lift up your heads. Your redemption is nigh" (Luke 21:28).

# 17

# *Further Signs the End is Near*

In this chapter we will examine a number of additional biblical prophecies that point to the return of Jesus Christ in the last days. Each of these prophecies is unique in that none of these predictions were fulfilled in any previous generation. The unusual nature of several of these specific predictions suggests that it is unlikely they will be fulfilled again in any following generation. Remember that Jesus Christ warned, "Now when these things begin to happen, look up and lift up your heads, because your redemption draws near" (Luke 21:28). Let's examine several of these other fascinating predictions that indicate that our generation will witness the return of Christ in our lifetime.

## 1. The Rebirth of Israel

"Now learn a parable of the fig tree; When his branch is yet tender, and putteth forth leaves, ye know that summer is nigh: So likewise ye, when ye shall see all these things, know that it is near, even at the doors. Verily I say unto you, This generation shall not pass, till all these things be fulfilled. Heaven and earth shall pass away, but my words shall not pass away" (Matthew 24:32-35).

The rebirth of Israel in 1948 is one of the most extraordinary of all the prophecies in the Bible. Jesus Christ foretold the rebirth of

Israel in his famous prophecy of the budding of the "fig tree" as recorded in Matthew's gospel. No other nation in history has ever ceased to exist for centuries and then returned as a nation to take its place once again on the stage of world history. The prophet Isaiah predicted the rebirth of Israel in these words: "Who hath heard such a thing? Who hath seen such things? Shall the earth be made to bring forth in one day? or shall a nation be born at once? For as soon as Zion travailed, she brought forth her children" (Isaiah 66:8).

Most nations evolved gradually over the centuries until they became nation-states, such as Egypt or France. At the time these ancient prophecies were given, no one had ever witnessed a nation being created "in one day." Yet, in his prediction, Isaiah prophesied twenty-five hundred years ago that Israel would become a nation in "one day." Incredibly, the prophecies of Isaiah and Ezekiel were fulfilled precisely as predicted on May 15, 1948 (see chapter 3).

2. *The Miraculous Restoration of the Hebrew Language*

Twenty-five hundred years ago the prophet Zephaniah predicted the miraculous revival of the Hebrew language in the last days. This prediction was as unlikely and impossible in human terms as the rebirth of Israel. The prophet Zephaniah, writing around 520 B.C., predicted that, in the last days, the Jewish state would restore the ancient dead language of Hebrew to become the spoken language of Israel. The language of Hebrew had ceased to be the common, spoken language of the Jews long before the days of Jesus Christ. The priests in the Temple were the only Jews who still used the ancient Hebrew language. "For then will I turn to the people a pure language, that they may all call upon the name of the Lord, to serve him with one consent" (Zephaniah 3:9). A study of historical records confirms that no other nation has ever lost its language and later recovered it as a living language. There are no nations in the Middle East speaking ancient Egyptian, Summerian, or Chaldee today. A Jewish scholar by the name of Eliazar ben Yehuda awoke one night with the distinct vision that God was calling him to restore the ancient Hebrew "tongue of the prophets."

Eliazar ben Yehuda is certainly the only person in history who has restored an ancient language single-handedly. He began working earlier in this century in Palestine under the British Mandate to revive the dead language of Hebrew. He examined the original seven thousand Hebrew words related to Temple worship that were used by the priests in the time of the Second Temple. From these basic Hebrew words, he created thousands of new, modern Hebrew words, for fountain pen, airplane, et cetera, using the Hebrew roots and the rules of biblical Hebrew grammar to guide his efforts. Ultimately, Eliazar created the modern Hebrew language that has become the living language of five million Israelis. The Jews began to return from seventy different nations to their Promised Land in 1948 after two thousand years of exile. The Israeli government and army used the Hebrew language classes in the army to unify these widely divergent peoples into a united people by teaching them the revived Hebrew language as the common language of Israel. Finally, in fulfillment of the ancient prophecies of Zephaniah, the inhabitants of Israel can now call "upon the name of the Lord, to serve him with one consent," in the Hebrew language of the prophets.

### 3.  *Ancient Biblical Predictions about the Present Arab-Israeli Conflict*

The ancient prophets predicted the animosity and hatred of the surrounding Arab nations in the years following the rebirth of the nation of Israel in the last days. The Lord inspired King David to predict almost three thousand years ago that the rebirth of Israel would trigger a bitter conflict in which the Jewish state would be immediately surrounded by its enemies, including the Arab nations of Jordan, Lebanon, Egypt, Saudi Arabia, and Syria. Incredibly, the ancient prophecy by King David precisely described the modern alliance of Arab states in the Middle East that is determined to destroy the Jewish state. By prophetically naming the ancient nations that are today represented by modern Arab states, King David identified those nations that have joined with the Palestinians in their vain attempt to destroy the Jewish state in the last days.

God's prophetic promise to Hagar, Abraham's concubine, was that she should call her son Ishmael: ". . . because the Lord hath heard thy affliction. And he will be a wild man; his hand will be against every man, and every man's hand against him; and he shall dwell in the presence of all his brethren"(Genesis 16:11–12). Unfortunately, this prophecy has been tragically fulfilled in the thousands of years of hatred between the Arabs, the descendants of Ishmael, and the Jews, the sons of Isaac. The Arab peoples are the descendants of Ishmael. They have travelled as nomads from place to place throughout thousands of years of the history of the Middle East. Significantly, at no time did the Arabs ever set up an independent nation or capital in Israel. The apostle Paul declared in his letter to the Galatians that the Arabs have an age-old hatred of the Jews: "But as then he that was born after the flesh persecuted him that was born after the Spirit, even so it is now" (Galatians 4:29). Although Egypt is often listed as an Arab nation because it uses the Arab language, its population is not Arab. As Max Dimont reported in his excellent book, *Jews, God and History* (p. 390), "Strictly speaking, Egypt, of course, is not an Arab nation, though 90% of its people profess the Moslem faith. The vast majority of today's Egyptians are of Hamitic descent, with the Arab Bedouins composing the largest minority group. Only a small minority, the Copts, are true descendants of the ancient Egyptians." King David prophetically listed the enemies of Israel in the last days.

> For, lo, thine enemies make a tumult: and they that hate thee have lifted up the head. They have taken crafty counsel against thy people, and consulted against thy hidden ones. They have said, Come, and let us cut them off from being a nation; that the name of Israel may be no more in remembrance. For they have consulted together with one consent: they are confederate against thee: The tabernacles of Edom, and the Ishmaelites; of Moab, and the Hagarenes; Gebal, and Ammon, and Amalek; the Philistines with the inhabitants of Tyre; Assur also is joined with them: they have holpen the children of Lot. Selah.
>
> (Psalm 83:2–8)

This ancient prophetic list of nations is fascinating, as it enumerates virtually every one of the nations in the Arab confederacy that oppose Israel's existence today:

| | |
|---|---|
| Edom | from Esau, brother of Jacob (Jordan)) |
| Ismaelites | descended from Ishmael, son of Hagar (Arabs) |
| Moab | son of Lot, (Jordan, east of Dead Sea) |
| Hagarenes | descended from one of the 12 sons of Hagar |
| Gebal | ancient Byblus, (north of today's Beirut) |

| Ammon | son of Lot, (capital of Jordan) |
| Amalek | descended from Esau (southern Jordan) |
| Philistines | from Ham, (throughout Palestine, Syria) |
| Tyre | a Phoenician city (Lebanon) |
| Assur | founded Assyria; (Iraq - Iran) |
| Children of Lot | Moab and Ammon, (Jordan) |

The prophet Ezekiel described in his great vision both the hatred of Israel's enemies, her exile from the Promised Land, and her final, miraculous return from the "valley of dry bones" in the last days leading to the return of the Messiah. In chapter 35, in the same section where we find the prophet Ezekiel's prediction of the restoration of the captives, the Lord describes the coming judgment of God against these Arab nations, including Edom (Mount Seir) in Jordan, because of their centuries-old hatred of the Jews.

> Moreover the word of the Lord came unto me, saying, Son of man, set thy face against Mount Seir, and prophecy against it, And say unto it, Thus saith the Lord God; Behold, O Mount Seir, I am against thee, and I will stretch out mine hand against thee, and I will make thee most desolate. I will lay thy cities waste, and thou shalt be desolate, and thou shalt know that I am the Lord. Because thou hast had a perpetual hatred, and hast shed the blood of the children of Israel by the force of the sword in the time of their calamity in the time that their iniquity had an end: . . . Because thou hast said, These two nations and these two countries shall be mine, and we will possess it; whereas the Lord was there.          (Ezekiel 35:1–5, 10)

The expression "two countries" refers to Ephraim and Judah, the two parts of the divided Jewish kingdom, Israel and Judah, following the death of King Solomon.

### The PLO's Struggle Against Israel

Since its creation in 1967, the Palestine Liberation Organization has been dedicated to the total destruction of the state of Israel and its Jewish population. During the last few years, PLO president Yasser Arafat has publicly promised that his organization has renounced terrorism. Meanwhile, the PLO and its allies in Hamas and Islamic Jihad have launched hundreds of terrorist acts against Jews both inside and outside of Israel. The PLO demands that Israel accept the proposition that every Arab related to anyone who claimed they lived in Palestine in 1948 be allowed to return to Palestine.

It is worthwhile to note that, despite the fact that more than 40 million refugees were dislocated as a result of World War II, neither the UN nor the media ever demanded the return of these refugees to their former lands. Historically, the UN plan for refugees has always suggested the settlement of these refugees in new nations so that they can begin to rebuild their lives. In the case of Poland, Germany, Vietnam, Cambodia, and dozens of other nations, the solution for refugees has always involved their resettlement in new countries. Significantly, it is only in the case of the Palestinians that the United Nations has demanded that common sense, normal practice, and natural justice be reversed. The UN and the Arab states have forced the Arab refugees and their children to remain in refugee camps for five decades. The hopeless claim was that they should be allowed to return to the original home in Israel that their relatives fled from half a century ago in 1948. The vast majority of living "Palestinians" were born in Arab countries outside Israel in the years since 1948. However, the PLO demands that Israel agree to resettle these hundreds of thousands of Palestinians (born in Arab countries since 1948) in the land of Israel. This "return," demanded by the PLO is obviously intended to destroy the Jewish state of Israel.

### 4. *The Return of the Ethiopian Jews to Israel in 1991*

The prophet Zephaniah predicted another seemingly improbable event when he declared that the Lord would return the Ethiopian Jews to the land of Israel. These Ethiopian Jews were separated from their Jewish brethren for almost three thousand years, as described in chapter eight. In the days of King Solomon, approximately three thousand years ago, a group of Jews from each of the twelve tribes immigrated to Ethiopia with Prince Menelik, the son of King Solomon and the Queen of Sheba, as documented in chapter eight of this book. The prophet Zephaniah foretold the return of these Jews to their Israeli homeland in the last days: "From beyond the rivers of Ethiopia my suppliants, even the daughter of my dispersed, shall bring mine offering" (Zephaniah 3:10). The prophet Isaiah confirms the prediction of

Zephaniah: "I will say to the north, Give up; and to the south, Keep not back: bring my sons from far, and my daughters from the ends of the earth" (Isaiah 43:6). Thousands of years ago Isaiah predicted the miraculous return of the Jews from both Russia (the north) and from Ethiopia (the south). In the period from 1989 to 1991, over 85,000 black Ethiopian Jews, known as Falasha, flew home to Israel from Ethiopia in fulfillment of the ancient prophecy of Zephaniah. Numerous other prophecies, including Ezekiel 37:21, foretold the return of Jewish exiles from foreign lands to the Holy Land in the last days.

### 5. *The Astonishing Fertility of Israel*

In addition to prophesying the recovery of the Jewish homeland, the rediscovery of the lost language of Hebrew, and the return of hundreds of thousands of Ethiopian Jewish exiles, the prophet Isaiah predicted twenty-eight centuries ago that Israel would become fertile again. "He shall cause them that come of Jacob to take root: Israel shall blossom and bud, and fill the face of the world with fruit" (Isaiah 27:6). The returning Jews have transformed the Promised Land, previously deserted and desolate, into the most agriculturally efficient land on earth, according to the United Nations. Today Israel supplies over 90 percent of the citrus fruit consumed by almost five hundred million Europeans.

The prophet Joel declared that the desert nation of Israel would experience tremendous increases of rain during the last days. "Be glad then, ye children of Zion, and rejoice in the Lord your God: for he hath given you the former rain moderately, and he will cause to come down for you the rain, the former rain, and the latter rain in the first month" (Joel 2:23). The rainfall in Palestine has increased dramatically by over 10 percent every single decade during the last century because the returning Jewish exiles planted more than two hundred million trees, transforming the complete environment of the Promised Land. "And the parched ground shall become a pool, and the thirsty land springs of water: in the habitation of dragons, where each lay, shall be grass with reeds and rushes" (Isaiah 35:7). As a result of this unprecedented reforestation, Israel's climate is beginning to return to the original conditions of the ancient past when Israel was truly a land of "milk and honey."

## 6. Israel's Plans to Rebuild the Temple

The prophet Isaiah wrote, "And it shall come to pass in the last days, that the mountain of the Lord's house shall be established in the top of the mountains, and shall be exalted above the hills; and all nations shall flow unto it" (Isaiah 2:2). In the book of Revelation (11:1–2), the prophet John tells us that the angel took him into the future to measure the Third Temple, which will exist during the seven-year tribulation period. Numerous other prophecies describe the rebuilding of the Temple in the last days. The apostle Paul confirmed that the Antichrist would occupy the future Temple. "Let no man deceive you by any means: for that day shall not come, except there come a falling away first, and that man of sin be revealed, the son of perdition; Who opposeth and exalteth himself above all that is called God, or that is worshiped; so that he as God sitteth in the temple of God, showing himself that he is God" (2 Thessalonians 2:3,4). The prophet Ezekiel described his vision of the final Temple, cleansed and cared for by minsitering Levites and priests worshiping God in the millennial kingdom. "And thou shalt give to the priests the Levites that be of the seed of Zadok, which approach unto me, to minister unto me, saith the Lord God, a young bullock for a sin offering" (Ezekiel 43:19).

## 7. The Oil of Anointing

The sacred oil of anointing was one of the most unusual aspects of the ancient Tabernacle and Temple worship service. This oil of anointing was specially prepared by the priests using five specific ingredients to anoint the Temple, the Ark, and the High Priest. Moses described God's specific commandment to Israel as follows: "And thou shalt make it an oil of holy ointment, an ointment compound after the art of the apothecary: it shall be an holy anointing oil. And thou shalt anoint the tabernacle of the congregation therewith, and the ark of the testimony" (Exodus 30:25–26). One of the five ingredients required to prepare the sacred oil of anointing for the Tabernacle was the rare and precious plant known as "sweet cinnamon," or "afars'mon" (Exodus 30:23). However, this special oil and one of its ingredients was lost, seemingly forever, almost two thousand years ago. When the Romans destroyed the Temple in A.D. 70, the retreating Jewish rebels burned the only two groves in Israel, in Jericho and Engedi, where these rare afars'mon trees grew. The Jewish sages taught that the Jews could never reinstitute the Temple services without this special oil of anointing because they had lost forever the missing ingredient of afars'mon. As a result of this loss, the Jewish sages believed they could not properly obey God's command to anoint the rebuilt Temple.

It is significant that the prophet Daniel foretold that, when the Messiah returns, He will be anointed with this special oil of anointing. "Seventy weeks are determined upon thy people and upon thy holy city, to finish the transgression, and to make an end of sins, and to make reconciliation for iniquity, and to bring in everlasting righteousness, and to seal up the vision and prophecy, and to anoint the most Holy" (Daniel 9:24). How could these prophecies about anointing the Most Holy be fulfilled when one of the key ingredients of the anointing oil was lost forever? Incredibly, several years ago, archeologists in Israel found a clay flask buried near the Dead Sea caves that was filled with the ancient oil of anointing. Scientists confirmed with carbon 14 dating that the oil is two thousand years old and determined that it is composed of the precise ingredients described in Exodus 30:25–26.

## 8. *Vessels For the Future Temple Worship*

Ezekiel foretold that the sacred vessels and linen robes would be prepared for use in the future Temple in the Millennium. "They shall enter into my sanctuary, and they shall come near to my table, to minister unto me, and they shall keep my charge. And it shall come to pass, that when they enter in at the gates of the inner court, they shall be clothed with linen garments; and no wool shall come upon them, while they minister in the gates of the inner court, and within" (Ezekiel 44:16–17). It is significant that the Temple Institute in the Old City of Jerusalem has prepared over eighty of the special sacred objects, vessels, and linen priestly garments required for future Temple services. Several Orthodox yeshivas, or Jewish Bible colleges, in Jerusalem have trained five hundred young Jewish men who are descended from the tribe of Levi to fulfill their future duties of Temple worship and sacrifice. Many have been trained in the Temple worship rituals and have learned to play the restored biblical musical instruments.

The predictions of the prophet Ezekiel (chap. 36:25) suggest that Israel will accomplish the resumption of the sacrifice of the "ashes of the red heifer" in the last days. This sacrifice is required to produce "the waters of purification" (Numbers 19) that are needed to cleanse the defiled Temple objects, the priests, and the stones on the Temple Mount, in preparation for the rebuilding of the Third Temple. The prophet Ezekiel confirmed that the waters of purification from the red-heifer sacrifice will be used to cleanse the future Temple and the Jewish people. "Then will I sprinkle clean water upon you, and ye shall be clean: from all your filthiness, and from all your idols, will I cleanse you" (Ezekiel 36:25). In this matter, it is fascinating to note that Israeli newspapers have recently reported (May 1997) that a pure "red heifer" has been born in Israel that meets the qualifications described in Numbers 19. This development may prepare the way for Israeli Jewish authorities to begin planning for a future Temple.

## 9. *The Revival of the Roman Empire*

The prophet Daniel and the apostle John, as the writer of the book of Revelation, both foretold the revival of the Roman Empire in the final generation when the Messiah would return to establish His eternal Kingdom:

> And the fourth kingdom shall be strong as iron: forasmuch as iron breaketh in pieces and subdueth all things: and as iron that breaketh all these, shall it break in pieces and bruise. And whereas thou sawest the feet and toes, part of potter's clay, and part of iron, the kingdom shall be divided; but there shall be in it of the strength of the iron, forasmuch as thou sawest the iron mixed with miry clay. And as the toes of the feet were part of iron, and part of clay, so the kingdom shall be partly strong, and partly broken. And whereas thou sawest iron mixed with miry clay, they shall mingle themselves with the seed of men: but they shall not cleave one to another, even as iron is not mixed with clay. And in the days of these kings shall the God of heaven set up a kingdom, which shall never be destroyed: and the kingdom shall not be left to other people, but it shall break in pieces and consume all these kingdoms, and it shall stand for ever.     (Daniel 2:40–44)

Daniel's prophecy (Daniel 7) and the apostle John's predictions (Revelation 13 and 17) confirmed that the Roman Empire will miraculously be revived in the final days of this generation in the unique form of a powerful ten-nation superstate. Following the devastation of two world wars, the leaders of Europe created a conference in 1957 to plan the creation of a confederate form of a European superstate, bringing the major nations of western Europe together for the first time since the time of the Roman emperors. In 1957, six European countries signed the Treaty of Rome and laid the foundation for the future United States of Europe. As reported in a BBC documentary on the European Union, Belgian Foreign Minister Henri Spaak, the former secretary-general of NATO, admitted, "We felt like Romans on that day. . . . We were consciously re-creating the Roman Empire once more." Since then, the Maastricht Treaty has consolidated the fifteen nations of the European Union into the world's first superstate. It is now an economic, political, and potentially, a military colossus that will dominate world events in the near future. However, recent reports from Europe reveal a plan to unite the first five nations of the European Union into a true European superstate, with the ten additional nations surrendering their autonomy in future years as they consolidate their union with the European Union.

### 10. The Rebuilding of Babylon

One of the most unusual of the Bible's prophecies reveals that the ancient city of Babylon will be rebuilt and will play a significant role in the events of the last days. The Scriptures reveal that the rebuilt city of Babylon will be destroyed by supernatural fire from heaven in a manner similar to the destruction of Sodom and Gomorrah. The prophet Isaiah foretold this destruction as follows: "Howl ye; for the day of the Lord is at hand; it shall come as a destruction from the Almighty/. . . And Babylon, the glory of kingdoms, the beauty of the Chaldees' excellency, shall be as when God overthrew Sodom and Gomorrah" (Isaiah 13:6, 19). In this remarkable prediction, the prophet declared that the city of Babylon will not only exist again but it will be destroyed by God on the Great Day of the Lord.

As unlikely as it seems, the Iraqi government of Saddam Hussein has spent over one billion dollars rebuilding the ancient city of Babylon. They intend to make it the center of their future renewed Babylonian Empire. Interestingly, the whole city of

Babylon was built over an underground lake of asphalt and oil. God has already provided the fuel for its final destruction. In another prophecy, God foretold that the wicked city will burn forever. "For it is the day of the Lord's vengeance, and the year of recompenses for the controversy of Zion. And the streams thereof shall be turned into pitch, and the dust thereof into brimstone, and the land thereof shall become burning pitch. It shall not be quenched night nor day; the smoke thereof shall go up for ever: from generation to generation it shall lie waste; none shall pass through it for ever and ever" (Isaiah 34:8–10). Several years ago during the Gulf War, we had a foretaste of this future burning of Babylon when President Saddam Hussein of Iraq set hundreds of Kuwaiti oil wells on fire and covered the desert with smoke and fire.

### 11. One World Government

Over two thousand years ago the prophets Daniel and John described that there would be a global world government led by the Antichrist in the last days (Daniel 7:14). "And it was given unto him to make war with the saints, and to overcome them: and power was given him over all kindreds, and tongues, and nations. And all that dwell upon the earth shall worship him" (Revelation 13:7–8). The prophecy by John and parallel predictions in the book of Daniel reveal that the population of earth will be placed under the control of one government led by the Antichrist in the last days. For the first time in history, one man, the future Antichrist, will have power "over all kindreds, and tongues, and nations." Despite the rise and fall of countless empires throughout history, there has never been a world government during thousands of years of human history. However, as I outlined in my book, *Final Warning*, the elite are moving behind the scenes to produce a world government as quickly as possible. The rising power of the United Nations, the International Monetary Fund, the World Trade Organization, and the World Court are moving us quickly beyond the days of national sovereignty and individual nations.

The elite who are planning a one-world government have embarked on a program to subvert and diminish the sovereignty of nation-states, including America and Canada. Henry Morgenthau, a former treasury secretary for President Roosevelt and a member of the Council on Foreign Relations (CFR), declared, "We can hardly expect the nation-state to make itself superfluous, at least not overnight. Rather, what we must aim for is recognition in the minds of all responsible statesmen that they are really nothing more than caretakers of a bankrupt international machine which will have to be transformed slowly into a new one." He stated that the key ingredient to this formula is their plan to "financially bankrupt the international machine." Nations will be forced to turn to the International Monetary Fund (IMF) and World Bank for a financial bailout, but only under the condition that borrowers abandon their national sovereignty to the UN. It is disconcerting that the IMF and the World Bank, the very institutions that can trigger a worldwide financial collapse, admit that the key event that will allow them to seize control of the nations is an international financial collapse.

The Ford Foundation financed a provocative United Nations study in 1994 called *Renewing the United Nations System*, written by two former UN officials, Sir Brian Urqhart and Erskine Childers. The study recommended massive changes to streamline UN operations. The report suggests that the United Nations General Assembly, the Security Council, the International Monetary Fund, the World Health Organization, and the International Labor Organization be transferred to one central location to improve efficiency and to centralize political control. The study suggested the possibility of Bonn or New York as the new headquarters. The authors called for the abolition of the present voting system of the International Monetary Fund. Their recommendation is that it be replaced with a radical new system that will allow impoverished Third World nations to dictate where and when loans would be made from rich countries to poorer ones.

This far-reaching proposal is obviously intended to lay the foundation for a one-world government. Consider this quote: "While there is no question, at present, of the transformation of the UN system into a supranational authority, the organization is in a transitional phase, basically shaped and constrained by national sovereignty, but sometimes acting outside and beyond it." Notice the phrase, "at present." Repeatedly, this document used terms such as "gradual limitation of sovereignty"; "notable abridgements of national sovereignty"; "chipping away at the edges of traditional sovereignty"; and "small steps towards an eventual trans-sovereign society." Throughout this extensive UN document, the authors discuss their plan to progressively erode our nation's cherished sovereignty. However, the authors recommend that the transition proceed step by step to avoid awakening a political backlash by the citizens of the western democracies who will be forced to forever surrender their freedom and sovereignty.

Some of the UN report's recommendations are very significant steps toward world government. Throughout the document, the authors talk about interim steps that must be taken "until the world is ready for world government." The authors suggest that the United Nations should raise funds for its own budget by assessing a global surcharge tax on "all arms sales," on "all transnational movement of currencies," on "all international trade, or on the production of such specific materials as petroleum," or "a United Nations levy on international air and sea travel." Other recommendations include assessing a "one day" income tax on all people of the planet every year. A proposal to have the UN apply a global tax on the citizens of the world is just one more indication of the UN's gradual transformation from an international consultative body into a governing power of a one-world superstate. The United Nations group has also called for a one-time global tax to be used to reduce government deficits and stimulate economic activity. This incredible precedent represents a major step towards the coming world government.

The study, *Renewing the United Nations System,* lays out the necessary steps to establish a powerful new world parliament. This is obviously a key step to build global public support for replacing the sovereignty of our individual nations with a newly enhanced United Nations that will ultimately become the nucleus of a powerful world government. There is an enormous difference between the present UN system of an assembly of representatives of national governments and the recently proposed plan that would have UN parliamentarians directly elected by all citizens throughout the planet. Using the example of the directly elected European Parliament, representing the citizens of the European Union, many are now calling for a "world people's assembly."

Unfortunately, for those who truly love democracy, the example of the European Parliament is not promising. Despite the trappings of democracy, the European Parliament does not possess the democratic power to choose the executives, set laws, or establish taxes. Most real power in the European Union remains in the hands of the twenty-one-member appointed Executive Commission. The directly elected European Parliament remains nothing more than a showpiece "debating society" with no real power or substantive influence when compared to the powerful, but unelected, Executive Commission. The pattern of all international institutions is that power is exercised by the members of the elite group from behind locked boardroom doors. Then, their decisions are sold to the public through slick public relations and media manipulation. History suggests that real democracy can only function practically at the local or national level. Once we move to the arena of international politics between nation-states, true democratic government is replaced by sophisticated trade-offs negotiated behind the scenes between the power brokers of these international organizations. The situation in the European Union is a preview of where the true power will lie in a future world government. In such a situation, a powerful individual will inevitably arise to seize power and rule this future world government. He will become the Antichrist prophesied thousands of years ago by the ancient prophets.

### Plans to Enlarge the Powers of the United Nations

Former British Foreign Secretary Douglas Hurd claimed in an interview that the United Nations needs to prepare itself to take on an "imperial role." He stated that the UN must usurp national sovereignty and take control as the occupying power when governments collapse, as in Somalia and Cambodia. During an interview held at the UN in New York, Secretary Hurd drew attention to what he called "a new phase in the world's history." There is a need for the UN to intervene in crisis situations earlier to "prevent things getting to the stage where countries are run by corrupt war lords, as in Somalia," he said. Douglas Hurd warned that since the breakup of the former Soviet Union — resulting in three or four "crisis areas" — the United States was the lone superpower and it had no wish to become "policeman of world."

The United States is calling for a more unified and efficient UN structure, arguing there is an urgent need to better organize the world body to deal with global hot spots like Bosnia, Haiti, and Rwanda. This is part of a trend of a powerful elite encouraging a new variation of neocolonialism. They propose that the UN establish some kind of "trusteeship" over nations whose governments are in disarray due to famine or civil war, such as recently occurred in Somalia and Rwanda. These tragic situations are ready-made for those who have an underlying goal of establishing the United Nations as the nucleus of the coming world government.

One of the key goals of the globalists is to create a permanent standing army of significant size that would allow the Security Council to enforce the will of the world body against any nation or group of nations who oppose its agenda. In the last seven years alone, the UN has engaged in more peace-keeping operations than it did in its first forty years. In the last decade the UN's peacekeeping budget has increased over 1000 percent, with a staggering 7000 percent increase in military personnel in UN police operations. In addition, there are now one hundred times as many civilian personnel involved in UN peacekeeping operations as there were during previous decades. The UN Security Council has deployed troops in nineteen countries around the globe at an annual cost of over $3 billion in the last few years.

### Plans to Build a Permanent United Nations Army

Significantly, an article in *Newsweek* magazine (September 26, 1994), called for the creation of a standing army for the New World Order to respond to future crises anywhere in the world. "The United Nations needs its own army, accountable not to national governments but to the United Nations itself. The rich nations would have to donate equipment to such an army; real live soldiers would be recruited from volunteers. Some would be trained mercenaries, like the Nepalese Gurkhas; others would be units from the armies of the western world."

Recent articles have also appeared in the *New York Times*, *TIME* magazine, and the *Economist* magazine calling for the creation of a permanent standing army for the United Nations under the control of the UN Security Council. The August 1994 issue of the respected *Economist* magazine wrote about the continuing disasters in Somalia and Rwanda as the UN tried and failed to create a professional peace-keeping force assembled from the disparate units of dozens of military forces provided by UN member states. Often the ammunition did not match the weapons, the troops were not trained for the equipment they had to use, and the soldiers were commanded by foreign officers who did not speak the languages of the troops they led.

As the tragedy of Rwanda unfolded, the United Nations saw disaster coming but found itself paralyzed into inactivity by competing political agendas and general indifference. When the UN finally sprung into action, after the horrible pictures of genocide filled our television screens, it was a case of "too little too late." As one commentator noted, "Never has intervention been needed more quickly than in Rwanda; never has it materialized more slowly. A prompt response when the slaughter began in April could not have saved all the victims, but it might have saved a great many . . . . Their foot-dragging over Rwanda is the best argument yet for the UN to have a small flexible peacekeeping force of its own." The *Economist* argued, "A standing force would respond to emergencies only when the Security Council told it to. . . it would be ready to try at once, not after UN officials had gone cap in hand to umpteen governments. The idea bristles with tricky questions: command, recruitment, training, pay, nationality, transport, supply, and support back-up. But it should be possible to create a brigade-sized force of this kind. And it is what the UN needs if it is to be a peacekeeper worthy of its name." The creation of a permanent United Nations armed force will be one of the key milestones on the road to world government.

The UN Secretary General has repeatedly called for the creation of a special UN rapid-deployment military force of sufficient size to defeat any potential opponent. He wants member states to provide trained soldiers and equipment and necessary funding on a permanent basis, supported by each member state's defense budget. He is committed wholeheartedly to the concept of the coming new world order that plans to replace national sovereignty with a world government led by the United Nations.

### 12. *Preparations for the Mark of the Beast*

The Book of Revelation describes the creation of a cashless society in the last days where the possession of a certain number, "666," will be essential to enable you to "buy or sell." This was an astonishing prophecy when John proclaimed it in the first century:

> And he causeth all, both small and great, rich and poor,
> free and bond, to receive a mark in their right hand, or in

their foreheads: And that no man might buy or sell, save
he that had the mark, or the name of the beast, or the
number of his name. Here is wisdom. Let him that hath
understanding count the number of the beast: for it is the
number of a man; and his number is Six hundred threescore and six.                         (Revelation 13:16–18)

However, in the final years of this century, we are already 95
percent cashless in North America. Studies reveal that less than 5
percent of the total money in our economy still exists as paper
currency or coins. The book of Revelation prophesies that the
number 666 will be placed beneath the skin on the right hand or
forehead in order to control people in the Antichrist's empire. For
the first time in history, we are developing technology that would
allow tiny computer chips holding your complete medical and
financial records to be placed beneath the skin of the right hand or
forehead. Recently, scientists developed a miniature computer
chip so powerful that it will hold up to five gigabytes of information in a chip the size of a large grain of rice. This tiny chip will
hold as much information as contained in thirty complete sets of
the *Encyclopedia Britannica*. This chip could easily be configured in
a shape that could be injected beneath the skin. Your complete
financial life records could be contained in such a chip, which
could then be scanned and read from a distance by electronic
scanners. *Business Week* magazine reported on June 3, 1996
(p. 123), that MasterCard International is testing a "smart card"
computer chip that includes information about your fingerprint
and identity that can be embedded in a credit/debit card. Card
scanners in stores and banks will scan your fingerprint and compare it to the information on the card to verify your identity. How
could the apostle John have known that the future would hold
such incredible cashless technology unless God inspired him to
write the words recorded in Revelation 13:16–18?

### 13. Worldwide Television Communications

Another incredible prophecy relating to our era, found in the
book of Revelation, describes worldwide television communications. The prophet John prophesied that in the future Tribulation
the Antichrist will kill two of God's witnesses who will have
stopped the rain for three and one-half years. The prophet John,

declared that the people living throughout the world will see the deaths of these two people and observe their bodies lying unburied for three and one-half days in Jerusalem. The whole world will hold a party, exchanging gifts in their relief that their tormentors are dead. Then these people will watch in astonishment as God resurrects His two witnesses to heaven (Revelation 11:9–10). How could the news that these men were killed travel instantaneously around the world in only three and one-half days in any other generation than today? Only seventy years ago it would have taken a week for news to travel from Israel to Japan or New York. However, today CNN instantly transmits pictures and sound about any important event worldwide. Over two billion people around the world simultaneously watched the Olympic events in Atlanta. For the first time in history, this prophecy about the whole world watching an event as it unfolds in Jerusalem can literally be fulfilled in our generation.

### 14. *Knowledge and Travel Shall Increase in the Last Days*

Twenty-five centuries ago the Book of Daniel predicted that there would be an explosion of knowledge and a huge increase in travel in the last days. Daniel wrote these words: "But thou, O Daniel, shut up the words, and seal the book, even to the time of the end: many shall run to and fro, and knowledge shall be increased" (Daniel 12:4). Throughout thousands of years of history the level of knowledge only increased incrementally. In some generations the level of general knowledge actually decreased. Yet, in the last century and a half, there has been an explosion of knowledge beyond anything ever experienced in human history. There are more scientists alive today than have lived in all of the rest of history. Recently, it was calculated that the sum total of human knowledge is growing so quickly that it literally doubles every twenty months. This is staggering in light of Daniel's inspired prediction from the ancient past that "knowledge shall be increased." In addition, Daniel stated that a characteristic of the last days would be an awesome increase in mobility as "many shall run to and fro."

The speed of transportation has also exploded in the last century. For thousands of years, until 1900, most people never traveled faster than a galloping horse. Currently hundreds of millions of people travel every day at sixty miles per hour or more in their cars, while others travel in planes at six hundred miles an hour. Our astronauts have travelled at over eighteen thousand miles per hour in the U.S. space shuttle *Discovery*. In addition, while most people in past centuries seldom traveled more than twenty miles from the place they were born, millions of people now travel across the globe as part of their normal course of daily business or for their annual vacation.

## 15. *Armies Preparing for the Battle of Armageddon*

Numerous biblical prophecies deal with the climactic Battle of Armageddon, which will occur at the end of this age when Christ will defeat the Antichrist's armies. This ultimate victory of Jesus Christ will establish His Kingdom on earth forever. The prophet John described the location of the final battle in this war between the western armies of the Antichrist and the armies of the kings of the East. "And he gathered them together into a place called in the Hebrew tongue Armageddon" (Revelation 16:16). John also stated that the army of the eastern nations from the "kings of the east" would consist of an astonishing two hundred million soldiers. This statement appeared to be impossible in light of the fact that the entire population of the Roman Empire in the days of John was only two hundred million people. "And the four angels were loosed, which were prepared for an hour, and a day, and a month, and a year, for to slay the third part of men. And the number of the army of the horsemen were two hundred thousand thousand: and I heard the number of them" (Revelation 9:15-16). Some writers have mistakenly suggested that the Bible referred to 200 million horsemen. However, there are only approximately thirty-five million horses throughout the world. A careful reading of Revelation 9:16 reveals that John's use of the word "horsemen" refers to the four horsemen of the Apocalypse (Revelation 6:1–8). Therefore the prophet is indicating that the size of the future army of the four horsemen, representing God's wrath, will be two hundred million soldiers.

The populations of the nations of Asia are growing so quickly that they could field an army in the next few years that would contain two hundred million soldiers. As a result of the cruel and evil one-child policy, Chinese couples frequently abort unborn babies whenever ultrasound tests indicate the unborn child is a female. A Chinese couple will continue to abort female fetuses until a test reveals that the woman is carrying a male fetus. Then the couple allow the male child to be born. Numerous reports by human rights organizations reveal that China, India, and North Korea are involved in the selective abortion of unborn female infants. In addition, many families in these nations admit to killing or abandoning their young female children. The *Toronto Star* newspaper reported in 1995 that Chinese officials admitted that they now have a staggering imbalance between boys and girls. This unprecedented sexual imbalance will result in an excess of over seventy million young men in China by the year 2000, with no women for these men to marry. This growing imbalance of sexes throughout Asia will produce an available manpower of up to two hundred million excess young men of military age in the next decade. This unprecedented situation could fulfill the prophecy of John about the two-hundred-million-man army from the kings of the East that will fight against the Antichrist in the climactic Battle of Armageddon.

### 16. *God's Warning to Those Who Destroy the Earth*

"And the nations were angry, and thy wrath is come, and the time of the dead, that they should be judged, and that thou shouldest give reward unto thy servants the prophets, and to the saints, and them that fear thy name, small and great; and shouldest destroy them which destroy the earth" (Revelation 11:18).

In the midst of the great judgments of the Great Tribulation, the prophet John recorded Christ's warning that He would "destroy them which destroy the earth" (Revelation 11:18). God commanded man to have dominion over the earth and to be a steward of the world's resources. Since then, man has destroyed large areas of the planet. One of the final judgments of God may involve a specific punishment to mankind for the devastation of this planet that has been committed in the last century.

### 17. *A Military Highway Across Asia and the Drying Up of the Euphrates River*

Another prophecy in Revelation declares that the Euphrates River will dry up to allow this enormous army of two hundred million soldiers to cross from Asia into the Middle East to invade Israel: "And the sixth angel poured out his vial upon the great river Euphrates; and the water thereof was dried up, that the way of the kings of the east might be prepared" (Revelation 16:12). Throughout history the Euphrates River has been an impenetrable military barrier between East and West. However, the government of Turkey recently constructed the huge Ataturk Dam that can now dam up the headwaters of the Euphrates River for the first time in history. The prophet John also foretold a future military highway across Asia that would allow this astonishing army to march toward the final battle in Israel. John appears to refer to the building of this highway in these words: "The way of the kings of the east might be prepared" (Revelation 16:12). The Chinese government has spent enormous sums and expended the lives of hundreds of thousands of construction workers to build a military super-highway across Asia heading directly toward Israel. This highway has no economic purpose, and no foreigners are allowed anywhere near this road. The highway has been completed, at a staggering cost of money and lives, through the rugged terrain across the south of China and through Tibet, Afghanistan, and Pakistan. The prophet John's unusual prophecy about "the way of the kings of the east" is being fulfilled in our day in a manner that sets the stage for the final battle of this age.

### The Staggering Odds against These Prophecies Being Fulfilled in Our Lifetime

In this chapter we have examined a number of significant prophecies pointing to the Lord's return in this generation that have been fulfilled, or are in the process of being fulfilled, in our lifetime. Almost two thousand years have passed from the time of Christ until our generation. At its simplest level we can ask, *What are the odds that even ten of these specific prophecies would be fulfilled by chance or coincidence during our lifetime?* If these prophecies have not come to pass as a result of random chance, then their fulfillment in our lifetime is overwhelming evidence that God inspired the writers of the Bible to correctly predict these future events!

The Bible uses the word "generations" in reference to three distinct time periods. The most common use of the word *generation* found in the Bible is the average length of life of most humans

— usually seventy or eighty years. King David wrote: "The days of our years are threescore years and ten; and if by reason of strength they be four score years, yet is their strength labour and sorrow; for it is soon cut off, and we fly away" (Psalms 90:10).

The second use of the word *generation* occurs in the Scripture's reference to the duration of the period before the Flood in Genesis 6:3. This generation lasted one hundred and twenty years. However, the third use of the word *generation* is often used in the Bible in reference to a period of judgment or of governing. This scriptural use of the word usually referred to a period of forty years, such as the thirteen different forty-year periods described in connection with the rule of Joshua, Gideon, King Saul, King David, King Solomon, et cetera.

During the span of the last two thousand years from the time of Christ, there have been fifty such forty-year generations. One way to analyse these prophecies is to ask the question, *What is the probability that this series of fascinating prophecies would all occur by coincidence in a single generation — our generation from 1948 until today?* Since there are fifty possible generations during which these predictions could have been fulfilled, the odds are only one chance in fifty that any one of these specific prophecies will happen by chance in our generation rather than in some other generation. Consider Jesus Christ's prediction about the rebirth of Israel (Matthew 24:32) as just one example. There was only one chance in fifty that Israel would become a nation in our generation, rather than in any one of the other fifty generations in the last two millennium, such as A.D. 350, or A.D. 1600.

According to the laws of combined probability the chance that two or more events will occur in a given time period is equal to the chance that one event will occur multiplied by the chance that the second event would occur. If the odds are fifty to one against Israel being reborn in our lifetime by chance, and if the odds are also fifty to one against the Roman Empire being revived in our generation, then the combined probability of both events occurring in our lifetime is fifty times fifty, which equals one chance in twenty-five hundred. To calculate the probability of just ten of these prophecies being fulfilled in our lifetime by chance or coincidence, consider the following analysis.

## What Are the Odds That These Prophecies Were Fulfilled by Chance in Our Generation?

There are 40 years to a generation.

There were 50 generations from Christ till today.

Therefore, the odds are 1 chance in 50 that any one of these specific prophecies will occur by coincidence in our lifetime.

The odds against these ten specific prophecies occurring by random chance all in one generation are as follows:

|  | *Chance* |
|---|---|
| 1 prophecy fulfilled = 1 × 50 | 1 in 50 |
| 2 prophecies fulfilled = 50 × 50 | 1 in 2,500 |
| 3 prophecies fulfilled = 50 × 50 × 50 | 1 in 25,000 |
| 4 prophecies fulfilled = 50 × 50 × 50 × 50 | 1 in 6.25 million |
| 5 prophecies fulfilled = 50 × 50 (5 times) | 1 in 312.5 million |
| 6 prophecies fulfilled = 50 × 50 (6 times) | 1 in 15.6 billion |
| 7 prophecies fulfilled = 50 × 50 (7 times) | 1 in 780 billion |
| 8 prophecies fulfilled = 50 × 50 (8 times) | 1 in 39 trillion |
| 9 prophecies fulfilled = 50 × 50 (9 times) | 1 in 1,950 trillion |
| 10 prophecies fulfilled = 50 × 50 (10 times) | 1 in 97,500 trillion |

Obviously, the odds against the fulfillment of even ten of these prophecies by coincidence alone in one generation are simply staggering: one chance in 97,500 trillion! Another way of looking at this is that the odds against the prophets of the Bible correctly guessing the details of these ten specific prophecies is also one chance in 97,500 trillion. If we calculated the odds against all twenty of these prophecies occurring by chance, the enormous odds would be astronomical. In other words, it is simply impossible that men alone could have written these biblical prophecies without the supernatural assistance and inspiration of God. In addition, the staggering odds against these predictions occurring in our generation by coincidence strongly suggests that Jesus Christ will return to earth in our lifetime.

This analysis demonstrates the truly incredible odds against even ten specific prophecies being fulfilled by chance in our generation. The odds against even ten prophecies occurring by random chance was 50 × 50 × 50 × 50 × 50 × 50 × 50 × 50 × 50 × 50, or one chance in 97,500 trillion!! This number is so large that it is hard to conceive of it. However, to illustrate these incredible odds, consider the following. The odds of "97,500 trillion to one" are equal to the estimated number of grains of sand that would fill the volume of our entire planet. Imagine that we take a single grain of sand out of this staggering number of grains of sand filling the globe and paint it blue. Then we blindfold you and let you randomly search the planet for this single buried blue grain of sand for as long as you wish. Remember that the entire globe consists of grains of sand and that you must consider the possibility that the blue painted grain of sand was buried ten miles or, possibly, a thousand miles deep beneath the planet's surface. When you think you have found the right place, reach down and pick up a random grain of sand. If you are lucky enough to pick up the only blue grain of sand in the whole planet, you have equalled the odds of one chance in 97,500 trillion — the same astronomical odds against these ten prophecies being fulfilled by chance in our generation. Frankly, I don't think you would find that grain of sand. Likewise, it is virtually impossible that all of these prophecies were fulfilled by random chance.

The Scriptures teach that the final generation of this age will witness the fulfillment of a staggering number of prophecies pointing to the imminent return of the promised Messiah. The material presented in this chapter also provides astonishing evidence that it was God who inspired the writers of the Scriptures to accurately predict the startling number of prophecies already fulfilled in our lifetime. Our generation has witnessed more fulfilled prophecies than any other in history. The Old Testament visions of the ancient prophets of Israel, together with the New Testament prophetic words of Jesus and His apostles, testify with one voice that our generation will see the triumphant victory of Jesus the Messiah over Satan. The establishment of the righteous Kingdom of God is at hand. In light of the astonishing fulfillment of prophecy in our day, we need to heed the words of Jesus Christ that speak especially to our generation: "And when these things begin to come to pass, then look up, and lift up your heads; for your redemption draweth nigh" (Luke 21:28).

The Lord has not left Christians in darkness concerning the general time of Christ's return. Although we cannot know "the day nor the hour in which the Son of Man is coming" (Matthew 25:13), the fulfillment of dozens of specific prophecies in our lifetime indicates that Jesus Christ's Second Coming will occur in our generation. Someday soon the heavens will open "with a shout, with the voice of an archangel, and with the trumpet of God" (1 Thessalonians 4:16) announcing to the Church the awesome news that our time of waiting is finally over. At that moment Jesus Christ will appear in the clouds to receive His Bride, His faithful Church composed of hundreds of millions of saints, rising supernaturally in the air to meet their Lord and King. Despite the dangers that lie ahead for mankind, those who love Jesus Christ as their Savior can rest in the knowledge that all these events are in the Lord's hands. The apostle John concluded his great book of Revelation with the final promise of Jesus Christ. "He who testifies to these things says, 'Surely I am coming quickly.' Amen. Even so, come, Lord Jesus!" (Revelation 22:20).

# 18

# *Your Personal Appointment with Destiny*

The apostle Paul said that God "Now commandeth all men every where to repent: because he hath appointed a day, in the which he will judge the world in righteousness by that man whom he hath ordained; whereof he hath given assurance unto all men, in that he hath raised him from the dead" (Acts 17: 30–31).

In light of the astonishing precision of God's fulfillments of past and present appointments with Israel and the nations, it is logical to conclude that the Lord will also fulfill Paul's prophecy about the final judgment of every one of us, " because he hath appointed a day." Jesus warned His disciples, "When ye shall see all these things, know that it is near, even at the doors. Verily I say unto you, This generation shall not pass, till all these things be fulfilled" (Matthew 24: 33–34). In the preceding pages, attention has been focused on impending world events. As we turn to examine our personal future, we can see that these same incredibly accurate Scriptures prophesied that every one of us faces a personal appointment with God. The writer of the book of Hebrews wrote about our personal destiny: "It is appointed unto men once to die, but after this the judgment" (Hebrews 9:27).

Our individual appointment with destiny with God cannot be postponed or evaded. Every person on earth will someday come face to face with Jesus Christ to give an account of what decision we have made regarding our relationship with Him. Every one of us has rebelled against God and sinned throughout our lives. The apostle Paul wrote, "For all have sinned, and come short of the glory of God" (Romans 3:23). The consequences of our choice to sinfully rebel against God is that we have all walked away from God's holy presence and have become unfit to enter heaven. God's Word declares, "For the wages of sin is death; but the gift of God is eternal life through Jesus Christ our Lord" (Romans 6:23). The Scriptures declare that our sinful rebellion has alienated each of us from the holiness of God. Continued rebellion and rejection of Christ will prevent us from ever entering heaven until our sins are forgiven by God. The sacrificial death of Jesus Christ on the cross is the key to bringing us to a place of true peace in our hearts. The death of our old sinful nature as we identify with Christ's death on the cross is the key to finding true peace with God. The only way we can be filled with the grace of God is to approach Him as we would bring a container to a well. It must be empty. It is only then that God can begin to fill us with His grace and spirit.

Jesus asked His disciples this vital question, "'Who do you say that I am?" Simon Peter answered and said, 'You are the Christ, the Son of the living God'" (Matthew 16:15–16). Every one of us must answer that same question for ourselves. If the Bible truly is the Word of God, your answer to that question will determine your eternal destiny. Ultimately, each of us must answer that question. We cannot evade it. If we refuse to answer, we have already rejected Christ's claims to be our Savior as the Son of God. According to God's Word, the choices we make in this life will have eternal consequences in the next.

The apostle Paul wrote, "For it is written, As I live, saith the Lord, every knee shall bow to me, and every tongue shall confess to God. So then every one of us shall give account of himself to God" (Romans 14: 11–12). Someday every human will bow their knee to Jesus Christ and acknowledge Him as Almighty God. The question is: Will you choose to repent of your sins now and bow your knee willingly to your Savior and Lord? Or, will you reject His offer of salvation today and finally be forced by His majesty to bow your knee before your final Judge as you are sent to an eternity in hell.

When we meet Jesus Christ on Judgment Day, we must

acknowledge whether we accepted or rejected His precious gift of salvation. When Jesus was crucified on the cross, He paid the complete price of your sins and mine. One of His final statements on the cross was "It is finished." As the sinless Lamb of God, Jesus allowed Himself to be offered as a perfect sacrifice to pay the price of our sins and to reconcile each of us to God. However, in a manner similar to a pardon offered to a prisoner awaiting execution, each of us must repent of our sins and personally accept Christ's pardon for His salvation to become effective. The New Testament declared, "We shall all stand before the judgment seat of Christ" (Romans 14:10). The basis of God's judgment following our death will be our personal relationship with Jesus Christ — not whether we were better or worse than most other people — and this alone will determine whether you and I will spend an eternity with God in heaven or an eternity without Him in hell.

Some people suggest that if God is truly a God of love, then somehow He will be "kind" and bend the rules to allow "good" people into heaven, despite their lifelong rejection of Jesus Christ's gift of salvation. Consider the implications of this proposition for a moment. If God allowed sinners who refused to repent of their sins into heaven, He would have to deny His nature as a holy and just God. Admitting unrepentent sinners into heaven would turn Paradise into an annex of hell. If an unrepentent soul was allowed into heaven, his sinfulness would destroy the holiness of heaven. In addition, a unrepentent sinner would hate the holiness and worship of God. The sinless nature of a holy heaven and the evil nature of sin make it absolutely impossible for God to forgive men's sins unless they wholeheartedly repent and turn from sin. Only then can God forgive and transform us as those saved by the grace of Jesus Christ, who cleanses us from our sinful rebellion. Although we can cleanse our bodies with water, the cleansing of our souls requires the spiritual application of the blood of Christ to our hearts.

When Nicodemus, one of the righteous religious leaders of Israel, came to Jesus, he asked Him about salvation. Jesus answered in these words, "Verily, verily, I say unto thee, Except a man be born again, he cannot see the kingdom of God" (John 3:3). It isn't simply a matter of intellectually accepting the facts about Christ and salvation. To be "born again" you must sincerely repent of your sinful life, asking Him to forgive you and to wholeheartedly trust in Christ for the rest of your life. This decision will transform your life forever. God will give you a new purpose and meaning to your life. The Lord promises believers eternal life in heaven: "This is the will of Him who sent Me, that everyone who sees the Son and believes in Him may have everlasting life; and I will raise him up at the last day" (John 6:40). The moment a person commits his life to Christ, he receives eternal life. Though your body will die, you will live forever with Christ in heaven. Jesus explained to Nicodemus, "For God so loved the world, that he gave his only begotten Son, that whosoever believeth in him should not perish, but have everlasting life" (John 3:16). Every sinner stands condemned by God because of his lifelong sinful rebellion against God's commandments as revealed in the Scriptures.

Jesus said, "He that believeth in him is not condemned: but he that believeth not is condemned already, because he hath not believed in the name of the only begotten Son of God" (John 3:18). After thirty years of studying the precision of fulfilled prophecy in the Bible, I am convinced that the Bible is the inspired Word of God. Therefore, I believe the words of Jesus Christ, "I am the way, the truth, and the life. No one comes to the Father except through Me" (John 14:6). God declares in these inspired words that there is no other road to salvation than accepting the "way," the "truth," and the "life" of Jesus Christ.

The sole entrance requirement to heaven will be our relationship to Jesus Christ, who changes His disciples so that they are now righteous and holy before God, in light of Christ's forgiveness of their sins. God demands perfect holiness and righteousness. However, it is obvious that no one can meet these requirements on their own merit. Since God could never ignore the fact that we have all sinned against Him, it was necessary that someone who was perfect and sinless should pay the penalty of physical and spiritual death as a substitute for us. The only person who could qualify was Jesus Christ, the Holy Son of God.

Christ's sacrificial gift of His life on the cross paid the price for our sins. Every one of us, by accepting His pardon, can now stand before the judgment seat of God clothed in Christ's righteousness: "For he hath made him [Jesus] to be sin for us, who knew no sin; that we might be made the righteousness of God in Him" (2 Corinthians 5:21). This fact of Christ's atonement is perhaps the greatest mystery in creation. Jesus is the only one in history who, by His sinless life, was qualified to enter heaven. Yet He loved each one of us so much that He chose to die upon that cross to purchase our salvation. In a marvelous act of God's mercy, the righteousness of Jesus is placed to our account with God.

The astonishing truth, difficult for many to believe, is that all that is required for Jesus Christ to become your personal Savior from the guilt and power of sin is that you turn from your sin and pride in true repentance. Accept Him as your Lord and Savior and share your faith with others. The apostle John wrote, "But as many as received him, to them gave he power to become sons of God, even to them that believe on his name" (John 1:12). The decision to accept Christ as your personal Savior is the most important one you will ever make. Your decision will change your eternal destiny, but it will also give you peace today as your guilt from sin will be removed forever.

However, it will cost you a great deal to live as a committed Christian today. Many people will challenge your new faith in the Bible and in Christ. The Lord Jesus Christ asks His disciples to "follow Me." Your decision and commitment to Jesus Christ will change your life forever. However, your commitment to Christ will unleash His supernatural grace and power to transform your life into one of joy and peace beyond anything you have ever experienced. While the decision to follow Christ will cost you a lot, it will cost you far more if you do not accept Him as your Savior before you die. Jesus challenges us with these words, "For what shall it profit a man, if he shall gain the whole world, and lose his own soul?" (Mark 8:36).

All those who have accepted Christ are called to be "witnesses" of Christ's message to our world. To be a faithful witness to Christ demands an active, not passive, involvement in the life of our Christian brothers and sisters. It requires a willingness to pay the price of a personal commitment to our coming Messiah. In addition, our belief in the imminent Second Coming of Christ should motivate us to a renewed love of Christ and a willingness to witness to our unsaved brothers and sisters about His salvation. This belief in the Second Coming will also purify our walk before the Lord as the apostle John wrote, "And everyone who has this hope in Him purifies himself, just as He is pure" (1 John 3:3). If you are a Christian, I challenge you to share the evidence in this book to witness to your friends and family about your faith in Jesus Christ.

The Scriptures reveal that we will be judged by God as to what we have done with His Son, Jesus Christ. Will you accept Him as your personal Savior and find peace with God throughout eternity? Or, will you reject Him forever? The decision is yours. Every one of us has our own personal "appointment with destiny." On some appointed day, at the end of your life, you will stand before Jesus Christ. The choice is entirely up to you as to whether you will meet Him as your returning Savior or as your final Judge. As the Jewish people prepared to enter the struggle for the Promised Land, their great leader Moses addressed all of Israel with words that also apply to us as we hear the approaching hoof beats of the Four Horsemen of the Apocalypse: "I call heaven and earth to record this day against you, that I have set before you life and death, blessing and cursing: therefore choose life" (Deuteronomy 30:19).

As the prophetic clock ticks on toward the final midnight hour, the invitation of Christ is still open: "Behold, I stand at the door, and knock: If any man hear my voice, and open the door, I will come in to him, and will sup with him and he with me" (Revelation 3:20).

# APPENDIX A

# *The 360-Day Prophetic Year of the Bible*

It is vital that, if we are to correctly understand the precision of Bible prophecy, we must determine the precise length of the biblical (or prophetic) year which is used in the Scriptures.

Our modern world calendar is based on the solar cycle and consists of 365.25 days. The modern Jewish calendar is calculated according to both the lunar and solar cycles. Their twelve months are currently calculated as containing 354 days, which leaves their year eleven and one-fourth days short of the true solar year. This is corrected by adding a "leap month," known as Ve-Adar, seven times during a nineteen-year cycle.

However, when we turn to the Scriptures, we discover that the biblical-prophetic year consisted of 360 days. Abraham, the father of Israel, used the 360-day year, the same calendar cycle of his ancient home in Ur of the Chaldees. The Genesis account of the Flood in the days of Noah illustrates the use of this 360-day year by recording the 150-day interval till the waters abated from the earth. The 150 days began on the seventeenth day of the second month and ended on the seventeenth day of the seventh month (Genesis 7:11, 24 and 8:3–4). In other words, the five months consisted of thirty days each; therefore, twelve months would equal 360 days (12 × 30 = 360 days).

Sir Robert Anderson, in his book *The Coming Prince* (p. 68) quotes Sir Isaac Newton regarding this fact:

All nations, before the just length of the solar year was known, reckoned months by the course of the moon, and years by the return of winter and summer, spring and autumn; and in making calendars for their festivals, they reckoned thirty days to a lunar month, and twelve lunar months to a year, taking the nearest round numbers, whence came the division of the ecliptic into 360 degrees.This was not a new discovery by Sir Isaac Newton in the late 1600s or even by Sir Robert Anderson in 1895. It had been discussed centuries earlier in detail by the Christian writer Julias Africanus in *Chronography* (A.D. 240), in which he gave an explanation of the fulfillment of Daniel's Seventy Weeks.

The book of Esther (1: 4) reveals the same use of a 360-day length of year by indicating that the six-months-long feast of King Xerxes continued exactly 180 days.

The prophet Daniel prophesied that the time of the absolute power of the Antichrist over the nations will last three and one-half years (Daniel 7:25). John, in the book of Revelation, described this same three-and-one-half-year period (Revelation 13:5–7) as consisting of forty-two months of thirty days each, totaling 1260 days (Revelation 11:2–3; 12:6). Both biblical writers, John and Daniel, used the ancient 360-day biblical year in both the historical and prophetic parts of Scripture.

## THE BIBLICAL CALENDAR

| Jewish month | | Our equivalent month |
|---|---|---|
| Order | Name | |
| 1. | Nisan | Mar – April |
| 2. | Iyar | April – May |
| 3. | Sivan | May – June |
| 4. | Tammuz | June – July |
| 5. | Ab or Av | July – Aug |
| 6. | Elul | Aug– Sept |
| 7. | Tishri | Sept – Oct |
| 8. | Bul | Oct – Nov |
| 9. | Chisleu | Nov – Dec |
| 10. | Tebeth | Dec – Jan |
| 11. | Sebat | Jan – Feb |
| 12. | Adar | Feb – Mar |

Ve - Adar: Intercalary Month in Leap Years

# APPENDIX B

# The Date of Christ's Nativity, Ministry, and Crucifixion

## The Date of Christ's Nativity

Our current system of numbering years (e.g., A.D. 1997) was developed in the sixth century by a monk named Dionysius Exignus. He calculated that the birth of Christ occurred in the Roman calendar year 754. He computed that the new year, beginning January 1 of the year following Christ's birth as recorded by Luke, was the year A.D. 1 of his new calendar (*anno Domini*, "year of our Lord"). He based this calculation on the historical records available to him in Rome and on the clear chronological statements of the historian Luke (3:1–2). The Christian historian Eusebius, in A.D. 315, appealed to existing Roman government records (the census of Cyrenius and Caesar Augustus) to prove that Christ was born in Bethlehem when Joseph and Mary went there to be enrolled in the census, as mentioned in Luke 2:16. Justin Martyr also stated that census records were still available (in the second century of the Christian era) to prove the truth of Christ's prophesied birth in Bethlehem (*Apology*, chapter 1, verse 34). It is therefore probable that the monk, Dionysius, had access to accurate government records to determine that the birth of Christ occurred in the year before A.D. 1, which would be the fall of the year 1 B.C., since there was only one year between 1 B.C. and A.D. 1.

Scholars discovered evidence several hundred years ago that motivated them to adjust the date of Christ's nativity back to 4 B.C., or even 6 B.C. One piece of evidence dated the rule of the governor of Syria, Cyrenius (who administered the taxation in Luke 2:1–3), from 7 B.C. to 4 B.C. However, more recent archeological evidence has proved that Cyrenius was governor of Syria twice; he was also governor of Syria from 4 B.C. to 1 B.C.

This fact is also supported by Sir Robert Anderson (*The Coming Prince*, p. 92):

> In his Roman history, Mr. Merivale . . . says (vol. iv, page 457), 'A remarkable light has been thrown upon the point by the demonstration, as it seems to be, of Augustus Zumpt in his second volume of Commentationes Epigraphicae, that Quirinus (the Cyrenius of St. Luke II) was first governor of Syria from the close of A.U. 750 (B.C. 4), to A.U. 753 (B.C.1).

Therefore, there is no contradiction with the time of Cyrenius's second Syrian governorship (4 B.C. to 1 B.C.) and the census of Luke 2:1–3 occurring during 1 B.C., as stated by the early Christian writers.

Another factor that caused the date of Christ's birth to be adjusted back several years to 4 B.C. was the fact that some scholars believed that King Herod's death (which followed Christ's birth) must have occurred in 4 B.C. The reason for assigning 4 B.C. as the date of the death of Herod was that the Jewish historian, Flavius Josephus, recorded that Herod died just before Passover in the same year that there was an eclipse of the moon. Astronomers in past centuries knew of a partial lunar eclipse in Jerusalem that occurred on March 13, 4 B.C.; therefore, scholars were certain this proved that Herod's death and Christ's birth both occurred in 4 B.C.

Recently, however, additional astronomical evidence has revealed that the date of Herod's death could have been as late as 1 B.C. or A.D. 1, allowing Christ's birth to have occurred in 1 B.C. We now know that a full (not a partial) lunar eclipse took place on January 9, 1 B.C., which could well be the one referred to by Josephus in *Antiquities of the Jews* (book xvii, chapter 6). Astronomical records reveal that several eclipses of the moon were visible in Jerusalem during several years from 5 B.C. to A.D. 4; for example, March 23, 5 B.C., September 15, 5 B.C., March 12, 4 B.C. and January 9, 1 B.C. (*Bible Encyclopedia and Scriptural Dictionary*, by Rev. Samuel Fallows, p. 423).

In the light of these facts, Christ's nativity could have occurred as early as 4 B.C. or as late as 1 B.C. This author believes the weight of evidence leans toward the fall of 1 B.C., which agrees with Luke's gospel and the tradition of the early Church.

The traditional date set for Christmas, December 25, is almost certainly an error. Around A.D. 320, the church adopted the date of December 25 to officially celebrate the nativity, under the direction of the first Christian Roman emperor, Constantine. Apparently, one reason for picking this particular day was to replace the existing pagan festival to the sun, known as Saturnalia. The information given in Luke 2:8, about the "shepherds abiding in the field, keeping watch over the flock by night," indicates that Christ's birth could not have been in late December because the cold weather would have forced the flocks and the shepherds to take shelter during that season.

The Scriptures give a hint that the actual date of Christ's birth may have been the fifteenth day of Tishri, the Feast of Tabernacles, which occurs in our September–October. The gospel of John (1:14) states, "And the Word was made flesh, and tabernacled [dwelt] among us." John would certainly be in a position to know Jesus' birthday, and it is probable that he is hinting at the Feast of Tabernacles as the actual date by using the unusual word "tabernacled" in the Greek text to describe Christ's birth. The fact that some forty other key events in the spiritual history of Israel have occurred on biblical anniversaries of feast days would indicate a high probability that the birth of the Jewish Messiah would also occur on a feast date (in this case the Feast of Tabernacles, 1 B.C.).

The Feast of Tabernacles was one of the annual feasts on which all Jewish males were required to go to the Temple in Jerusalem to worship. This would cause a huge pilgrimage and thus a temporary increase in the population close to Jerusalem, accounting for the fact that "there was no room in the inn" in Bethlehem on the night of Christ's birth. Also, the census would contribute to the overcrowding. It is interesting to note that if we are correct about Jesus' birth in the fall, on the Feast of

Tabernacles, then Mary would have conceived on December 25th (280 days earlier).

## The Date of Christ's Ministry and His Crucifixion

In all of Scripture the clearest, most definitive chronological statement is found in the beginning verses of Luke (3:1–2), which describe the actual year in which John the Baptist began his ministry. Luke also recorded that the beginning of Christ's teaching ministry started with His baptism (Luke 3:21–22), and that Jesus, when He began His ministry, "was about thirty years of age" (Luke 3:23, RSV).

Luke's chronological statement is this: "Now in the fifteenth year of the reign of Tiberius Caesar, Pontius Pilate being governor of Judaea, and Herod being tetrarch of Galilee, and his brother Philip tetrarch of Ituraea and of the region of Trachonitis, and Lysanias the tetrarch of Abilene, Annas and Caiaphas being the high priests, the word of God came unto John the son of Zacharias in the wilderness" (Luke 3:1–2).

The Roman emperor, Tiberius Caesar, ascended his throne as emperor on the nineteenth day of August, A.D. 14 — a date as well known in Luke's day as the date of the assassination of President John F. Kennedy is known in our day. Therefore, the fifteenth year of Tiberius Caesar began on the nineteenth day of August, A.D. 28. Historical records confirm that all of the officials named in the statement by Luke ruled in the year A.D. 28. It thus approaches historical certainty that Christ's ministry began in the fall of A.D. 28.

It is obvious that many Bible commentators have assigned several earlier dates for the commencement of Christ's ministry, from A.D. 24 to A.D. 27. The reason they ignore the clear date of A.D. 28, described with such precision by the gospel historian Luke, is probably due to their previous commitment to an early (7 B.C. to 4 B.C.) dating of the nativity of Christ.

Since Christ was "about thirty years of age" at the time of his commencement of public ministry, they are forced to ignore Luke's clear historical dating. The way they accomplish this is to imagine that the first year of the reign of Tiberius Caesar refers to A.D. 12, the year that Caesar Augustus promoted General Tiberius for his victories in Germany, instead of the official coronation of Tiberius Caesar as Emperor on August 19, A.D. 14, following the death of Caesar Augustus. They imagine a kind of co-regency of the two men for the last two years of the reign of Caesar Augustus. However, there is no historical basis for this interpretation.

An analogy would be for a historian to count the years of President Johnson's presidency from January 1960, when President Kennedy was inaugurated, instead of from the date of the death of President Kennedy on November 22, 1963, when Vice President Johnson became president. Such a calculation would be a total distortion of historical dating and no reasonable person, let alone a historian, would do it.

The problem with such an interpretation of a co-regency from A.D. 12 is simply that there is not one single shred of evidence in any other contemporary historical writing that the reign of Tiberius Caesar began on any date other than the true date of his reign, August 19, A.D. 14. It is inconceivable that an accurate historian such as Luke, in writing to Theophilus (Luke 1:14), would have used a method of counting the years of Tiberius Caesar's reign so peculiar as to have caused Theophilus confusion about the correct date of the beginning of Christ's ministry.

Our conclusion, therefore, is that Christ's public teaching commenced in the fall of A.D. 28. The first Passover of His ministry would have then taken place six months later on the fourteenth of Nisan, A.D. 29 (John 2:12–23).

There is a further confirmation that Christ's public ministry began in the fall of A.D. 28. The apostle John records that while attending the Passover Feast six months later in the Temple, Christ prophesied that He would be killed and would rise again in three days. The Jews, not understanding that He was referring to Himself, not the Temple, replied to Jesus, "Forty and six years was this temple in building, and wilt thou rear it up in three days?" (John 2:19–20).

The historical records of that time, including *The War of the Jews* by Flavius Josephus, tell us that Herod the Great began the restoration of the Temple in 18 B.C. The year of Christ's first Passover in His public ministry, A.D. 29, is exactly forty-six years from the commencement of Herod's restoration program in 18 B.C. (Note: only one year exists between 1 B.C. and A.D. 1.)

Jesus continued His ministry over a period of approximately three and one-half years. Dr. Pusey, in his excellent book, *Daniel*, (pp. 176–177) states, "It seems to me absolutely certain that our

Lord's ministry lasted for some period above three years." According to the gospel of John, Jesus attended at least three Passovers, and if the Feast mentioned in John 5:1 is also a Passover, then it is certain that the Crucifixion occurred on the date of His final Passover in A.D. 32. The Feast described in John 5:1 must be either the Feast of Passover or Purim and, since Purim was a social feast celebrating the events described in the book of Esther, it is unlikely in the extreme that Jesus would specifically go up to Jerusalem for a nonreligious holiday. The evidence supports the contention that this Feast was also a Passover. Thus, Christ's ministry extended from the fall of A.D. 28, for three and one-half years, to His final Passover and crucifixion in A.D. 32.

# SELECTED BIBLIOGRAPHY

Anderson, Robert. *The Coming Prince.* London: Hodder & Stoughton, 1894.

Auerbach, Leo. *The Babylonian Talmud: In Selection.* New York: Philosophical Library, 1944.

Barnes, Albert. *Notes on the Book of Daniel.* New York: Leavitt & Allen, 1855.

Baylee, Rev. Joseph. *The Times of the Gentiles.* London: James Nisbet & Co. 1871.

Besant, Walter and E. H. Palmer. *Jerusalem.* London: Chatto & Windus, 1908.

Blackstone, Wm. E. *Jesus is Coming.* London: Fleming H. Revell Co., 1908.

Blackstone, Wm. E. *The Millennium.* New York: Revell Publishing Co.

Bloomfield, Arthur. *Where Is the Ark of the Covenant and What Is Its Role in Bible Prophecy?* Minneapolis: Dimension Books, 1976.

Bradley, John. *World War III: Strategies, Tactics and Weapons.* New York: Cresent Books, 1982.

Bullinger, Ethelbert W. *Numbers In Scripture.* Grand Rapids: Kregel Publications, 1978.

Burnett, Bishop. *The Sacred Theory of the Earth.* London, 1816.

Butterfield, Herbert. *Christianity and History.* New York: Charles Scribner and Sons, 1949.

Calder, Nigel. *Unless Peace Comes.* Victoria: Penguin Books, 1968.

Chaldler, Bishop Edward. *A Defence of Christianity from the Prophecies of the Old Testament.* London: James and John Knapton, 1725.

Culver, Robert Duncan. *Daniel and the Latter Days.* Chicago: Moody Press, 1954, 1977.

Cummings, John. *Lectures on the Book of Daniel.* Philadelphia: Lindsay and Blakiston, 1855.

Cummings, John. *Apocalyptic Sketches.* London: Hall, Virtue and Co., 1850.

Davidson, John. *Discourses on Prophecy.* London: John Murray & Co., 1825.

Dimont, Max I. *Jews, God And History.* New York: New American Library, 1962.

Edersheim, Alfred. *The Temple.* London: The Religious Tract Society, 1912.

Edersheim, Alfred. *The Life and Times of Jesus the Messiah.* 2 vols. New York: Longmans, Green, and Co., 1896.

Edersheim, Alfred. *Bible History, Old Testament.* Grand Rapids: W.B. Eerdmans Publishing Co., 1982.

Eusebius. *Eusebius' Ecclesiastical History.* Oxford: The Clarendon Press, 1881.

Fabun, Don. *The Dynamics of Change.* Englewood Cliffs: Prentice-Hall, Inc., 1967.

Freeman, Hobart E. *An Introduction to the Old Testament Prophets.* Chicago: Moody Press, 1968.

Gaster, Theodor H. *Festivals of the Jewish Year.* New York: Morrow Quill Paperbacks, 1953.

Gilbert, Martin. *The Arab-Israeli Conflict: Its History in Maps.* Jerusalem: Steimatzky Ltd., 1985.

Graham, Billy. *Approaching Hoofbeats: The Four Horsemen of The Apocalypse.* Waco: Word Books, Inc., 1983.

Guinness, H. Grattan. *The Approaching End of the Age.* 8th ed. London: Hodder & Stoughton, 1882.

Hallifax, Dr. Samuel. *Twelve Sermons on the Prophecies Concerning the Christian Church.* London: T. Cadell, 1776.

Harrison, William K. *Hope Triumphant: Studies on the Rapture.* Chicago: Moody Press, 1966.

Hawley, Charles A. *The Teaching of Apocrypha and Apocalypse.* New York: Association Press, 1925.

Heinisb, Dr. Paul. *History of the Old Testament.* St. Paul: The North Central Publishing Co., 1952.

Jarvis, Rev. Samuel F. *The Church of the Redeemed.* Boston, 1950.

Josephus, Flavius. *Wars of the Jews.* Kingston: N. G. Ellis, 1844.

Jones, Alexander, ed. *The Jerusalem Bible.* Garden City: Doubleday & Co., 1968.

Kellogg, Dr. Samuel. *The Jews or Prediction and Fulfillment.* New York: Anson D. F. Randolf & Co., 1883.

Kidron, Michael and Dan Smith. *The War Atlas.* London: Pan Books Ltd., 1983.

Larkin, Clarence. *The Book of Daniel.* Philadelphia: Clarence Larkin, 1929, 1949.

Lewis, David Allen. *Magog 1982: Cancelled.* Harrison: New Leaf Press, 1982.

Lindsay, Hal. *The Late Great Planet Earth.* Grand Rapids: Zondervan Publishing House, 1970.

Lockyer, Herbert. *All The Messianic Prophecies Of The Bible.* Grand Rapids: Zondervan Publishing House, 1973.

Ludwigson, R. *A Survey of Bible Prophecy.* Grand Rapids: Zondervan Publishing House, 1951.

Marsh, Rev. John. *An Epitome of General Ecclesiastical History.* New York: J. Tilden and Co., 1843.

McCall, Thomas S., and Zola Levitt. *The Coming Russian Invasion of Israel.* Chicago: Moody Press, 1976.

McDowell, Josh. *Evidence That Demands a Verdict.* San Bernadino: Here's Life Publishers, Inc., 1979.

Mesorah Publications. *Daniel: A New Commentary Anthologized from Talmudic, Midrashic and Rabbinical Sources.* Brooklyn: Mesorah Publications, Ltd., 1980.

Mesorah Publications. *Ezekiel: A New Commentary Anthologized from Talmudic, Midrashic and Rabbinical Sources.* Brooklyn: Mesorah Publications, Ltd., 1980

Messing, Simon D. *The Story of the Falashas.* Brooklyn: Balshon Printing, 1982.

Newton, Bishop Thomas. *Dissertations on the Prophecies.* 2 vols. London: R & R Gilbert, 1817.

Payne, J. Barton. *Encyclopedia of Biblical Prophecy.* Grand Rapids: Baker Book House, 1980.

Pentecost, Dwight. *Things to Come.* Grand Rapids: Dunham, 1958.

Peters, Joan. *From Time Immemorial: The Origins of the Arab-Israeli Conflict Over Palastine.* New York: Harper & Row, Publishers, 1984.

Pusey, E. B. *Daniel the Prophet.* Plymouth: The Devonport Society, 1864.

Rosenau, Helen. *Vision of the Temple.* London: Oresko Books Ltd., 1979.

Sale-Harrison, L. *The Remarkable Few.* London: Pickering & Inglis, 1928.

Schell, Johnathan. *The Fate of the Earth.* New York: Avon Books, 1982.

Scofield, C. I. *The Scofield Reference Bible.* Oxford: Oxford University, 1909.

Seiss, Joseph. *The Apocalypse.* Philadelphia: Approved Books, 1865.

Siegel, Richard, and Carl Rheins. *The Jewish Almanac.* New York: Bantam Books, Inc., 1980.

Smith, Wilbur M. *Israeli/Arab Conflict and the Bible.* Glendale: Regal Books, 1967.

Suborov, Victor. *Inside The Soviet Army.* London: Granada Publishing Ltd., 1984.

Szyk, Arthur. *The Haggadah.* Jerusalem: Massadah and Alumoth, 1960.

Taylor, Gordon R. *The Biological Time Bomb*. London: Thames and Hudson, 1968.

The Ante-Nicene Fathers. 10 vols. Grand Rapids: Eerdmans Publishing Co., 1986.

Tinbergen, Jan. *Reshaping The International Order: A Report to the Club Of Rome*. Scarborough: The New American Library Of Canada, 1976.

Ussher, Archbishop Jacob. *Chronology of the Old and New Testaments*. Verona, 1741.

Walvoord, John F. *Daniel, The Key to Prophetic Revelations: A Commentary*. Chicago: Moody Press, 1971.

Walvoord, John F. *The Rapture Question*. Findlay: Dunham Publishing Co., 1957.

Strassfeld, Michael. *The Jewish Holidays: A Guide And Commentary*. New York: Harper & Row, Publishers, 1985.

Weber, Timothy P. *Living in the Shadow of the Second Coming*. New York: Oxford University Press, 1979.

West, Gilbert. *Observations on the History and Evidences of the Resurrection of Jesus Christ*. London: R. Dodsley, 1747.

White, John Wesley. *World War III*. Grand Rapids: Zondervan Publishing House, 1977.

Yadin, Yigael. *Masada*. London: Sphere Books Ltd., 1973.

Zlotowitz, Rabbi Meir. *Bereishis Genesis: A New Translation with a Commentary Anthologized from Talmudic, Midrashic, and Rabbinic Sources*. Brooklyn: Mesorah Publications, Ltd., 1980.

18075565R00193

Made in the USA
Middletown, DE
20 February 2015